EDUCATING FOR THE ANTHROPOCENE

EDUCATING FOR THE ANTHROPOCENE

Schooling and Activism in the Face
of Slow Violence

PETER SUTORIS

The MIT Press
Cambridge, Massachusetts
London, England

The MIT Press would like to thank the anonymous peer reviewers who provided comments on drafts of this book. The generous work of academic experts is essential for establishing the authority and quality of our publications. We acknowledge with gratitude the contributions of these otherwise uncredited readers.

This book was set in Adobe Garamond and Berthold Akzidenz Grotesk by Westchester Publishing Services. Printed and bound in the United States of America.

Library of Congress Cataloging-in-Publication Data

Names: Sutoris, Peter, author.
Title: Educating for the anthropocene : schooling and activism in the face
    of slow violence / Peter Sutoris.
Description: Cambridge, Massachusetts : The MIT Press, 2022. | Includes
    bibliographical references and index.
Identifiers: LCCN 2021057614 | ISBN 9780262544177 (paperback)
Subjects: LCSH: Education—Social aspects—India. | Education—Social
    aspects—South Africa. | Poor—Education—India. | Poor—Education—
    South Africa. | Marginality, Social—India. | Marginality, Social—South Africa. |
    India—Environmental conditions. | South Africa—Environmental conditions.
Classification: LCC LC191.8.I4 S87 2022 | DDC 370.954—dc23/eng/20220302
LC record available at https://lccn.loc.gov/2021057614

10 9 8 7 6 5 4 3 2 1

We learn from history that we do not learn from history.
—Hegel

Some have said that my father was ahead of his time, but the truth is he was on time and perhaps we were late.
—Attallah Shabazz, in the foreword to *The Autobiography of Malcolm X*

Tree, water, and smokestacks, Durban, 2017.

Dedicated to all young people who keep dreaming of different futures.

Contents

Acknowledgments

The research presented in this book would not have been possible without the help and kindness of many strangers, family, mentors, and friends. At Cambridge, Jo-Anne Dillabough and Phil Gardner made important contributions to my intellectual growth and the growth of this project. I owe much to the educational institutions that shaped me—especially United World College of the Atlantic and Dartmouth College—and friends and mentors from my undergraduate days—Doug Haynes, Andrew Garrod, Sienna Radha Craig, and Jerry Auten—who have continued to guide me through the vagaries of academic research, and life more broadly.

The participants in this study are too many to list; many are anonymized. The staff and students at Seema Primary (a pseudonym for the school in India where I undertook my research) and Durban South Primary (a pseudonym for its South African counterpart) welcomed me into their communities and shared life-changing perspectives and insights, and for this I cannot thank them enough. Environmental activists working with the South Durban Environmental Community Alliance—in particular, Des D'Sa and Bongani Mthembu—and their colleagues at groundWork Bobby Peek and Rico Euripidou, as well as antidam activists in Pashulok and other activist figures in India and South Africa, including Medha Patkar, Oupa Lehulere, Patrick Mkhize, and Chris Albertyn, generously shared their time and experience with me. Scholars, journalists, and artists in both countries, including Ramachandra Guha and Mahesh Rangarajan, provided important insights that helped me contextualize my research.

During the pilot phase of this work, a large number of organizations and individuals helped me map out the ideology and practice of education for sustainable development (ESD). The staff at the Centre for Environment Education (CEE) in Ahmedabad, India, including director Kartikeya Sarabhai, was particularly helpful, as was the staff at the ESD section of UNESCO in Paris, at the Environmental Education Research Centre at Rhodes University in Grahamstown, South Africa, at the Wildlife and Environment Society of South Africa (WESSA; Dr. Jim Taylor, in particular) and at Jeevan Shala in Maharashtra (especially Yogini Khanolkar). The staff and students at the numerous schools I visited during the pilot phase helped me understand their concerns and lived realities, which aided me in shaping my research questions.

Dr. Manish Jain at Ambedkar University in Delhi and Dr. Rob O'Donoghue at Rhodes University shared valuable contacts and provided feedback in the early stages of my analysis. University of KwaZulu-Natal provided me with a research affiliation that helped me immerse myself in South African academia, and scholars there, particularly Kathy Sutherland, Shauna Mottiar, Jane Quin, and Moraig Peden, generously shared their contacts in South Durban.

Many friends, colleagues, and strangers made my research in India and South Africa possible through their advice, research assistance, translation, and logistical support. In particular, I would like to thank Tarini Manchanda, Poorvi Gaur, Kent Buchanan, Obakeng Molelu, Richa Shivhare, Skikha Pandey, Trisha Mahajan, Adam Cooper, Rone McFarlane, and Kim Harrisberg. Others provided support and guidance remotely, in particular David and Judy MacDougall, Georgina Drew, and Radhika Iyengar. At Cambridge, Arathi Sriprakash, Elsa Lee, Susan Robertson, Nigel Meager, and Karen Pinkus provided valuable support and intellectual guidance.

The research behind this book would not have been possible without financial support from the Gates Cambridge Trust, Clare Hall College's Boak Student Support Fund, the Cambridge University Faculty of Education's Fieldwork Fund, and a British Association for International and Comparative Education (BAICE) Student Fieldwork Grant, for which I am deeply grateful. These institutions also supported me in other ways. My college tutors—Dr. Rosie Luff and Dr. Iain Black—were there for me in times of doubt. The Faculty of Education's IT staff entrusted me with their professional camera equipment and were extremely helpful throughout the filmmaking process. The staff of University Library and Faculty of Education Library at Cambridge and the British Library in London provided invaluable assistance and guidance in locating sources.

My thanks also go to those who tirelessly helped with proofreading this book at various stages, including Dody Riggs, Nuith Morales, Ben Kahn, Amanda Mata-Mei, Maria Khwaja, and Andy Foust. Various versions were presented at conferences and symposia between 2016 and 2019, where participants provided valuable feedback. At The MIT Press, Susan Buckley, Noah Springer and Lillian Dunaj saw this book through completion with great professionalism and generosity.

Finally, I would like to express my gratitude to my family—Ivan, Helena, Ivan Jr.—and a number of friends who supported me through this research—Eileen Brody, Fr. Greg Sharkey, Arif Naveed, Maria Khwaja, Ellora Adam, Chris Adam, Swojan Newa, Max Last, Renata Snow, Andrea Grant, Jose Saavedra, Abhijit Acharya, and many more. Others helped to shape my intellectual trajectory prior to this project—Ray and Angie Silkstone, Agnesa Mojžišová, Tamara Greenstone, Newton LaJuan, and Ingrid Ahlgren. Last but not least, the family dog Asha deserves an honorable mention for her unconditional love and companionship during the writing process.

London, August 2021

Abbreviations

ANC	African National Congress
BJP	*Bharatiya Janata Party* (Indian People's Party)
CAPS	Curriculum Assessment Policy Statements
CEE	Centre for Environment Education
DA	Democratic Alliance
EE	environmental education
ESD	education for sustainable development
ESE	environmental and sustainability education
GDP	gross domestic product
HIV/AIDS	human immunodeficiency virus/acquired immunodeficiency syndrome
INC	Indian National Congress
IPCC	Intergovernmental Panel on Climate Change
LO	life orientation
MK	*uMkhonto we Sizwe* (Spear of the Nation)
NCERT	National Council of Educational Research and Training
NGO	nongovernmental organization
RSS	*Rashtriya Swayamsevak Sangh* (National Volunteer Association)
SDCEA	South Durban Community Environmental Alliance
SDG	Sustainable Development Goal
STEPWISE	Science and Technology Education Promoting Wellbeing for Individuals, Societies and Environments
STSE	Science, Technology, Society, and Environment

TBVSS	*Tehri Bandh Virodhi Sangharsh Samiti* (Tehri Dam Opposing Struggle Committee)
THDC	Tehri Hydro Development Corporation
TNC	Trans-National Corporation
TRC	Truth and Reconciliation Commission
UKZN	University of KwaZulu-Natal
UCIL	Union Carbide India Limited
UCT	University of Cape Town
UN	United Nations
UNESCO	United Nations Educational, Scientific and Cultural Organization
WESSA	Wildlife and Environment Society of South Africa

I LEARNING TO LIVE IN THE ANTHROPOCENE

Mpophomeni Township, Eastern Cape, South Africa, 2016.

DILEMMA 1 THE SHOCK OF RECOGNITION: (DE)POLITICIZING EDUCATION

It was May 2016 in South Africa, a beautiful autumn day in a township near Grahamstown, and children were outside learning about planting saplings during their science lesson. The teacher, Helen, was kind and warm-hearted and clearly knew what she was talking about.[1] She commanded respect without shouting or hitting students, which was common practice in other South African township schools I visited. Her face, lined with wrinkles, wore a constant smile as she moved seamlessly from student to student. Her rapport with each of them was amazing. After the class, she proudly showed me the different products her students had made from recycled materials. The beautiful colorful doormats made of bits of plastic bags were unforgettable.[2]

At first, I was captivated by the hands-on environmental education I had just witnessed, but that began to shift as I interviewed Helen. "Do you ever connect planting trees to climate change in your classes?" I asked. She gave me a pained look, and I detected a pinch of amazement at my ignorance. "The students would not be able to follow. They are just cognitively not there." I gasped. Suddenly I saw everything in a different light. This White teacher seemed to be implying that Black township children were unable to understand the concept of global warming.

As I walked out of the tool shed where we were talking, all I could see was how tangled hands-on environmental education was in a web of racism, paternalism, and apartheid. My thoughts ran away with me: those plastic mats were not about empowerment but about giving the kids the skills to become "petty entrepreneurs." And that fun, engaging lesson I had witnessed? It clearly was a way to give the Black children the illusion that they were doing their bit without granting them agency: "Don't ask questions about the environmental mess we are in, how we got into it, who is responsible, or how we can get out of it. Just plant your tree."

I realized only much later, as I was looking over my notes, that this episode took place in a special needs school and that I had no idea about the disabilities the students suffered from or what they were or were not capable of, and therefore I could not sit in judgment of the teacher. That I forgot this important detail told me something about my own political orientation, about the hypotheses I brought with me to the field and for which I hoped to find empirical support.[3] I was looking for simple answers that could be translated directly into policy and finding it frustrating that the field was not yielding such solutions. But even though I may have misread the situation, the shock of recognizing environmental and sustainability education (ESE) as a potentially apolitical space, and the associated grave implications, stayed with me. It was the impulse that led to the research behind this book.

Up until the encounter with Helen and her students, my research was all about the idea of sustainably developing (the core concept of education for sustainable development, or ESD) and trying to understand how best to "optimize" education to support this effort more effectively in low-income settings. But that morning my thinking started to change. What if I turned ESE[4] on its head and focused on "developing sustainability" instead? How do we define, promote, and strengthen sustainability in individuals, systems, and societies? What dangers may the depoliticization of ESE—an effort to deprive young people of the ability to imagine different futures and to limit their political agency in bringing these into being—pose to environmental sustainability?

This was my initial dilemma: Should I keep working on researching the effectiveness of ESE interventions, a subject that might appeal to practitioners but one I was becoming increasingly convinced did not get to the heart of the issue of sustainability? Or should I shift my focus to the (de)politicization of ESE, a seemingly vague and quite possibly "useless" subject?

I chose the latter, reasoning that I needed to go where the ethnographic journey was taking me. The politics of the interface between education and the environment became the unintended subject of my research.[5] I started seeing a pattern in the South African and Indian schools in which I was conducting research: planting trees, fixing leaking taps, or cleaning a river was seen as making a contribution to the sustainability of communities. But other actions—writing a letter to a local politician, for example—were often discouraged. Individual apolitical deeds were what the ESE interventions I was encountering seemed to stand for, and maybe this was something they shared with other development projects.

I soon found, however, that simply changing the research question did not resolve the dilemma between "sustainably developing" and "developing sustainability." To study depoliticization, we must understand what politicization may mean, and I soon discovered that my research was pulling me into spaces outside the school context. I encountered environmental activists and learnt about their radical knowledge-making practices and political imaginations[6] that contrasted sharply with what I was witnessing in schools. The pivot in the subject of my research necessitated refining my research sites, too, as I concluded that doing an ethnography of the (de)politicization of ESE necessarily meant stepping outside the realm of institutionalized education. Schooling and activism became the two spaces of my exploration.

While discussing my research with a colleague later on, I received an unexpected response that seemed to reveal the useless, disconnected-from-practice nature of my project. This scholar was uncomfortable bringing politics into the conversation about environmental decay and felt that politicizing the environment only means that we argue and fail to act, which there is no time for anymore. They asked me, "Shouldn't all the educators in the world focus on one thing and one thing only—preparing the future generation for the massive challenge of sequestering carbon from the atmosphere so that humanity survives?"

I was speechless for a moment, then thought back to my time in South Africa in 2016. On the last day of that trip, I talked to two academics from the University of KwaZulu-Natal in Pietermaritzburg. These two scholars told me that schoolchildren clean up trash from the local river every year as part of their environmental education and that every year more rubbish made its way into the river. "There's no point in cleaning up if you don't fix the real issues upstream," one of them told me. Surely there was more to ESE than this? And surely there is more to education than learning how to capture carbon from the atmosphere?

While I continue to ponder how my research—a slow, ethnographic exploration of schooling and activism in two different contexts—squares up with the urgency of the environmental multicrisis,[7] I do not doubt that studying the politics of education and the environment is worthwhile. Encountering the activist knowledge base has taught me that "politics" is not an abstract concept but can indeed be a radically practical idea. This is especially so in the Anthropocene.

1 INTRODUCTION: EDUCATION'S TASK IN THE ANTHROPOCENE

> The greatest challenge we face is a philosophical one: understanding that this civilization is already dead.
> —R. Scranton, *Learning to die in the Anthropocene*, p. 23

The ancient Greek root of the word "Anthropocene" has a peculiar origin. According to some translations, *anthropos*—human—means "he who has the face of a man."[1] The gender bias aside, this interpretation implies it is possible to be a person and not be human. And conversely, if we grant personhood to the nonhuman, as many cultures around the world do, it is also possible to have the face of a (wo)man without being human. We live in an age marked both by human beings dehumanized in the name of progress, and the nonhuman earthly landscapes simultaneously transformed into the face of man[kind],[2] being deprived of the fecundity that had sustained life, at the time of this book's publication still the only known life in the universe, for millions of years. It is as if the cultural lens of our age blinds us to humanity's suffering and instead propels us to put our face on the very landscapes that nourish and sustain us. The Anthropocene, the new geological era in which people are the primary force shaping our planet in ways that only geological, deep time can undo, is the ultimate manifestation of this fixation. Rather than seeing the "other" as human, we want to build monuments to humanity on Earth (and in space), unaware that what we are really building is our own gravestones. This paradox is what this ethnography is about. More precisely, it is about the ways in which education helped us get here, and the ways in which it might help us survive.

The multiple environmental crises we are facing have brought us to a crossroads unlike any before—we are in the process of deciding whether we sacrifice both our history and our future for the sake of the present. The Anthropocene is an age marked by what Rob Nixon (2011) describes as "slow violence," the gradual, "invisible" destruction of the planet and its "marginal peoples"[3] that lacks the spectacle of the blatant violence we see in daily news. It signifies both the ability of humankind to become a force of stupendous magnitude and its fundamental fragility (as Roy Scranton intimates in the epigraph of this chapter). It is not only a time of technological advancement but also an era of catastrophic climate change, mass extinction, ocean acidification, and increasingly technocratic, depoliticized educational institutions that threaten to eliminate criticality. Can education escape the trap of instrumentalization and help transform rather than maintain the status quo? What does it mean to educate generations of people whose decisions and actions will determine the habitability of the planet and the survival of human beings as a species? How do young people make sense of the environmental burdens of history they carry? How may education enhance or hinder their ability to imagine and bring about alternative futures?

In this book, I explore these questions through the story of schooling and activism in two communities I researched between 2016 and 2018—Pashulok in India and Wentworth in South Africa. Pashulok is a periurban patch of land that lies south of the religiously significant town of Rishikesh in the state of Uttarakhand and is found along the Ganges, just west of Nepal's border. It is a rehabilitation site for about five thousand of the people forcibly displaced by the construction of the nearby Tehri Dam in the Garhwal Himalayas (figure 1.1). This reservoir holds four cubic kilometers of water, under which lie the homes of more than one hundred thousand people—entire towns, villages, songs, stories, and ways of life. It is hard not to be awestruck when visiting this monument to modernity, whose sheer scale is an imprint on the face of the earth, a seemingly infinite body of water.

The Anthropocene's slow violence takes a very different shape in Wentworth, a community of Coloured people[4] living in the heart of the South Durban Industrial Basin, one of the most heavily polluted places on Earth (figure 1.2). Dante's "Inferno" comes to mind in South Durban—smokestacks

Figure 1.1
Tehri Dam, curving around a mountain.

Figure 1.2
The "Inferno" of South Durban.

upon smokestacks, golden flares of burning chemicals reaching into the sky, factories, warehouses, trucks, pipes, the vomit-inducing smell of a freshly sanitized hospital room that has been put on fire, a round-the-clock symphony of revving engines, clouds of smoke covering the horizon, hiding the sun, the moon, the clouds, and the heavens.[5]

Why look for answers in Pashulok and Wentworth? These are communities "of the future," where the accelerating slow violence is found in the face of an environmental refugee or in the odor of carcinogenic air inhaled every day by marginalized people of color. But they are also places of the past, artifacts of colonial, racialized histories, of modernity's underbelly.[6] Pashulok and Wentworth are "behind" on their supposed development trajectory but also ahead of their time; they are already experiencing levels of environmental decay awaiting much of the rest of the world as humanity moves further into the Anthropocene, or what we may call the "high Anthropocene." (This latter term, to which I refer throughout this book, roughly corresponds with the twenty-first century and is characterized by an acceleration in slow violence, a deepening environmental multicrisis, and the global dominance of techno-capitalism. I say more about the high Anthropocene later in this introduction.)

Yet Pashulok and Wentworth are located within countries whose progressive constitutions guarantee their citizens a right to a clean environment, a contradiction not lost on the activist groups that sprang up in both places. The young people in these communities are pulled both into the past by activist narratives about the origins of environmental decay in their communities and into the future by confronting the dystopia of accelerating slow violence in real time. In other words, they are being educated for (or perhaps by) the Anthropocene by the virtue of living on the cultural and social frontier of the high Anthropocene.

This book, then, is an ethnographic exploration of schooling and activism in relationship to slow violence in the context of intergenerational legacies of colonialism, racism, and environmental degradation. What is the relevance of such an exploration to the discussion of education's role in the Anthropocene? In this ethnography, we learn about the ways in which state-run schooling seeks to depoliticize the environment, co-opting environmental and sustainability education (ESE) efforts in service of (post) colonial and neoliberal agendas. These ethnographic accounts of schooling cast doubt on the idea that we can educate ourselves out of unsustainability so long as education means state-sponsored social reproduction. They highlight a contradiction at the heart of global ESE policy—we are, as the British saying goes, putting the cat among the pigeons by trusting political regimes, built on environmentally unsustainable ideologies, to oversee and finance the effort to bring about sustainability through education. Such political systems have no real incentive to encourage young people to question the regimes' fundamental values, such as infinite growth.[7] This volume takes us into activist communities where such values are challenged, illustrating the ways learning for environmental justice and sustainability occurs outside formal education systems.

The emphasis on context and historicization within this ethnographic study also enables tracing the global origins of the locally observed (de)politicizing effects of schooling and activism. This is not a story of a privileged academic traveling to spaces of socioeconomic deprivation and finding the schooling in these spaces lacking; it is rather a story of the academic recognizing the impact of centuries of Western colonialism, globalized neoliberal capitalism, and ideologies of infinite growth (and hence infinite extraction) on these spaces.[8] The phenomenon of depoliticization is highly visible across the schooling systems of the so-called "developed countries," and much of the global ESE discourse, curricula, and policy is formulated in spaces of Western(ized) privilege.

While I try my best to be sensitive to the colonial pasts and presents in the pages that follow, I also bring my own biases and assumptions to the narrative. These are associated with various aspects of my identity and my life experience, including my previous work as a development practitioner in South Asia, during which I had the opportunity to spend much time in schools in India and Nepal. In telling the story of Pashulok and Wentworth, I try to be transparent about the assumptions I am conscious of as I write these pages, guided by the tradition of self-reflectiveness and positionality in ethnographic scholarship (Behar, 1996; Geertz, 1988; Rabinow, 1977).

Crucially, and in contrast to much of the existing literature about environmental learning[9] in the Anthropocene, this ethnography attempts to channel the voices of the young people living on the high Anthropocene's frontier. As we listen to them and consider the short observational films about their environments they made as part of the research presented in this book (figure 1.3), we learn of significant discrepancies between their imaginations of possible futures and the curriculum they are exposed to in their schools. It is tempting to see young people as passive absorbers of knowledge, as blank slates to be filled by the political pedagogies of schooling (or activism). But this is not accurate. This book illustrates that young people are political agents in the here and now, not merely yet-to-become future adult citizens, as they are often seen. In doing so, it seeks to challenge the ageism of much of mainstream development and ESE discourse.

But *Educating for the Anthropocene* does not simply aim to provide an empirical illustration of arguments about ESE and politics, a number of which have been expressed in some form in the existing literature (as discussed in chapter 2). It seeks to bring ethnographic nuance to the idea of "educating for the Anthropocene" in the tradition of public anthropology. In the pages that follow, we encounter expansive activist imaginations of

Figure 1.3
Making an observational film in Pashulok.

"the promise of politics" (Arendt, 2007) in the high Anthropocene. We meet characters whose life experience of slow violence shaped their understanding of the "horizons of the possible" (cf. Ricœur, 1984) and ponder how these visions contrast with the everyday practices of state learning in schools.

We put these narratives in conversation with the ideas of several thinkers, including Hannah Arendt. While Arendt's ideas have been sparsely applied to education and environment (they have been more influential in political science), she has a lot to contribute to how we think about educating for the Anthropocene. Her ideas allow us to ponder the parallels between the slow violence of the Anthropocene and the fast violence of twentieth-century totalitarian regimes (particularly Nazism and Stalinism) that she studied, illuminating cultural and political landscapes that enable violence in modern societies.

Thanks to the nuance of the ethnographic method, we observe the ways individual characters seize their agency despite the systemic headwinds they face. We come across activists who, while suspicious of schooling, nevertheless work to build bridges with educators in schools. We meet "outlier" teachers who deal in the risky business of actively questioning the postcolonial, neoliberal structures in which they are forced to operate. We encounter children between the ages of eleven and fourteen whose imaginations of future worlds are a direct product of neither schooling nor activism, not even of popular culture, but rather reflect a reimagining of elements of the past in creating a temporal arc (Ricœur, 1984) linking past and future worlds. The lesson from the high Anthropocene's frontier is that educating for the Anthropocene is neither a black-and-white affair nor, despite appearances, a hopeless endeavor. As this book shows, it is a complex effort, operating within a fragmented space and shaped by a wide gamut of political ideologies.

Surprisingly, ethnography—a form of immersive, highly nuanced research that lends itself particularly well to studying this complexity—has been used sparsely in the context of ESE (Sutoris, 2019). But this book aims to go beyond simply bringing a set of unorthodox methods to ESE; it also seeks to turn research into an activist intervention by exploring the ways it may help mediate the political fragmentation within the field. In particular, the participatory filmmaking techniques explored in this volume are intended as both a research method and an experimental intervention into young people's sense-making around historical responsibility and environmental futures.[10] The filmmaking workshops were premised on the idea that children may possess knowledge that we as adults could not fully understand through a verbal exchange. They were inspired by similar workshops organized by the ethnographer and filmmaker David MacDougall in India, Australia, and elsewhere (MacDougall, 2006; Potts, 2015). This interventionist edge also aims to demonstrate one way public anthropology could enrich the field of ESE, and vice versa (Sutoris, 2021).

The book is organized around three parts. Each one begins with a dilemma and contains two chapters. The first part has opened with an account of the idea of educating for the Anthropocene from philosophical, anthropological, and sociological perspectives. Having covered this broad outline of the book's themes, we are now about to move into the next section of the introduction, which helps the reader decode the book's title (including critically examining the word "Anthropocene" and its hidden meanings). In the following section we take a closer look at the links between slow violence and bureaucratization. I argue that Hannah Arendt's theoretical frames for studying totalitarianism can help us make sense of education's role in the Anthropocene. In the final section, we return to the idea of bridging ESE with public anthropology, exploring how such a bridge may be built and how it may enrich both fields. In the final section, I provide an introduction to the history of Pashulok and Wentworth, and with the help of this narrative, define the concept of the "frontier of the high Anthropocene." By extension, this discussion establishes the wider significance of Pashulok and Wentworth as sites of environmental learning. The theoretical discussion continues in chapter 2, which summarizes existing research about ESE in the Anthropocene and (de)politicization and further discusses the significance of the work of Hannah Arendt and Paul Ricœur to this field.

The tone shifts in the book's second part, where we pick up the ethnographic narrative in earnest, exploring the histories of slow violence in the two sites (chapter 3) and how schooling (chapter 4) engages with this slow violence. Finally, the third part focuses on environmental activism as a space of education (chapter 5) and the potential for bridging it with schooling (chapter 6).

DECODING THE BOOK'S TITLE

Before we proceed any further, it is worth looking at the three words in the book's title in some detail. Let's start with "educating." In colloquial language and in much of public policy, "educating" usually refers to "schooling." This is not so in the title of this volume. Indeed, one of the arguments of this book is that engaging in an ethnography of education in the Anthropocene means going outside the institutional spaces of schooling. During my time in the field I came to believe that activism is crucial to the conversation about education in the Anthropocene (an argument I explore in more depth in chapter 2). But this is not to suggest that other spaces—religion, family, work, community exchange, Indigenous knowledge/practice, and others— are any less important (a point I revisit in the conclusion). Schooling and activism are, however, the main focus here.

The second word, "for," could also carry multiple meanings. Doesn't educating *for* something imply relegating education to a means to an end when true education is an end in itself? Bob Jickling, one of the stalwarts of ESE research, made this point in his influential 1994 piece "Why I Don't Want My Children to Be Educated for Sustainable Development": "[E]ducation is concerned with enabling people to think for themselves. Education for sustainable development, education for deep ecology . . . or education 'for' anything else is inconsistent with that criterion," he wrote (Jickling, 1994, p. 116). "Educating for the Anthropocene" is, however, not a matter of promoting any particular idea or achieving any instrumental aim; it is about the recognition of the historical moment we are in. It means preparing for life at a time of unprecedented precarity, a life marked by immense historical responsibility that perhaps no other generation has ever faced.

This does not mean that it should be education's purpose to make up for the flaws in other policy domains. We cannot expect education to solve the environmental crisis just as we cannot put the responsibility for solving the crisis on the shoulders of young people alone. This would be neither fair nor realistic. Education is not, nor can it ever be, the panacea, but it does have a role to play. As the material in this book suggests, we might serve the agenda of environmental sustainability better if we see education as an end in itself—a process of self-discovery and discovery of the world—as opposed to trying to turn education into a fix for the failures of policy, markets, or human behavior. This might seem illogical; surely, education will make more difference to sustainability if we actually resolve to make education a force in service of sustainability? But the apparent contradiction can be resolved if we consider that noninstrumentalized education is more likely to bring us closer to our own humanity—including sensitivity to the world around us and our ability to imagine different futures—than education designed to advance any specific political agenda.

This is also one of the reasons why this volume does not aim to be a manual for either educators or activists. The goal of ethnographic research, after all, is not to provide conclusive answers but to make readers feel they are right alongside the ethnographer, sensing the ethnographer's movements and finding themselves inside the affect of the narrative tale. Whether readers choose to embrace the practices and ideas of the characters they encounter along the way is not for the author to decide. It is my hope, however, that a teacher or an activist who reads this book will come away with a sense of shared purpose, an understanding that each has a lot to learn from the other. Further, in addressing the challenge of "educating for the Anthropocene," they can enrich each other's practice as activist educators and educational activists.

Finally, the word "Anthropocene" is perhaps the most "loaded" word in this book's title. It was famously used by geologist Paul Crutzen, who exclaimed at a conference of the International Geosphere-Biosphere Programme in Cuernavaca, Mexico, in February 2000, "We're no longer in the Holocene but in the Anthropocene!"[11] He followed up with an article in *Nature* (Crutzen, 2002), in which he argued that "the stratigraphic scale had to be supplemented by a new age, to signal that [hu]mankind had become a force of telluric amplitude" (Bonneuil and Fressoz, p. 3).[12]

One way to visualize the sheer scale of human impact on the planet is to picture four hundred thousand Hiroshima-sized bombs being detonated every day, or *four each second*—that is how many explosions it would take to produce the amount of additional heat stuck near the planet's surface as a result of the excessive carbon dioxide pumped into the atmosphere by humans (McKibben, 2019, p. 22). Even though the 2015 Paris Agreement called for limiting anthropogenic climate warming to 1.5°C, this could happen only if "rapid," "unprecedented," and "far-reaching" changes were made worldwide across all sectors (Intergovernmental Panel on Climate Change [IPCC], 2018, p. 15). We are, however, on track for considerably greater warming of the atmosphere, which would have truly existential threats to humanity (D. Klein et al., 2017). The Sixth Assessment Report of the IPCC published in 2021—which many pundits came to refer to as "code red for humanity"—reaffirmed this (IPCC, 2021). Even if the world remained at the decreased level of emissions during the pandemic of COVID-19—a 7 percent decrease in 2020 compared to 2019 (Friedlingstein et al., 2020)—this would not be sufficient to limit the global temperature increase to 1.5°C. In fact, if we continued lowering emissions at the same rate every year, we would not get to zero net emissions until 2035, and even that may not be enough to remain within 1.5°C (Matthews & Tokarska, 2021).

Humans are not the only ones in peril: one-third of reef-building coral, a quarter of all mammal, a fifth of all reptile, and one-sixth of all bird species are expected to become extinct during the ongoing, human-made "sixth mass extinction" (Kolbert, 2015, pp. 15–17).[13] Neither is climate change the only environmental crisis we face. Biodiversity loss and ecosystem collapse are caused by a myriad of reasons other than the warming of the atmosphere, from chemical pollutants released into the environment to the damming of rivers to invasive species transported around the world through global trade and travel. And there's more—the crisis of phosphate and nitrogen cycles, overdraft of water reservoirs, overfishing, deforestation . . . the list goes on and on (cf. Bradshaw et al., 2021). This is a crisis unprecedented in human history, a crisis of the Anthropocene, as opposed to "merely" of the climate.

Crutzen was not the first person to notice the scale of human-induced environmental change; in fact, the idea had been around for decades, if not centuries.[14] In the twenty-first century, however, the scientific community started taking the notion seriously and went looking for the beginning of the Anthropocene, trying to identify "golden spikes," the traces of human activity that are identifiable across the earth's crust. Many possible starting points have been proposed, some going back thousands of years. While a decision has not been reached by the International Commission on Stratigraphy, three contenders seem to be in the lead:[15] 1610, a year that marks the lowest recorded levels of carbon dioxide as a result of the reduction in farming in the wake of the genocide of some 50 million Indigenous people in the Americas; 1776, the year James Watt invented the steam engine; and 1945, which brought the Trinity test, the first detonation of a nuclear bomb (Barker, 2013) and the beginning of the "Great Acceleration" of human activity on Earth (McNeill & Engelke, 2014).

All three years are intimately linked to colonial forms of extraction, and the debate remains influenced by Cold War ideologies.[16] Rather than a critical analysis of the power dynamics that led to the kind of Anthropocene we are now faced with, the debate revolves around who gets to claim primacy in "winning" over nature (Yusoff, 2018). For this reason, the controversy around the beginning year of this new age is of little relevance to my argument. What is more pertinent is how we got to this point and how we can get out of here. About the latter, Crutzen says, "A daunting task lies ahead for scientists and engineers to guide society towards environmentally sustainable management during the era of the Anthropocene. This will require appropriate human behavior at all scales, and may well involve internationally accepted large-scale geo-engineering projects, for instance, to 'optimize' climate" (as cited in Bonneuil & Fressoz, 2017, p. 81).[17] This may seem to be common sense in the context of the current obsession with technology as a panacea for all of humanity's problems, but there is, in fact, nothing self-evident about Crutzen's proposed solution. The Anthropocene represents people's desire to control nature, and "optimizing" climate or large-scale geoengineering are ways to further increase control.

The Anthropocene is not just about hard science; it is a cultural and political phenomenon too. The answers as to why control is at the heart of it can be gleaned from Amitav Ghosh's incisive analysis of twentieth-century literary trends:

> Jawaharlal Nehru's passion for dams and factories and Mao Zedong's "War on Nature" had their counterparts also in literature and the arts. . . . In Asia, as elsewhere, this meant that the abstract and the formal gained ascendancy over the figurative and the iconographic; it meant also that many traditions,

including those that accorded the non-human a special salience, were jettisoned. Here, as elsewhere, freedom came to be seen as a way of "transcending" the constraints of material life—of exploring new regions of the human mind, spirit, emotion, consciousness, interiority: freedom became a quantity that resided entirely in the minds, bodies, and desires of human beings. (2016, p. 161)

This literary imaginary also has its counterpart in twentieth-century political regimes across the world that, as James Scott (2008) pointed out, revolved around "high modernism," which meant achieving total human control over nature, including human nature. The Anthropocene is not accidental; it was willed into being through an imagining of anthropogenic hegemony.

This context allows us to tackle the question of responsibility for the Anthropocene's onset. Seeing a homogeneous *anthropos* as the reason behind the planet's new geological era would be a massive oversimplification. "This explanation might be sufficient for polar bears or orangutans seeking to understand what species was disturbing their habitat,"[18] but it is hardly sufficient for people who understand what is at stake and wonder what to do about it. Besides, claiming that humanity at large is responsible for the destructiveness of the Anthropocene is not merely simplistic but a form of epistemic violence. Kathryn Yusoff writes, "To be included in the 'we' of the Anthropocene is to be silenced by a claim to universalism that fails to notice its subjugations . . . legitimat[ing] and justif[ying] the racialized inequalities that are bound up in social geologies" (2018, p. 12). The Anthropocene is a seductive idea: while invoking apocalyptic visions, it also conveys a certain pride, a recognition of humankind's (but, really, just a small part of humanity's) ability to subjugate and transform that which it views as "sub-human"[19] (non-White people,[20] other life forms, the natural environment).

We may marvel at the Anthropocene in the same way that we marvel at the ingenuity of a skilled criminal. However, at least those of us who consider ourselves part of the "White liberal communities" are likely to, consciously or unconsciously, also feel a sense of racial pride and dominance, which is part of our socialization and cultural programming. The Anthropocene is an idea that can lead us down the path of imagining a White savior rescuing the planet—arguably the dream of many in Silicon Valley with their plans to solve the environmental crisis through technology alone, including by colonizing deep space. Elon Musk's article, "Making Humans a Multi-Planetary Species" (2017), is just one example of this trend. Such efforts to "fix" the Anthropocene signal "a desire to overcome coloniality without a corresponding relinquishing of the power it continues to generate in terms of who gets to formulate, implement, and speak to/of the future" (Yusoff, 2018, p. 27). Put simply, it is more of the same.

Multiple alternative labels have been put forward. For example, as the cumulative emissions by Great Britain and the United States amounted to "60 per cent of cumulative total emissions to date in 1900, 57 per cent in 1950 and almost 50 per cent in 1980," some have proposed renaming the Anthropocene to "Anglocene" (Bonneuil & Fressoz, 2017, p. 116). Another alternative term is Erik Swyngedouw's "Oliganthropocene," "a geological epoch caused by a small fraction of humanity" (Bonneuil & Fressoz, 2017, p. 71). The "Capitalocene" is another alternative proposed by Jason Moore (2017), who sees the environmental crisis as a consequence of the rise of capitalism, which began centuries before the industrial revolution (cf. Hickel, 2020a). What these alternatives have in common is that they focus on the unequal contribution of different groups of people (or economic systems/ ideologies) to the current crisis, highlighting the Anthropocene's lack of emphasis on the causes of and responsibility for environmental decay.

Although this is an apt critique, the concept of the Anthropocene is still pertinent to this book. "The Anthropocene" conveys the sheer magnitude of global, irreversible environmental change caused by humankind. Generally, I am not concerned with the hard science of environmental change nor the debates about when the Anthropocene began; those topics are exhaustively covered elsewhere.[21] What matters for the arguments presented in this book are the unprecedented urgency and unparalleled magnitude of responsibility young people are facing. To convey this gravity, a singular shared conception of the Anthropocene (one that acknowledges its imperial genetic makeup and the differential contributions of different peoples and economic/political systems) is a helpful metaphor. In this respect the "we" of the Anthropocene is truly all-encompassing of those living through the current historical moment (as well as all those not yet born).

Given my focus on the magnitude of the crisis, it may appear that I am using the term "Anthropocene" uncritically. However, its analytical power becomes clear when comparing the idea of "educating for the Anthropocene" to its much more famous and influential cousin that also refers to the current historical moment, "educating for the twenty-first century." The idea of twenty-first-century skills—information and communication technology competence, media literacy, critical thinking, and teamwork, among others (Voogt & Roblin, 2012)—has permeated many of the conversations about education reform, curriculum, and teacher training in the last two decades (C. Williams et al., 2013). This is an educational agenda informed by a technovision of the world, designed to produce workers for a global system of neoliberal capitalism that abides by the gospel of infinite growth and sees the natural environment as a resource to be exploited.

We can conceive of an "education for the Anthropocene" along parallel lines—as an instrumentalized form of education that is concerned with further cementing humankind's dominance over the planet and for which environmental degradation is merely a bump along the road of progress to be solved through technological innovation. This could not be *further* from what I mean when I put the four words—"educating," "for," "the Anthropocene"—together in the title of this book. So what *do* I mean by this title? Let's return to the story of Pashulok and Wentworth before I answer this question.

THE ANTHROPOCENE, BUREAUCRATIZATION, AND EDUCATION

The kind of depoliticization I observed during my interactions with Helen (the teacher we met in the dilemma preceding this introduction) is not constrained to South African townships; it is a transnational phenomenon, as I learned through my research in India. During an interview in Delhi in March 2017, Arnab, one of the environmental activists who tried to stop construction of the Tehri Dam, explained to me how India came to be obsessed with these megaprojects: "Water resource bureaucracy was developed and it became totally not only non-transparent and non-participatory and unaccountable but they actually justified it [by] saying it is a very techni-cal issue and only we know it and engineers know what needs to be done," he began. "The people" were unable to understand the highly technical nature of these projects, so only the views of the "experts" mattered. "Pandit Jawaharlal Nehru, by calling these projects 'temples of modern India,' actu-ally allowed them to be immune and outside the whole democratic set-up and democratic accountability," Arnab concluded. Damming India's rivers was, he noted, a bureaucratized process that undermined the civic equality among Indians that was needed for meaningful participation in shaping the country's development trajectory—a dynamic I explored extensively in my previous book *Visions of Development* (Sutoris, 2016).

Let's compare Arnab's views on dams with those of Trisha, a science teacher at Seema Primary, a government school in Pashulok where I did the bulk of my research in India. Trisha believed that "[Tehri] Dam is extremely beneficial for the entire Uttarakhand as well as for entire India . . . The elec-tricity which is being generated is being used in Uttarakhand and being sold to Uttar Pradesh and Delhi . . . The dam is a blessing as it will help in development."[22] When asked about the project's potential downsides, she commented, "There has been no harm and even if many trees were cut, the only harm was that people were resettled. But they have got land, houses and money. So, even if they earned their entire lives, they would not have been able to earn the amount of money they have received." Trisha was not alone in this view; all the teachers at Seema Primary expressed the belief that the environmental and human costs of Tehri Dam were negligible and could not begin to compare with the benefits. This was a closed matter and there was nothing to debate. The school seemed to be spreading the very ideology Arnab identified as the cause of India's state-sponsored destruction of the natural environment and the oustees'[23] ways of life.

Arnab's and Trisha's perspectives allow us to draw a parallel between the twenty-first century high-Anthropocene moment and the European totali-tarian regimes of the twentieth century. Hannah Arendt (1970), who studied these regimes, has argued that totalitarianism was possible because of the bureaucratization of entire swathes of population. People who unquestion-ingly follow in the blueprints designed by others, who may unwittingly become cogs in bureaucratic machines, often make for docile subjects that authoritarians need to succeed. Arendt famously wrote that "the sad truth is that most evil is done by people who never make up their minds to be good or evil" (1984, p. 28). This is certainly true of our era. If there are still historians writing centuries from now, they may well see our generations as culpable for the greatest violence and greatest evils in all of human history. Yet few of us wake up every morning and decide to destroy the natural environment and, with it, humanity's future.

There are indeed common denominators between the "fast violence" of Hitler's concentration camps or Stalin's gulags and anthropogenic slow violence. Arendt warns us that the most modern and most despotic of tyrannies is the rule of bureaucracy, "or the rule of an intricate system of bureaus in which no men, neither one nor the best, can be held responsible, and which could be properly called rule by Nobody" (1970, p. 38). Or, as Amos Elon summarized in his introduction to *Eichmann in Jerusalem*, "Evil comes from a failure to think. It defies thought for as soon as thought tries to engage itself with evil and examine the premises and principles from which it originates, it is frustrated because it finds nothing there. That is the banality of evil" (2006, p. xiv). If "banality of evil" was an appropriate description of the Nazi system of bureaucratization, it is just as apt to apply it to present-day slow violence. It is not that we are witnessing a worldwide conspiracy that seeks to turn schooling into a neoliberal brainwash (cf. Jain, 2013); rather, education itself has become bureaucratized, or at the very least it has failed to stand up to the self-destructive tendencies toward bureaucratization within the wider society.

This becomes clear when we consider the contemporary landscape of globalized formal education. It is marked by the often extrajudicial globalization of the models and practices of education governance (Ball, 2012).[24] This is linked to the advance of privatization and new financial models for managing state life (Nambissan, 2010),[25] transnational neoliberalism (Au & Ferrare, 2015; Ferguson & Gupta, 2005; Thapliyal, 2016), and testing regimes (Morgan, 2016; Morris, 2015). All of these phenomena represent a rapid global technocratization of schooling, often under the guise of seemingly benign labels like "evidence-based education."

With these thoughts in mind, let's return to the meaning of "educating for the Anthropocene." Against the backdrop of widespread bureaucratization as an enabling force for slow violence, the role of education must go far beyond social reproduction, beyond helping humanity develop new technologies, even beyond cultivating critical thinking among young people. What is needed is nothing short of a wholesale reimagining of the future, and this requires education that helps us envisage alternative futures and gives us tools to communicate our visions and agonize with others over their visions, helping us realize our agency as *political* beings. Critical thinking envisioned by proponents of twenty-first-century competencies may be a helpful skill, but if it is limited to thinking about a limited set of possible futures, it may not save us from becoming cogs in the Anthropocene's destructive processes, just as the educational accomplishments of Weimar Germany did not save millions of Germans from becoming complicit in the Holocaust. In other words, by de-instrumentalizing education and putting it out of service to the larger economic/political system, we may have a greater chance to succeed in confronting slow violence.

Educating for the Anthropocene encapsulates three key ingredients: radical imagination, agonistic pluralism, and intergenerational dialogue. I am not going to define these terms here; their definitions are grounded in the ethnographic narrative and articulated more fully in the conclusion. It is helpful, however, to ask what these concepts represent and to explain why I do not believe their inclusion is at odds with this book's goal to avoid being prescriptive.

These three ideas about education emerged from the accumulated ethnographic co-creation of knowledge with the many South Africans and Indians I was privileged to work with and learn from in the course of this project and the repeated, iterative bridging of this field knowledge with existing academic literature. There is no single interlocutor, event, sociocultural pattern, or scholarly perspective I can point to as their source. These three concepts are not meant to be comprehensive, definitive, nor generalizable, but they are intended to illuminate, guide, and stimulate. I hope they capture the insights that emerged from my research even if applying them to policy, curriculum design, or pedagogy in a particular place and at a particular time may require further layers of sociocultural translation.

EDUCATING FOR THE ANTHROPOCENE THROUGH THE LENS OF PUBLIC ANTHROPOLOGY

Now that we have looked at this book's purpose, let's examine its method. Why use ethnography? What can this approach add to existing research? Why should educators and activists care about what an anthropologist has to say about ESE?

Ethnography enables cultural translation. Through sustained, immersive field research, the ethnographer attains a level of depth that is rarely achieved in "fast" qualitative research. Ethnography relies on building real relationships with real people in the field, gaining their trust, and appreciating the complexities of their lived realities. Ethnographic immersion illuminates not only cultural and social patterns but also the underlying symbolic worlds of human beliefs, practices, rituals, relationships, hopes, and imaginations.

Equally important, ethnography allows meaningful co-creation of knowledge (R. Rosaldo, 1994) between the researcher and the interlocutors. Unlike in much quantitative and qualitative research, the field is not seen merely as a data source, where raw data are collected (and knowledge created elsewhere), but a site of knowledge production in its own right (cf. Connell, 2007). Put differently, ethnography allows us to tell a story that brings together many voices in what Van Maanen (2011, p. 8) calls "jointly told tales." This is particularly important in the context of the "Global South"[26] and postcolonial societies with a long and tragic history of exploitation and extraction of resources, including intellectual resources, by the West.[27]

The kind of ethnography that underpins this book—one that anthropologists refer to as multisited ethnography (Marcus, 1995)—also creates possibilities for multiple shifting frames of reference. Sometimes insights about the nature of particular phenomena may only come into view when looked at from the perspective of another "worlds-apart" location. An intergenerational trauma of displacement, as in Pashulok, shapes the cultural landscapes of imagination. Studying Pashulok's rupture is enriched when considered alongside a different trauma, such as the legacies of environmental racism and deadly air pollution in Wentworth. The two sites together also tell a story about global forces that may impact each of them differently but share important underlying characteristics, such as the hubris of (neo) colonialism-fueled global neoliberalism.[28]

Let me share an example of how the ethnographic journey shaped the narrative in this book. When my colleagues and friends asked me about my research in Pashulok and Wentworth in between my research trips to the sites, I would tell them it had two parts. The first sought to show the ways mainstream, state-run schooling in my research sites (and, arguably, around the globe) failed to respond to the challenges of the Anthropocene. Despite the optimism of the United Nations Educational, Scientific, and Cultural Organization (UNESCO) and other institutions that view education as a path toward sustainability, I would say to them, in some ways mainstream ESE made the world *less* sustainable. The second part explored the ways activist movements operating within the same communities may be able to fill the gaps left by schooling (e.g., through their efforts to encourage young people toward a politicized environmental agenda) and suggested ways that schooling may find inspiration in activism. The first part was the critique and the second part was the proposed solution.

But the more immersed in my field sites I became, the more this clear-cut distinction between activism and schooling seemed like a caricature of the research I was doing. I realized that the two phenomena interacted with each other and with countless social, cultural, economic, and historical factors and that neither impacted young people's imaginations of the future in predictable, linear ways. The filmmaking component of my research showed this very clearly. For example, in one of the student films shot in South Africa, *Wentworth Changing to Progress,* the children included a scene about "Dance Moves," a modern dance class for young people in South Durban (figure 1.4). In this sequence, the viewer gets to see young people of different ages and skin colors dancing, smiling, and apparently having a good time. These shots are interwoven with segments of interviews with the organizers, who are not much older than the participants. These facilitators talk about

Figure 1.4
"Dance Moves" in Wentworth through the lens of a student film.

their hopes for the community, which lie in the potential they see in young people. When I spoke to Mimi, one of the student filmmakers, she told me she hoped the viewer would take away from the film that "Wentworth is not only a bad place, that people care about our community." This contestation of stereotypes about Wentworth implied a recognition of a kind of politics in which the "horizons of the possible" can be extended through collective action. The aesthetics of the sequence mirrored this: the images are carefully composed with wide shots focusing on natural scenery very different from Wentworth's industrial landscape. As a result, the sequence may appear out of place, and the activity does indeed take place on nearby Treasure Beach, a seaside area over the hill from Wentworth. It was as if, through their choice of subject and the deliberate framing and sequencing of shots,[29] Mimi and her friends were saying that the youth of Wentworth deserved to live in a space devoid of environmental threats and injustice.

I revisited each site multiple times over a period of three years, asking questions I would not think to ask initially and deepening relationships with my interlocutors. I witnessed changes in the community over time, adding to my understanding of the national and regional political, social, and economic developments as well as the history of the sites. This led to an iterative spiral of questioning that helped clarify my vision. One of the realizations that emerged from this process was that my research was about not just trying to understand the meaning of education in the face of unprecedented historical responsibility but also building a bridge between public anthropology and ESE.

Public anthropology, the effort to bring anthropology's tools and insights to the forefront of social change, has so far largely avoided ESE. Yet it is a field full of inspiration for how we may approach education in the Anthropocene anthropologically. Books like Seth Holmes' *Fresh Fruit, Broken Bodies* (2013) have demonstrated the great potential of public anthropology in the face of contemporary global challenges. Holmes' book is a fascinating story of Mexican migrant workers on US farms that engages both the mind (by exposing the reader to the complex calculus of economic incentives that migrants learn to compute instinctively) and the heart (by letting the reader experience the incredible hardships and injustices the workers suffer at the hands of a heartless political and economic system). Laurence Ralph's *Torture Letters* (2020) about police brutality against African Americans in Chicago, Claire Wendland's *A Heart for the Work* (2010) about what it is like to go through medical school in Malawi, Sienna Craig's *The Ends of Kinship* (2020) about Himalayan diasporic lives in Nepal and New York, and Ruth Behar's partly autobiographical *The Vulnerable Observer* (1996) are exemplars of a powerful integration of rigorous, slow, deeply illuminating research with the political project of addressing the big questions. While each of these ethnographers wrestles with issues of representation and ethnographic authority, this is engaged ethnography (Hale, 2006) in action—an effort that, in Philippe Bourgois's words, "combine[s] a practical politics of solidarity with reflexive theoretical critiques to engage the high stakes of everyday life" (2008, p. xii).[30] What this tradition of engaged public anthropology teaches us is that, however fraught with inequality and the researcher's inability to grasp fully the realities of the research participants, being "engaged" is what makes ethnography come alive, what imbues it with hope, and what makes it relevant. Shining the light of public anthropology on ESE is the most relevant research endeavor I can think of in the Anthropocene.

Such an endeavor seeks to make a difference not just to the theory but also to the practice of education in the Anthropocene. In this book, you will encounter multiple publics of educators, activists, young people, and community members. What the activists in Pashulok and in Wentworth had in common was their limited reach and a separation from formal education. I found in both countries that environmental educators and environmental activists were often two distinct camps that were suspicious of each other: educators often saw activists as radical antisystem agitators, while activists considered educators complicit in the status quo. In other words, even if activists had the resources to politicize the environmental, their potential was often untapped, at least when it came to formal education. The ethnographic project in such a fractured space represents a call to mend the fissures, helping to make possible a vision of a more unified public sphere by making conversations happen between unlikely groups of people. The bifurcation between schooling and activism in the context of ESE as portrayed in this book can serve as an impetus for anthropology to reflect on its social role and potential as a force for change beyond exposing readers to nuanced and deeply felt "thick descriptions" (Geertz, 1973) of the big issues of the day. The bridge between public anthropology and ESE is, in other words, a two-way street.

Having discussed the concepts behind this book's title and public anthropology's relationship with ESE, let's now refine the questions about the meaning of education in the Anthropocene. The countless ethnographic encounters in the field during the course of the five years I spent working on this project have led me to revisit and reimagine these questions many times: What are the degrees of politicization enacted by intergenerational knowledge transfer in the context of schooling and activism? Who, among teachers, activists, and community members in Pashulok and Wentworth, are the bearers of the "horizons of the possible"? What role do education spaces—schools, community narratives, social movements—play in this knowledge transfer? What are the mechanisms of state learning for young people and how do they shape or undermine their visions of alternative futures? How do young people understand and narrate their historical responsibility for the environment vis-à-vis the dead and the unborn? How do slow violence and the highly advanced marginality experienced by these young people mediate or mitigate their capacity for historical responsibility, and what can an ethnographer do to enhance the potential for a recognition of historical responsibility? And last but not least, how may this form of responsibility be realized or hindered as a consequence of their experiences on the "frontier of the high Anthropocene"?

ON THE HIGH ANTHROPOCENE'S FRONTIER: ENVIRONMENTAL LEARNING IN INDIA AND SOUTH AFRICA

What do I mean by the "frontier of the high Anthropocene"? It is being "ahead of time," experiencing in the here and now a level of environmental decay that the rest of the world has yet to experience, that puts a place on the high Anthropocene's frontier. Such places allow us to make informed forecasts about the future of the rest of the world. Identifying these spaces as high Anthropocene's frontiers can help us appreciate the broader significance of the ways in which environmental learning happens here.

These are liminal spaces visibly and viscerally affected by environmental destruction. The idea of liminality has been used in anthropology to describe in-betweenness, a place of ambiguity between the previous state and the next. For example, rites of passage in many cultures transform people's identities, leaving them in a state of confusion during the process (van Gennep, 2019; cf. Thomassen, 2013). But the concept of liminality has also been used to talk about the anticipation of a deepening crisis, a sense of impending gloom (Thomassen, 2016).[31] In Pashulok and Wentworth, development projects the modernist promise of prosperity while importing toxic by-products from the territories where modernity has already established its hegemony.[32] This push and pull keeps these spaces in what Thomassen calls the "permanentization of liminality" (2009, p. 22). In other words, Pashulok and Wentworth are torn between the unfulfilled promises of development and paying the price for others' development. This is a liminal predicament that may become the fate of entire future generations who will pay the price for the environmental degradation caused by (a fraction of) those who lived before them.

In understanding the idea of the "frontier of the high Anthropocene," it is also helpful to think with the anthropologist Anna Tsing, who speaks of friction—"the awkward, unequal, unstable and creative qualities of interactions across difference" (Tsing, 2005, p. 4) where local realities meet large ideas. The friction experienced in the high Anthropocene's frontier spaces such as Pashulok and Wentworth between globalized slow violence and the localized agency of communities manifests in activism. The "permanentization of liminality" and "friction of activism" in Pashulok and Wentworth are what futurologists call "weak signals" (Ansoff, 1975; Holopainen & Toivonen, 2012)—hints about the nature of likely future worlds that manifest in the present.

Pashulok and Wentworth show us that the high Anthropocene's frontier is a space of precarity, ambivalence, and permanent crisis. This condition is, to a large extent, caused by the historical context of the nation-states within which they are located. Let's now turn to a brief exploration of the history of these states in an effort to understand how Pashulok and Wentworth arrived at the frontier of the high Anthropocene.

As the sociologist Patrick Heller contends (2001, p. 150), India and South Africa are "arguably the most successful cases of democratic consolidation in the developing world."[33] He points out that "their respective transitions were driven by broad-based, encompassing, secular, pan-racial/pan-ethnic movements deeply rooted in civil society. Because political society was the domain of European elites, the liberation struggle in both countries evolved and mobilised through structures of civil society (unions, schools, communities, peasant associations, religious organisations) and relied heavily on rich, domestic narratives of resistance" (Heller, 2001, p. 153).

And yet, despite this history, democratic institutions that are formally in place in both countries often lack the corresponding participation of the disadvantaged "masses" in policy decisions, leaving these states in a kind of unfulfilled, liminal democracy. The gap between the freedom fighters' aspirations and the everyday lived realities of Indians and South Africans is one of the clues history gives us as to how these spaces arrived at the high Anthropocene's frontier.

In India, this gap can be partly traced to the history of colonialism and of uprooting millions of people in the name of development.[34] In South Africa, the racialized legacy of apartheid underpinned by a cultural and political heritage of settler colonialism is among the contributing factors. Imperialism and racism, which are inscribed in the histories of these two countries, represent two of the main forces Hannah Arendt (1962) identified as the causes of twentieth-century totalitarian regimes. These regimes have more in common with Anthropocenic dystopia than meets the eye, and the frontier of the high Anthropocene is where this convergence becomes most visible.

To a historian of India, widespread bureaucratization that interferes with the functioning of Indian democracy is not surprising. As Ludden (1992) has argued, the independent Indian state inherited a bureaucratic apparatus from the colonial period in which self-proclaimed experts determined the country's future on behalf of the "masses." Five-year plans inspired by the Soviet Union were seen as too complex to be grasped by the "average" Indian, which led to a lack of transparency and accountability in governance (Zachariah, 2005, 2012). Large dams, which were given the status of a secular religion (Khilnani, 2012), are perhaps the most grandiose manifestation of this authoritarian tendency (Jalal, 2009) of the Indian state. Since India's economic reforms of 1991, we can add neoliberalism to the list of bureaucratizing and antidemocratic forces in the country (Ganguly-Scrase & Scrase, 2008; Panagariya, 2005; Varshney, 1998), and since the 2014 elections, the takeover of the government by illiberal Hindu nationalists (Blom Hansen, 2019; Komireddi, 2019; Palshikar, 2019); both are examined in chapter 3.

The disconnect between the democratic promise and lived reality is perhaps even more pronounced in South Africa. Take the country's constitution: Section 24 reads, "Everyone has the right to an environment that is not harmful to their health or well-being; and to have the environment protected, for the benefit of present and future generations" (Republic of South Africa, 2015, p. 9).[35] And yet, South Africa "remains one of the world's most dangerous environments in which to live and work" (Bond & Hallowes, 2002, p. 45). This is due in part to the historical legacy of the eugenicist (Dubow, 1995; Klausen, 2018) and totalitarian apartheid regime of 1948 to 1993, in which non-White people were considered disposable; to the country's neoliberal economic orientation, which has seen a massive increase in unemployment and inequality (Russell, 2010); and to the

Figure 1.5
"Everyday life" in Wentworth.

successive governments' lack of attention to environmental issues (Bond & Hallowes, 2002).

This historical analysis rings true when you visit South Durban. The township of Wentworth (figure 1.5), my research site, is home to approximately forty thousand Coloured people and dates back to the early 1960s when, because of the implementation of the apartheid government's Group Areas Act of 1950, many Coloured people were forcibly relocated here from across the city and from places as far as the Eastern Cape (Anderson, 2009, p. 58). Subsequently, according to Chari (2006a, p. 123), the township "retreat[ed] into a local world that becomes increasingly parochial, trapping its itinerant population of labourers and their families in a local world of gangs, churches, artisans and a bittersweet affirmation of the ghetto."

Today, the township, like many others in South Africa, is notorious for crime, gang violence, drug use, teenage pregnancies, prostitution, and high human immunodeficiency virus (HIV) rates. Wentworth is located directly on the fence line of Engen, South Africa's oldest oil refinery, which has a dismal environmental record.[36] Along with other heavy industries situated in

South Durban's Industrial Basin, which have accounted for 8 percent of the country's gross domestic product (GDP) (Aylett, 2010a, p. 484), its emissions contribute to the "toxic soup" (Chari, 2006b, p. 428) in which people live. Apart from sky-high rates of thyroid cancer, leukemia, and asthma (Kistnasamy et al., 2008; R. N. Naidoo et al., 2013; Nriagu et al., 1999), frequent industrial accidents, including fires and explosions, threaten the residents (D. Scott & Barnett, 2009). The state's failures in Wentworth can also be seen in the area of education. Not only was Durban South Primary, the school where I undertook my research, made of "cardboard"[37] (figure 1.6) and lacking in basic amenities, but the kind of education it provided was more likely to help maintain the intergenerational cycle of poverty and exclusion than break it. While such schooling may be highly prevalent in low-income postcolonial states, the effects of the depoliticization and social reproduction are heightened and more visible on the frontier of the high Anthropocene, where environmental threats are imminent and ubiquitous.

It is perhaps here—at the intersection of "advanced marginality" (Wacquant, 2016, p. 1078), regional deprivation, and bureaucracy—that we find

Figure 1.6
The view from a school corridor, Wentworth.

some of the defining features of schooling on the high Anthropocene's frontier in Pashulok and Wentworth.[38] Both Seema Primary in Pashulok and Durban South Primary in Wentworth relied heavily on textbooks and teaching to the test, a rigid disciplinary regime was maintained in both, and neither seemed to encourage independent thinking. Students and their families saw education as a way to get a job that would allow for a barely-out-of-poverty existence. The natural environment was rarely mentioned, and even on those few occasions it was, teachers explored it through the lens of individual, depoliticized actions. The overarching political and cultural landscapes of schooling in Pashulok and Wentworth demonstrated a remarkable degree of similarity—an unfortunate testament to the globalization of the kind of education that not only is unfit to meet the challenges of the Anthropocene but in fact adds to them.

It is symbolic of the oustees' predicament that the school where I did my research in Pashulok sat, or perhaps more appropriately, squatted, inside a shopping complex (figure 1.7). In addition to their history of environmental

Figure 1.7
A shopping complex in Pashulok that hosted a school on its first floor.

activism together with the Chipko movement and its leader Sunderlal Bahuguna,[39] at the time of my research, the residents of Pashulok were engaged in protesting the government's handling of compensation for resettlement. Nakul, one man I interviewed, highlighted the many injustices of the process: "We were given ₹1.5 lakh, but that was spent on shifting. Now we are struggling to find ways to build a house. How is that compared to our house back in the village, which had six rooms, a cowshed, and a lawn with litchi, apricot, papaya, lemon, and jackfruit trees?" Perhaps even more troubling is that the oustees were seeing their communities fall apart, causing a breakdown of social cohesion and solidarity. Of the approximately five thousand oustees, some 60 percent had reportedly sold their houses and left by the time I conducted my field research.[40] Nakul continued: "Earlier there was unity among villages and villagers. There was a system of canals for irrigation. If there was some damage somewhere resulting from rain or other causes, we had a water guard, who would alert us and all the villagers would come together to repair any damage in the canal or river dam without any fee or without the help of the authorities." But the times have changed.

The new times brought not only social breakdown but also the rise of environmental community activism. As David, one of the activists in South Africa, told me, "We've come out of apartheid and the constitution says you will have economic development while protecting the environment, and the word is 'while,' not 'after.'" According to David, postapartheid governments did not deliver—not on the question of environmental protection or on a host of other issues. Desmond (Des) D'Sa, the leader of the South Durban Community Environmental Alliance (SDCEA)—an activist group I explore in depth in chapter 5—told me that the 1990s were marked by "a false sense of hope because little did we realize that the very same people that we had put into government is [sic] going to turn on its own people. So we got all the freedom, but we haven't got the jobs, we haven't got the services, we haven't got leaders that are capable of serving us, they are serving their own interest and cost of living has gone up."

The activists offered a notion of an engaged citizenry that collectively imagines a shared future and rectifies what they see as a lack of civic engagement in both countries. Some emphasized their concern for future generations and were seeking to mobilize an alternative understanding of development, state, and citizenship. Activism took different forms in the two sites, operating within an institutionalized framework in Wentworth and in a much less organized fashion in Pashulok. Its emphases in the two locations reflected the distinct historical, cultural, and socioeconomic context of each (explored in detail in chapter 5). But in both of these frontier spaces, activism exposed the liminal condition of being stuck between a promise of politics and reality of everyday life, a dynamic analogous to the Anthropocene's liminal condition between states' outward commitment to sustainability and the hard facts of irreversible environmental degradation. And in both sites, activists appeared to be in sync with the times, reminding me of a remark by Attallah Shabazz, one of Malcolm X's daughters, found in the epigraph of this book, in which she muses that perhaps it was not her father who was ahead of his time, but that the rest of us were late.

Clearly, activism and schooling on the frontier of the high Anthropocene are worlds apart. But is it possible to imagine a world in which education is no longer synonymous with depoliticization and bureaucratization and aligns itself with the "right side of the barricade"? In the next chapter I consider previous research and the theoretical tools that can shed light on this question, but for now I would like to bring Hannah Arendt back into the discussion. In her postmortem of the Nazi regime (and Eichmann's trial in Jerusalem), she asserted that totalitarianism sought to create "holes of oblivion into which all deeds, good and evil, would disappear. . . . The holes of oblivion do not exist. Nothing human is that perfect, and there are simply too many people in the world to make oblivion possible" (Arendt, 2006, pp. 232–233). The more time I spent at my research sites, the more I felt this sentiment, and the more potential I saw in the interface between education and activism. For all its gloomy content, this book seeks above all to illuminate the often unnoticed but important corners of hope where there is no space for oblivion. They just might help us survive the Anthropocene.

2 A BITTERSWEET LANDSCAPE

> Contemporary environmental education . . . has the revolutionary pur-
> pose of transforming the values that underlie our decision making . . .
> This contrasts with the traditional purpose of schools . . . of conserving the
> existing social order by reproducing the norms and values that currently
> dominate environmental decision making.
> —R. Stevenson, "Schooling and environmental education: Contradictions
> in purpose and practice," p. 145

Witnessing the scenes of the Tehri Dam and South Durban made the Anthropocene's environmental multicrisis seem palpable, prompting me to wonder how we got to this point. To achieve harmony and agreement on what is to be done with the Earth and its resources across so many countries, cultures, and languages is a feat that makes the Roman Empire's range seem trivial. The science and the engineering skill behind the megaprojects of modernity owe much to the phenomenon of mass schooling, as does the cultural sculpting that has been necessary to convert very different groups of people to a single gospel—that of endless economic growth within the context of neoliberal capitalism.[1] Formal education is not the only reason we are where we are, but it certainly is one of the main reasons.

Looking over the register of people considered to be the most influen-tial thinkers on the subject of education,[2] I wonder who called for formal education to help jumpstart the Anthropocene? Was it Socrates, with his dictum that the unexamined life is not worth living (Rembert, 1995, p. 98)? Immanuel Kant in his conception of moral education (Moran, 2009)?

Friedrich Nietzsche, who believed that education is meant to bring us "above the decadent values of mass culture" (Johnston, 1998, p. 74)? We could consider many such examples, but the pattern is clear: none of these ideas points in the direction of the environmental destruction unleashed on the planet in the last two centuries. All these thinkers would likely be horrified to see the Anthropocene we have created.

Still, we should not give up on education as one of the forces capable of transforming the future. That is this chapter's central argument. As much as education may have indeed been one of the main culprits in molding a "human monoculture" (M. S. Prakash & Esteva, 2008, p. 24) that is at the root of the unfolding environmental destruction, many of the ideas and practices associated with education—both within formal schooling systems and in noninstitutional spaces—show considerable promise in charting a different path forward. For all the bureaucratization and alignment with neoliberal (neo)colonial ideologies, the field also contains many gems of ideas and practices that can inspire a shift toward "educating for the Anthropocene." In this chapter, I explore this bittersweet, self-contradictory landscape to help us contextualize the ethnographic narrative that follows, to identify the points of resonance and dissonance between the stories of Pashulok and Wentworth and the existing research, debates, and theoretical frameworks. It is not necessary to read this chapter for the ethnographic narrative of the following chapters to make sense, and readers not interested in theory can feel free to skip ahead to chapter 3. However, I believe these ideas are helpful thinking tools for exploring the ways in which the story of Pashulok and Wentworth helps us understand what education in the Anthropocene may mean.

It is beyond this book's scope to provide a comprehensive overview of all the literature and theory pertinent to educating for the Anthropocene, and neither is this my goal. This book tells a story rather than providing a theoretical treatise, and I focus on several strands of research and theoretical thinking that are particularly relevant to this story and its wider implications. The first section highlights the contradiction between the expectation that education is a key part of the solution of the environmental multicrisis and a depoliticized, instrumentalized mainstream definition of sustainability. The second section considers the proposed alternatives, including critical perspectives about (de)politicization among ESE scholars, research about activist educators, ecopedagogy (an ESE alternative with roots in Paulo Freire's pedagogy of liberation), as well as deschooling and Indigenous knowledge. The third, final section ventures into deeper philosophical waters and builds on the discussion of the relevance of Hannah Arendt and Paul Ricœur's thought to the study of ESE in the Anthropocene. The section outlines ideas of historical responsibility and the "debt to the dead" and "debt to the unborn," which are, I argue, helpful theoretical frameworks for us to think with as we ponder the (de)politicizing effects of schooling and activism in Pashulok, Wentworth, and beyond. Together, these three sections can be read as a manifesto for the need for us to focus on how we educate in the Anthropocene, underscoring the relevance and urgency of the story told in the remaining chapters of this book.

THE PARADOX OF SUSTAINABILITY AND EDUCATION IN THE ANTHROPOCENE

How do we "fix" the environmental crises at the heart of the Anthropocene? Although scholars have proposed different solutions to different aspects of this multicrisis—climate change,[3] biodiversity loss, the acidification of the oceans—there are areas of agreement. Substantial changes in education systems underpin the theory of change of most proposed solutions, from curbing consumption (Ivanova et al., 2016; Wackernagel & Rees, 1998; Young et al., 2010), replacing economic growth by de-growth (Alier, 2009; Hickel, 2020b; Kallis, 2011; Kallis et al., 2020; Schneider et al., 2010)[4] and drastic population control (Dukes, 2011), to "ecosystemic reflexivity" of institutions (Dryzek, 2016, p. 937),[5] geoengineering (Crutzen & Stoermer, 2000; Vaughan & Lenton, 2011; Wigley, 2006), fostering "circular economies" (Lieder & Rashid, 2016), and inspiring a "fourth industrial revolution" aimed at creating more sustainable technologies (Schwab, 2016).[6] All these ideas rely on changing our methods for educating future generations. As Robert Stratford (2019, p. 149) said, "[I]n the process of more carefully considering our interconnected natural, social and intellectual systems [in the Anthropocene], it seems likely that new approaches to education need to be part of this process."

While the central role of education is indeed enshrined in the United Nations (UN) Sustainable Development Goals (SDGs)—a set of targets shaping much of the governmental, intergovernmental, philanthropic, and for-profit development work around the globe (United Nations, 2018)— this is not necessarily good news. Although the SDGs are often uncritically accepted among policy-makers and scholars alike as the desirable global direction of travel, they in fact represent a form of technocratic instrumentalization and bureaucratized rationality that can get in the way of educating for the Anthropocene. Their focus on largely predetermined, quantifiable outcomes mirrors the testing regimes that have come to dominate the global education landscape. As Derek Hodson said, such regimes are "philosophically unsound (because they are rarely, if ever, based on a valid model of science or scientific literacy), educationally worthless (because they trivialize teaching and learning), pedagogically dangerous (because they foster bad teaching), professionally debasing (because they de-skill teachers), socially undesirable (because they project a number of powerful messages about control and compliance) and morally repugnant (because they objectify people, regard knowledge as a commodity to be traded for marks)" (2011, p. 303). These are just some of the reasons why the SDGs, under whose banner these testing regimes are often promoted, are at odds with educating for the Anthropocene.

A key factor behind this fundamental incompatibility is the definition of "sustainability" at the root of the SDGs. While many earlier understandings of the concept reflected in religion and Indigenous cultures emphasized the importance of living in harmony with nature and preserving the natural environment (Mebratu, 1998, p. 498), such understandings of sustainability would be considered radical by many of today's standards. The 1987 Brundtland Commission's report, "Our Common Future," defined sustainable development as "development that meets the needs of the present without compromising the ability of future generations to meet their own needs" (The World Commission on Environment and Development, 1987) and called for a "5–10-fold increase in gross world industrial activity over the next century to meet the needs of the poor" (J. Robinson, 2004, p. 372). This definition, which departs from earlier ideas of environmental sustainability and calls for increased production rather than redistribution as a solution to inequality, continues to be influential well into the twenty-first century (Griggs et al., 2013; Sneddon et al., 2006).[7] Without a notion of sustainability that "accepts that there are critical ecological limitations that must be addressed, the crucial potential of education is missed because, under the weaker notion, nearly every status quo can be defended as sustainable" (Holfelder, 2019, p. 950)—and this is exactly what the SDGs are enabling.

The current SDG framework defines sustainability as relying on three pillars—"economic growth, social inclusion and environmental protection" (United Nations, 2015). Yet a close reading of the SDGs points to the primacy of the economic over the environmental and the social in the accepted notion of sustainability. As Hannah Weber (2017, p. 400) has argued, "the implementation of highly contested neoliberal policies is itself part of the explicit goals of the SDG framework," as reflected, for example, in SDG 10, whose targets are "revealing about the centrality accorded to economic growth—rather than a commitment to redistribution—as the means to reducing inequality" (p. 404). SDG 4, which concerns education, has been criticized along the same lines. According to Elena VanderDussen Toukan (2017, p. 296), "The language of 'quality education' and 'lifelong learning opportunities' is left ambiguous in the SDGs, seemingly open to interpretation." This is problematic, since, "as standardized testing regimes are justified as the primary indicator for 'quality' . . . measuring and ranking content proficiency belies any claim to curricular neutrality. Erosion of local systems, processes, possibilities—and education's role in it—continues today" (VanderDussen Toukan, 2017, p. 306). In other words, SDG 4 opens the door to (and offers a justification for) using education as a tool to maintain and reproduce a global economic (neoliberal) regime at the expense of the social and the environmental.

Education within the context of SDGs is thus paradoxical in that it claims to be aiming for a sociopolitical transformation but in fact reinforces the status quo. Or, as Richard Kahn, a scholar of ecopedagogy (about whose work I say more below), writes, environmental literacy has "in an Orwellian turn . . . come to stand in actuality for a real illiteracy about the nature of ecological catastrophe, its causes, and possible solutions" (2010, p. 9). As Smith (2005) points out, in the context of neoliberal sustainability, "the 'responsibilities' we are called on to exercise . . . involve little out of the ordinary—drive a few miles less, recycle plastic containers, compost organic waste, and so on. These 'acts' are, in fact, largely apolitical in an Arendtian sense . . . They usually do not initiate anything new, nor offer any real possibility for the individual to change the world; rather they become a means for ameliorating some of modernity's excesses" (p. 58).

Within the confines of "apolitical" ESE, these acts take place through an "individualization of responsibility." As Maniates (2001, p. 33) writes, "when responsibility for environmental problems is individualized, there is little room to ponder institutions, the nature and exercise of political power, or ways of collectively changing the distribution of power and influence in society—to, in other words, 'think institutionally.'" The transformative potential of education is subdued by recognizing only nonradical, individualized action as worth striving for, thus placing constraints on young people's imaginations of both their present and future political agency.

In light of these arguments, it is hard not to see the idea of sustainable development, in its SDG variety, as an oxymoron (Caradonna, 2017). If the goal of development is to convert all national economies to the gospel of endless economic growth and sustainability is disconnected from social and intergenerational justice, then the natural environment (and the sociocultural fabric of humanity) cannot be sustained under a "sustainable development" regime. This was made clear in the Club of Rome's 1972 seminal report, *The Limits to Growth* (Meadows, 1972), and in countless publications since (F. Hirsch, 1977; N. Klein, 2014; Meadows et al., 2006; Steffen et al., 2007, 2015), including Foster's (2002, p. 26) call to end the "ecological tyranny of the bottom line."[8] Echoes of a critical approach to the political and economic status quo can also be found in the Belgrade Charter of 1975, one of the foundational documents of ESE (United Nations Environment Programme, 1975).[9]

Current levels of consumption are unsustainable, suggesting that a net *de*growth of the global economy is needed to bring the world closer to sustainability (in its older, "radical" definition). Bond and Hallowes (2002, p. 30) made the issue with sustainable development clear: "Occasionally . . . this strand of thinking does actually grapple with capitalism's ability to consume and accumulate beyond the limits of the biosphere. Yet the main point behind the sustainable development thesis is a technical and reformist one, namely that environmental externalities such as pollution should, in the classical example, be brought into the marketplace." The advent of the "human age" makes such logic harder and harder to sustain. As Bonneuil and Fressoz (2017, p. 20) argue, "the concept of the Anthropocene challenges this separation [of growth and nature] and the promise to perpetuate our economic system by modifying it at the margin. In place of 'environment,' there is now the Earth system." The oxymoronic nature of the accepted notion of sustainable development, and the underlying neoliberal dynamics it aims to cover up, are growing ever more discernible.

What might an alternative to this global political regime look like, and what is the role of education in bringing it about? Much of the "radical" writing on the environmental crisis calls for "eco-socialism" (Angus, 2016; Barkdull & Harris, 2015) or a left turn in politics (Chomsky, 2016) as a solution. But the problem is not so trivial as to be fixed by simply replacing one economic system by another, as Shrivastava and Kothari (2012) aptly point out. Their argument is "not just against market capitalism, in which TNCs (Trans-National Corporations) compete for political influence and economic dominance. We stand as much against state socialism, in which nation states compete for economic influence and political dominance. Under the competitive conditions of industrial modernity, the race towards a socialist utopia paves the way to ecological dystopia no less than the paradise dreamt up by enthusiastic neo-liberals. The ecological debris left behind by the carcass of Soviet communism after its official end in 1990 stands as a testimony to this" (Shrivastava & Kothari, 2012, p. 243).[10] Socialism is not the antidote for capitalism, at least when it comes to anthropogenic slow violence.

This conclusion brings us to a larger point—educating for the Anthropocene is not about promoting any particular political regime. As Holfelder has argued, much of the mainstream ESE sees the future as "something which you cannot shape but which acts on you [. . .] rather than something formable which would give individuals an alternative other than submission" (Holfelder, 2019, p. 948). A necessary step toward educating for the Anthropocene is a departure from this fatalistic perception and seeing the future as "open" instead of "closed"; this means "tak[ing] current educational systems and today's society with their non-sustainable future-building practices into account, because otherwise ESD would not make any difference to the educational and societal status quo" (Holfelder, 2019, p. 943).

Another clue to possible alternatives can be found in a recent empirical study whose findings suggest that individualism gets in the way of actions that might help to "fix" the Anthropocene. Komatsu, Rappleye, and Silova (2019) showed that "individualistic" societies—that is, those where a belief in independent selfhood/autonomous competitive citizens is dominant, particularly Anglo-American countries—contribute to environmental decay more than less individualistic societies—those where a belief in interdependent selfhood prevails, such as some of the countries in Asia and Latin America.[11] The study also reported statistically significant findings confirming its subhypotheses: that people in more individualistic societies tend to believe less in human (anthropogenic) causes of environmental degradation, that this prevents people living in such societies from consciously organizing proenvironmental behavior, and that even among countries with similar levels of anthropogenic perception, the more individualistic ones have a larger negative environmental impact "due to less self-control when facing trade-offs between individual and social benefits" (Komatsu et al., 2019, p. 1). The study points to a potentially significant relationship between a society's cultural beliefs and practices and the way it deals with slow violence. While Komatsu et al. (2019) did not prove a causal effect of culture, they suggested that in less individualistic countries a perception of interdependence between people may extend to a recognition of interdependence between humanity and the natural environment. In such countries, they also suggested, deliberation and dialogue may be fostered more than in more individualistic societies, potentially making it easier to identify and address environmental issues.

This is consistent with Bruno Latour's contention that "the critic is not the one who lifts the rugs from under the feet of the naïve believers, but the one who offers the participants arenas in which to gather" (Latour, 2004, p. 246). Cultivating such arenas calls for "an understanding of how the political becomes pedagogical, particularly in terms of how private issues are connected to larger social conditions and collective force—that is, how the very processes of learning constitute the political mechanisms through which identities are shaped and desires mobilized" (Giroux, 2004, p. 62).[12] Arendt (1998, p. 188) asserts that it is in such spaces—and only in such spaces—that "action" emerges: "Action . . . is never possible in isolation; to be isolated is to be deprived of the capacity to act." Put differently, action is only possible through the multiplicity of perspectives inherent in the shared human condition. Cultivating the capacity to act—not in an instrumental sense with the aim of any predefined outcomes but with an openness to the promise of politics—whether through schooling, activism, or other modalities of education, has the potential to help us reimagine (and transform) the Anthropocene.

A TAPESTRY OF CRITICAL PERSPECTIVES

The idea that education is a key component of charting a different future resonates with scholarship across several areas. In this section, I will explore the work of ESE scholars, the research about activist educators, ecopedagogy, and the ideas of deschooling and Indigenous knowledge. The concept of "educating for the Anthropocene" builds on the insights from all of these fields, even as it seeks to chart a slightly different trajectory from each of the authors who have contributed to this "tapestry of critical perspectives" about environmental learning at a time of environmental multicrisis.

(De)Politicization of the Environment and ESE Research
A concern with politics has long resonated with the work of scholars who have theorized the interface between education and sustainability. Stephen Sterling argued in 1996 that education for sustainability that is suited to twenty-first-century challenges must be "ideologically aware and socially critical" (p. 23). A decade later, Vare and Scott (2007) made a distinction between "ESD (Education for Sustainable Development) 1," which promotes behavioral change among students, and "ESD 2," which lies in "building capacity to think critically about [and beyond] what experts say and to test sustainable development ideas . . . exploring the contradictions inherent in sustainable living" (p. 194). According to these authors, the two

approaches must be combined if ESD programs are to be effective. They argue that a dominance of ESD 1 approaches has, in fact, undermined the sustainability agenda—a view echoed by Sund and Ohman (2014), who argue that "unmasking the political dimension" (p. 639) of sustainability discourse is necessary for ESE to succeed. McKenzie (2012) goes further in her critique, pointing to the need to interrogate critically the influence of advanced neoliberalism on articulations of sustainability policy, including the SDGs and ESE. Recognizing the diverse understandings of "politics" in this literature, Håkansson, Östman, and Van Poeck (2018) developed a typology of four different categories of what they call the political tendency in ESE—democratic participation, political reflection, political deliberation, and political moment.

Several of these categories—political deliberation in particular—align with Arendt's definition of the "political." Levy and Zint (2013) suggest that the ESE field can learn from established research in political science and education in "prepar[ing] students to participate in political processes to address major environmental problems" (p. 568), a notion that supports civic equality and which Arendt emphasizes as a precondition for political action. Focusing less on participation and more on awareness, Räthzel and Uzzell (2009) argue for educating young people about the power structures underlying global production and consumption. This idea, too, would resonate with Arendt, who suggests that "the more we think of the political realm as concerned with matters of subsistence and material reproduction, the more likely we are to accept hierarchy in place of civic equality" (Villa, 2000, p. 10). Another concern prevalent in the ESE literature is the importance of conflict, disagreement, and dissonance in educating learners about the paradoxes of sustainability (Lundegård & Wickman, 2007; Sund & Ohman, 2014)—a theme aligned with Arendt's emphasis on agonistic pluralism. This literature recognizes many aspects of the kind of politics that I argue is necessary for ESE to contribute to environmental sustainability.

Much of recent ESE scholarship has focused on transformative social learning (Macintyre et al., 2018), which calls for varied modalities and transgressive pedagogies within education (Lotz-Sisitka et al., 2015, 2016). These larger themes within ESE resonate with critiques of the depoliticization of the field. Stevenson (2007), quoted in the opening of this chapter, has argued that the historical antecedents of contemporary school-based ESE— "nature study" and "conservation education"—were not intended to challenge the political status quo, which made them easily compatible with the social reproduction at the heart of schooling. This historically determined approach to ESE is in line with the "fact-based tradition" (Säfström & Östman, 2020): "This tradition is built upon the conviction that environmental and sustainability issues can be discovered and cured by scientific knowledge alone, although with the help of technology. The ethical-political dimension of these problems is perceived as something subjective and non-rational that should be avoided" (p. 991).

The fact-based tradition and socially reproductive, status-quo-preserving schooling systems go hand in hand with what Säfström & Östman (2020) call instrumentalization. What they mean by this term is "the tendency to treat the child as a student on which the nation-state projects its desires and goals regardless of how the student understands his or her own life: The student is thus understood as a means to achieve something other than what concerns the student him or herself" (Säfström & Östman, 2020, p. 992). This way, the child becomes a cog in a country's development machinery, with both the development of the child and of the country following linear, predictable trajectories toward end points based on "Western" discourses (cf. Sriprakash et al., 2019). What this literature teaches us is that projecting a set of desired outcomes that children do not themselves actively participate in defining is both unethical and unlikely to achieve those outcomes.

The traps of instrumentalization, fact-based tradition, and social reproduction that ESE can fall into are not necessarily intentional. They can be the consequences of bureaucratization that accompanies trends like "evidence-based education" and the increased use of testing regimes and easily quantifiable, measurable benchmarks in education systems. These policy trends rely on standardization of curricula and pedagogic practices that lead to "order" and predictable, linear learning in which a teacher's individual approach (or a student's uniqueness) play little role. Alternative approaches to ESE, in which teaching and learning processes involve "difficulty, ambiguity, contradiction, autonomy, and cognitive and psychological uneasiness[,] suggest a recipe for classroom disorder rather than classroom order" (Stevenson, 2007, p. 149). Consequently, "environmental education, which is often necessarily interdisciplinary, problem centered, and emergent, is often marginalized or becomes non-existent" (Hursh et al., 2015, p. 307). One antidote proposed by Säfström & Östman is a focus on creativity and artistic activities "through a transactive teaching approach that can extend grievability to all Life on our planet" (2020, p. 1000). The participatory filmmaking with young people explored in chapter 4 is one attempt at such an approach.

The ESE literature also teaches us that global changes in technology and culture of the last decades too have contributed to a fertile ground for depoliticization and bureaucratization. In his book *To Know The World*, the environmental educator Mitchell Thomashow has argued that the Anthropocene represents "the convergence of accelerating natural resource extraction and global communication networks" and that "the dynamic pace of these processes has profound implications for how the psyche perceives the biosphere" (2020, p. 71). Along with "global capitalist expansion," these developments cast what Thomashow calls a "collective spell," thus "creat[ing] proliferating demands for our immediate attention, yielding a quest for ubiquitous novelty." The challenge of environmental learning in the Anthropocene is to understand how the collective spell affects our perception of the natural world. The perceptual dynamics identified by Thomashow are, I would argue, a further factor in enabling slow violence and bureaucratization and another reason to pay close attention to how we do education in the Anthropocene.

But Thomashow also sees the Anthropocene as an opportunity for educators. This new era "can also be envisioned as a time of human awakening, an era when scientific knowledge and the prospects for global awareness are unprecedented, and a period for learning opportunities and discovery," he argues (Thomashow, 2020, p. 63). Others have made similar observations. According to Karen Litfin, "the dawning of the Anthropocene seems to compel us to ask ourselves not only, 'What on Earth are we doing' but even more fundamentally, 'What on Earth *are* we?' If nothing else, the new geological era highlights our species' paradoxical relationship to the rest of creation" (2016, p. 119). She suggests that humanity in the Anthropocene is less of a "cancerous scourge" and more of "an intriguing puzzle, a riddle whose solution must emerge from a place beyond business as usual. Surely a puzzle of this depth is antithetical to a quick fix," Litfin muses, "surely it is worthy of earnest contemplation. And surely, since we are (despite our varying levels of privilege and culpability) in the same boat, our reflections should have an intersubjective dimension—all the more so because the truly effective responses will be matters of collective action. . . . Contemplative inquiry is therefore the yin to the yang of collective action" (Litfin, 2016, p. 120). What Thomashow and Litfin seem to be suggesting is that the Anthropocene presents us with an opportunity to redefine what we mean by education.

Michael Maniates also considers what we can learn from the limitations of current educational practices as we move further into the Anthropocene. He identifies ways in which ESE can fuel despair and fatalism about the future. "[O]ur attention gravitates to political struggle at the national level, where the price of entry into the conversation seems impossibly high and environmental concerns are too often an afterthought," Maniates notes (2016, p. 139). He offers an alternative: "We must remember that complex systems also offer positive feedback loops and thresholds that can transform small and strategic interventions into large and positive systems changes" (Maniates, 2016, p. 140). Like Thomashow and Litfin, Maniates points to the potential of education to help us transform the Anthropocene, in spite of its (at best) patchy track record.

Activist Education

Another area of research that is important for us to consider is the literature about activist educators. While the dual focus on schooling and activism in Pashulok and Wentworth emerged organically through my ethnographic immersion in these communities, the two modalities of education have been previously researched together in the context of the environmental multicrisis. This literature offers both normative ideas about charting new directions for formal education and examples of practice we can look to for inspiration as we ponder the idea of "educating for the Anthropocene."

The Science, Technology, Society and Environment (STSE) field is one of the spaces where activist education has been discussed for decades. Within this field, we find a focus on politicization, debureaucratization, and action.

Teacher training is also a frequent subject of research. As Derek Hodson has pointed out, "if we are to politicize students we need to politicize teachers, too. Because teachers hold a pivotal position between the state, parental influence, media power and the dictates of institutional norms, they have enormous opportunities to foster the development of democratic values and influence the attitudes of students" (2011, p. 300). Hodson suggests that teachers' role is to be what Henry Giroux (1988) refers to as *transformative intellectuals*: "Central to the category of transformative intellectual is the necessity of making the pedagogical more political and the political more pedagogical. Making the pedagogical more political means inserting schooling directly into the political sphere by arguing that schooling represents both a struggle to define meaning and a struggle over power relationships" (Giroux, as cited in Hodson, 2011, p. 302). According to Hodson, this would in turn help students become what Mark Elam and Margareta Bertilsson call *radical scientific citizens*: "The radical scientific citizen is fully prepared to participate in demonstrations . . . street marches, boycotts, and sit-ins and other means of publicly confronting those ruling over science and technology . . . While the scientific citizen as activist may be taking a partisan position in defence of a particular individual or group in society, they are also understood as assuming a moral stance in defence of general ethico-political principles . . . which are accepted as existing through many different and conflicting interpretations . . . and subjecting them to continuous contestation" (Elam & Bertilsson, as cited in Hodson, 2014, p. 69).

Many of these ideas are reflected in the STEPWISE (Science and Technology Education Promoting Wellbeing for Individuals, Societies and Environments) education framework developed by Larry Bencze at the University of Ontario. This framework focuses on guiding students through "apprenticeship" lessons designed to enable them to self-direct research-informed projects that address harms they identify in STSE relationships (Bencze & Carter, 2020, p. 65). This approach also relies on actor-network theory to unpack power relationships and address the underlying sociopolitical causes by the issues identified by students. The theme of power relations is perhaps nowhere more present than in ecopedagogy, another approach that has a lot to teach us when trying to reimagine education in the Anthropocene.

Ecopedagogy

Rooted in the ideas of Paulo Freire and activist movements of Latin America, ecopedagogy focuses on the links between environmental decay and social conflict. "All environmental pedagogies advocate environmental change, but ecopedagogical models, through a problem-posing method, focus on the politics behind environmentally harmful actions, the normative system and structures of society guiding these actions, and the deeper, transformative steps needed to end these actions" (Misiaszek, 2016, p. 590).[13] One of the central tenets of ecopedagogy is deconstructing the idea of "progress" and its convergences and divergences with the Western-influenced models of development (Misiaszek, 2016, p. 596).

As the ecopedagogy scholar Richard Kahn points out, "Environmental movements engage pedagogically with society, with their own membership and with other movements. They thereby generate theories, new strategic possibilities, and emergent forms of identity that can be accepted, rejected, or otherwise co-opted by dominant institutional power" (2010, p. 27). This is where, according to Kahn, ecopedagogy meets activism in line with Herbert Marcuse's theory of "politics *as* education" (2010, p. 128). According to Kahn, "Education and revolution were largely synonymous forces, which struggled against their reified forms as one-dimensionalizing political apparatuses, corrupting professions, and dehumanizing cultural forms" (2010, pp. 137–138). Education, in the form of ecopedagogy, could therefore be seen, in Marcusian terms, as an activist reaction to the repressive tolerance of the political status quo (Marcuse, 1965).

While these ideas share much with the ingredients of educating for the Anthropocene explored in this book—radical imagination, agonistic pluralism, and intergenerational dialogue—I chose not to couch the discussion in ecopedagogical terms. I see ecopedagogy as somewhat of a normative model of education, and, as I explained in the introduction, my goal in this book is not to tell teachers or activists how to approach education but take the reader on an ethnographic journey. Nevertheless, the material in this book resonates strongly with many of ecopedagogy's key tenets, and it is helpful to think with ecopedagogy when we think about educating for the Anthropocene.

Deschooling and Indigenous Perspectives

While Indigenous peoples' "traditional ecological knowledge" is, according to Richard Kahn, one of the key elements of ecopedagogy (2010, p. 105), it is in fact also central to a number of other critiques of education and sustainability. As Thomashow points out, "Indigenous peoples live in tropical forests, boreal forests, deserts, and snow as well as on tundra, savannas, prairies, islands, and mountains, and occupy every remaining complex biotic community (or 'biome') on the planet. They are stewards of about 80 percent of the world's remaining biological diversity and account for 90 percent of its cultural diversity" (2020, p. 141). As many of the world's Indigenous peoples sustained their ways of life by learning to live within the boundaries of their ecological environments, sometimes over centuries, a return to these lifestyles can appear as a potential solution to the environmental crises of the Anthropocene.

Madhu Prakash and Gustavo Esteva are among the most vocal critics of mainstream education who highlight the importance of Indigenous knowledge transmitted outside institutionalized settings. Their work builds on the concept of deschooling advanced by Ivan Illich (2018), who saw the very idea of universal education through schooling as undesirable and detrimental. "Authentic cultural practices are necessarily taught outside the classroom," Prakash and Esteva write (2008, p. 25). In contrast, within the modern school, "The emphasis is on earning money in a provisional future that has nothing to do with place, commons, or community" (p. 3). They point out that all universalisms, "including the different brands or breeds of education—are nothing but arrogant particularisms" (p. 2). The idea of universal schooling, enforced as a human right by the state, is particularly problematic in that it often conflicts with local knowledge and culture, uprooting young people from their communities. Prakash and Esteva believe that, as a result, "monocultures of learning and living destroy the rich pluriverse of the diverse cultures of the social majorities" (2008, p. 24). The solution they point to is deschooling—decoupling learning from institutionalized education and helping young people learn in the world outside the classroom.

These arguments resonate with this book's focus on community activism and intergenerational transmission of knowledge as forms of environmental learning. It is, however, important to remember that not all communities have a strong activist presence and what Kahn (2010, p. 105) calls "traditional ecological knowledge" has not been preserved in all societies. It is also not clear whether such knowledge could in all cases serve as a model for facing the environmental challenges of the high Anthropocene. Simply put, we need to be mindful of romanticizing and instrumentalizing Indigenous knowledge as a solution to the complex problems faced by humanity. And while the arguments presented in this book certainly call for elements of "deschooling," a wholesale abolition of schooling does not appear to be warranted based on the data presented here. The idea of institutionalized learning does not seem to be, by itself, responsible for the problematic aspects of schooling discussed in the chapters that follow; rather, overarching cultural and political forces (e.g., coloniality, neoliberalism, consumerism) seem responsible. These forces are also present outside of schools and would likely still affect young people's learning even if schools were abolished. Nevertheless, the concerns raised by this literature are helpful in thinking about what educating for the Anthropocene may mean, particularly in contexts outside the school.

THINKING WITH ARENDT AND RICŒUR ABOUT EDUCATING FOR THE ANTHROPOCENE

These strands of criticism—the critique of depoliticization within ESE, activist education, ecopedagogy, Indigenous education, and deschooling—all resonate with the theoretical work of Hannah Arendt. Her ideas help us find the "common denominator" between these approaches and provide a language helpful to imagining what an alternative to education in the Anthropocene may look like. The instrumentalized nomenclatures of SDGs, ESD/ESE, and development discussed in the first part of this chapter are arguably unhelpful in thinking about educating for the Anthropocene; they represent a technocratic obfuscation of politics. We need to think with different concepts—ones that take us past the Anthropocene's scientism and that we can put to work in the field. In the introduction, we encountered Hannah Arendt's concepts of bureaucratization, agonistic pluralism, and politics. Before we launch into the ethnographic narrative proper in chapter 3,

I would like to introduce one more related idea—historical responsibility, as conceptualized by Paul Ricœur—which will help us understand the ways in which young people in Pashulok and Wentworth make sense of the past and the future as they navigate life on the high Anthropocene's frontier.

While many different definitions of historical responsibility have been proposed (Tillmanns, 2009), a particularly helpful way to think about this concept in the context of ESE is to engage Paul Ricœur's (1984) notion of debt. We can conceptualize human contribution to environmental decay in the form of a "debt to the dead" to be carried by future generations. Ricœur first articulated his theory of debt in *Time and Narrative* in the context of describing the process of writing history: "The historian's constructions have the ambition of being reconstructions, more or less fitting with what one day was 'real.' Everything takes place as though historians knew themselves to be bound by a debt to people from earlier times, to the dead" (p. 100). To the extent that all people are historians engaged in the task of interpreting past events, all are also bound by the recognition that we carry a debt to the dead or to people from the past we may never have known. Following this logic, we can conceptualize environmental degradation, caused by the pursuit of modernity at the expense of future generations, as a form of debt to the not-yet-born—a debt impossible to repay.

The theme of historicity, which lies at the root of ESE, links it to our imagination of the future. The "surplus of meaning," a core concept in Ricœur's hermeneutics, is key to the logic behind ESE interventions: by becoming aware of the historical causes of environmental degradation, we simultaneously become aware of the likely effects our actions will have on the future environment—our debt to those we will never know. ESE may therefore be seen as relying upon a "temporal arc" that links the past with the future through the present: "The temporal arc of our lives is such that the past (as collected in the present) throws a deep shadow over our future, and so the primarily retrospective (or recollective) character of narrating does not prevent it from having [a] prospective, indeed truly self-transformative, effect" (Dunne, 2007, p. 152). This idea of the "storied self" (Dunne, 2007) is especially applicable to ESE interventions: "Given the radically unsustainable nature of our current systems, environmentalism is first and foremost a critical endeavour. In criticizing an unsustainable status quo, environmentalists are engaged in imagining an alternative, even when they do not fully elaborate the proposed alternative" (Treanor, 2013, p. 161).

Global aspirations for development and modernity also carry burdens of history, but they must be conceptualized in different ways. Traces of colonial encounters and their legacies, as they shape education practice, often have meant that such aspirations are uneven and unpredictable, particularly among populations subjected to slow violence. The sacrifices previous generations made to achieve better living standards, particularly in the context of the (neo)colonial histories of many communities in the "Global South," act as a burden on those now alive and may not easily translate into the practical application of often utopian perspectives on ESE. The incompleteness of the development narrative, the belief that "we are still developing," seeks to render the present the latest stage in the struggle for development—a struggle whose temporal dimension is greater than individual lives, in which not participating means being seen to betray the moral and political obligation of honoring the dead. To understand the ways ESE interventions shape the perception of sustainable development among young people, it is first necessary to understand how such interventions interact with existing notions of historical responsibility that have been shaped by the cultural, political, and economic landscapes in the target communities. What "horizons of the possible" do young learners see for themselves and how do ESE interventions change these perceptions?

Neither debt—the debt of environmental degradation to the unborn or the debt to the dead of continuing the struggle for development—can be fully paid off. Ricœur (1984) addresses this insolvency paradox relative to historians, whose constructions "aim at being *re*constructions of the past. Through documents and their critical examination of documents, historians are subject to what once was. They owe a debt to the past, a debt of recognition to the dead, that makes them insolvent debtors" (p. 142). Yet, as Ernst Gerhardt (2004) noted in his analysis of *Time and Narrative*, Ricœur "does not consider insolvency a function of a structural impossibility as doing so would negate any ethical force the debt might possess" (p. 246). Not being able to *fully* repay the debt thus does not mean one lacks the ability to imagine oneself as a capable, willing subject; indeed, it means that the process of reconstructing narratives of empowerment is a lifelong project. Importantly, Ricœur (2010) does assume that we are capable of such acts of reconstruction and ought to be empowered to assert our capability.

Examining the concepts of environmental sustainability and the related concept of development through Ricœur's lens allows us to explore such questions as these: To what extent do young people envision their impact on the environment as a "burden of history" to be carried by future generations? How does ESE alter their perception of their personal and historical responsibility vis-à-vis the environment, as well as their obligation to reimagine the future, the dead, or the unborn? These questions link phenomenology with ethics in examining how students see the exteriority of their lives—their impact on imagined others—and the extent to which the production of subjectivities in ESE classrooms is influenced by positive projections into the future that are rooted in cultural learning about the past.

The debt to the unborn of sustainability and debt to the dead of material progress are not necessarily at odds with each other. The very concept of sustainable development at the heart of ESE assumes that the two debts are in tune; pursuing development does not have to come at the expense of future generations. However, the particular definition of sustainable development operationalized by the SDGs is oxymoronic, as we have seen in this chapter, and pits the debts against one another.

Promoting this paradigm as a sustainable form of human "progress" or failing to challenge its fundamentally unsustainable nature while engaging in the individualization of sustainability is where ESE can become a form of greenwashing. In the remaining chapters, we will consider the ways in which schools come to spread such antieducation for the Anthropocene and what we can learn from activism in articulating an alternative vision for education at this time of unprecedented crisis.

II SCHOOLING ON THE HIGH
   ANTHROPOCENE'S FRONTIER

Outside a gated community in India, 2016.

One morning at Durban South Primary, I found the campus deserted. It was a day like any other, with the refinery smokestack throwing up flares and the hipsters, gangsters(?), churchgoers, and other characters milling about, throwing curious looks in my direction across the school fence. It had slipped my mind that the seventh-grade students (whom I was primarily working with) had left for camp that morning, and it seemed there was nothing for me to do. I decided to check Megan's office; as one of the long-term teachers and a department head, she was someone I had been trying to interview for weeks but our schedules never aligned. Fortunately, she was in her office. The quiet of the morning allowed us to speak at length about the challenges facing both students and teachers, about the school's crumbling paper-thin walls, and about just how rough Wentworth was.

What really captured my imagination, however, was not Megan's words but the drawings and photographs on the wall of her office. I was not sure what I was looking at, so I asked her. She paused, let out a quiet sigh, and started telling me a story. "Did Johny come up in any of your interviews?" Megan asked me. I said he did; I had heard he was one of the notorious troublemakers at Durban South. But Megan was much more interested in cause than effect. "His mother died, his sister has HIV, he . . . I am not sure of his status. His father lives in Chatsworth and he lives with his uncle," she began.[1] Megan was more animated than I had ever seen her; she usually kept to herself and was rarely seen outside her office or the classroom. That morning I was talking to a different Megan.

I learned that Johny's uncle had three children of his own, all of whom received preferential treatment. Johny often was blamed for their mischief. If the children complained to their father, Johny would get "a beating with whatever the uncle has in his hand. And the uncle is a mechanic and Johny has been hit, I think, with every tool, every tool." The level of detail in this story was remarkable; I had not come across another teacher who knew so much about a child's life outside the school walls. "[Johny] is a bully of note because that's what he's exposed to, that's how he's treated and that's how he deals with things, 'cause that's how he's dealt with," Megan continued. She spoke next of her colleagues. "Some teachers just won't understand that, they won't accept it, they will not embrace him, they will not say to him, 'You have the potential to do extremely well, come and sit here,' no . . . I've had people come in [and say to me], 'Why do you have that scum on your wall? I just wait for him to leave the school and you still want to put his picture on your wall?'"

This did not surprise me. I spent a good deal of my time in the field talking to teachers who did not seem to believe their pupils had any curiosity, motivation to learn, nor individual agency. As I reflected on the mosaic of experiences that contributed to my perception of Durban South—the every-day rituals of discipline, listening to shouting and screaming, the normalization of violence against the pupils—in my ethnographic diary I compared the schools to Foucault's (1979) idea of the prison and panoptic society. But there was no denying that such comparisons were driven as much by my visceral reactions to what I was observing around me as they were the product of an intellectual effort to make sense of the field. And while emotional responses do not have to be the enemy of analytical thought, as Ruth Behar (1996) has so beautifully shown in her work on Latin American migrants in the United States, I wondered if the sympathy I felt for the children colored my understanding of their teachers; perhaps I had judged them harshly as a result. After all, both of my key informants—Pranay in Pashulok and Aruna in Wentworth—were highly motivated educators who appeared to care about their students' futures. Could it be that what I was interpreting as a manifestation of an oppressive, (post)colonial education was, at least in part, an expression of tough love? That perhaps these teachers believed, or even knew, that their methods had the potential to turn things around for these children? Where did the influence of bureaucratization and depoliticization end and caring individual agency begin?

Megan was now telling me how the drawings and photographs came to be on her wall. Johny's class was due to go on an excursion to the Durban Playhouse, a theater in the city's downtown. But another teacher, Aruna, told him he was not allowed to join because he had "bunked" school the day before. Johny told her he did not "bunk"; he went to see a doctor. Aruna did not believe him because she had passed by him that day as he was talking to a group of boys. Both stories were apparently true: Johny met his friends on the way to the doctor and chatted with them before going on, and that is when Aruna saw him. But then he crossed a line: not only was he speaking back to Aruna but he also clicked his tongue at her, a gesture considered very rude. "He's been accused of something he didn't do," Megan said emphatically, "so the agitation of what he's been through at home is coming through as being rude and aggressive. Now you being rude to me, you clicking your tongue at me . . . There are several more things that you have done now in this time than bunking school, so that's not even an issue now, we not even going to talk about that . . . A long story cut short, he wasn't allowed to go and he was crying because he wanted to react, but he couldn't react."

I looked at the picture (see figure) again. It seemed to be of a scene in Wentworth. Above the drawing there were three photographs of Johny as he made the drawing. The picture showed boxlike houses with flat roofs and narrow streets and a large sun in the sky. The drawing looked like it had been tinkered with, as if parts had been erased, and the house in the center had a peculiarly bright window. There was a rawness to the picture, with its dark colors, large plain areas, and the eerie absence of people. This was no realism and yet it felt very Wentworth-like.

When Megan saw Johny cry, she asked him to come to her office. "I gave him a piece of paper and some chalk and I got him to draw, and he drew this picture but he had lots of rain coming down, which he later on took away and he—the windows were broken here. It's a shop just down the road, and he had a caption at the bottom, 'Hate this shop, they are thieves.'" When Megan asked why he wrote this, Johny told her that he once bought

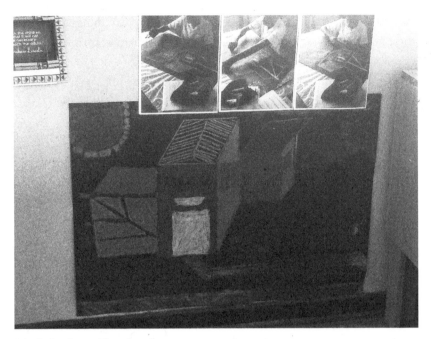

Johny's drawing on Megan's wall.

a loaf of bread at the store, worth R11, and paid for it with a R20 note. The shopkeeper said he did not have change, and Johny was "shoved out." Ever since, whenever it rains, Johny goes to the shop early in the morning when it is closed, picks up rocks, and breaks the shop window. Megan asked how many times he had done this, and Johny said four or five. She said to him, "You know, it costs them like R80.00 for every window you broke to have it fixed, maybe more than that if they not fixing it on their own. So let's just say R150.00 times four—that is R600.00. I think you've got back your R8.00 that they took and refused to give you, so it's time to stop doing that now." Johny said nothing in response, but the next day he came to Megan's office again and asked to see the picture he made. "He took the white chalk and he cleaned up the windows and he rubbed out his little caption there about them being thieves and rogues and whatever, and he—yeah, he changed the picture and he took away the rain. I said to him, 'Why you taking away the rain?' He said, 'Cause now I look at the shop as not something that I need to get back at. So I'm not going to wait for it to rain and go and break their windows anymore.'"

Apparently all it took for Johny to stop acting out was for a single teacher to offer him a way to tell his story. And, given the lengths to which I had seen teachers at Durban South go to push their students, I wondered if perhaps each of them had a "Johny" tale to tell, if underneath the shouting and verbal abuse, they truly cared. When Megan finished telling me the story, I asked her why she keeps the drawing and the photographs. "To me it symbolizes that there's hope for him. He has the potential to heal, but he has so much of pain." The children in Wentworth, she believed, "think that they have nothing to offer you, and they feel very small and inadequate in their capacities, but if our teachers would just open their mindsets to who these children really are, they are—I don't know, for me, phenomenal. They go through—if you see them dressed for school, you would not believe where they come out of. Where they come from. Little houses with mattresses in the kitchen, no electricity, no hot water, gas, a little gasket that they use for everything."

I did not have the detailed knowledge about these children's life circumstances that Megan had accumulated over the years, but my instinct was to empathize with them the best I could and—given the racialized history of South Africa, the colonial legacies of anthropology, and social science at large, and the fact that I am White—steer clear of judgment as much as possible. I nodded as Megan spoke; my dilemma was not whether to agree with her but how to square her words from that morning with the, in my view, harsh practices I witnessed at Durban South day after day. Could the apparent contradiction be due to the cultural lens with which I viewed empathy, a lens that prevented me from seeing these practices for what they truly were—expressions of tough love in the context of a rough township? Or were these words simply a rationalization for problematic practices? Were the teachers agents of an institution or activists in their own right, battling the legacies of apartheid by trying to bring out the best in these children?

The dilemma of choosing between these two interpretations points to a politics of representation fraught with the ethnographer's inevitably limited understanding of the informants' social realities. The dilemma, in other words, was not so much between choosing one interpretation over another as it was in deciding which claims I felt confident enough to include in this ethnography. As the pages of this book attest, the word "felt" in the previous sentence was important in this process because ethnographic confidence is often as emotional as it is intellectual. While it may appear that some of the conclusions I reached about schooling in Pashulok and Wentworth, as presented in chapter 4, were shaped chiefly by my understanding of the histories of these two spaces, the affective politics of delineating ethnographic truths from opinions played an equal part in how I navigated this dilemma. Like Johny, I kept coming back to what I knew. I did not always accept my informants' invitations into their realities; but, like Megan, they did often drag me out of my bubble. This made me realize that my interlocutors were citizens of postcolonial, liminal states, which had a profound influence over their worlds. In the next chapter, I examine the histories of these states and their ongoing ideologies and practices that regulated my informants' lives.

3 THE ORIGINS OF DEPOLITICIZATION

We accept what's happening because we're too lazy to go and actually sit and think about the long-term effects these things are going to have on us. And once you're educated enough to understand something better, then you take it on. You're not going to accept it.
—Grace, mother of a twelve-year-old boy in Wentworth

In his remarks at the Eleventh Hoernle Memorial lecture delivered in 1955 to the South African Institute of Race Relations in Johannesburg, T. B. Davie (1955), then vice chancellor of the University of Cape Town (UCT), called the situation of education for non-Whites in South Africa "depressing."[1] He remarked that "it is the intention of the framers of the [Bantu Education] Act [of 1953] that the education of the African child shall be different from that of the European and, further, that this difference shall establish and perpetuate an inferior status in the African in relation to the European" (Davie, 1955, pp. 15–16). According to Davie, this revealed the government's intention behind the act; the goal was not "to stimulate the development of [a child's] intellect and character, but to prepare it [*sic*] for a certain service to the state: a service which is primarily that of servant of the Europeans and secondly one which carries with it no promise of advancement toward the eventual social and political status which he [or she] covets in order to benefit to the full under western democracy." Davie's analysis is consistent with a historiography of apartheid (Field, 2012; Thompson, 2014) and suggests that the education systems of that era were not designed to politicize the population (in an Arendtian sense) or to help create the civic equality needed for agonistic pluralism and instead served as an "anti-politics machine," to borrow Ferguson's (1994) expression.

Three years later, in November 1958, India's Planning Commission, which was responsible for designing the country's all-encompassing five-year plans, was contemplating significant changes to the education system.[2] "Democracy requires above all that the citizens owe loyalty to the nation," it wrote in its report (Planning Commission of India, 1958, p. 2). Such loyalty, according to the commission, could "only spring from an awareness of and broad acceptance of the values inherent in our civilisation and faith in our future goals and present endeavour . . . In order to evolve as a classless society we will need to launch an all-out attack on casteism, communalism, linguistic fanaticism and religious intolerance". The idea of a "classless society" was a cornerstone of Nehruvian socialism that was at its height in the late 1950s (Guha, 2011). This regime sought to use education to relegate the vast majority of Indians to the position of docile subjects (Ludden, 1992; Sutoris, 2016; Zachariah, 2005), effectively turning them into the wheels of government-designed development machinery.[3]

In both countries, government-sponsored education contributed to the exclusion of citizens from the political sphere, as understood by Arendt. Smith (2005, p. 54) explains that "our appearance in the political sphere is not a matter of any functional role we might play in society, as, say, mechanic, chef or academic, but is envisaged as a locus of creative self-actualization in the presence of others. For Arendt, this is precisely what it should mean to be a citizen." However, the idea of citizenship in apartheid South Africa and in post-Independence India was lopsided: citizens were not to act, they were merely to follow predetermined patterns of behavior. Arendt (1970, p. 31) notes that actions differ from mere behavior in that they "interrupt what otherwise would have proceeded automatically and therefore predictably." The suppression of action—and its prerequisites, agonistic pluralism, and the promise of politics—appears to have been, despite very different histories, integral to both countries in the wake of World War II. And, as is evident in what follows, this convergence is not only spatial but temporal, for when it comes to depoliticization through formal education, the India and South Africa of today have much in common with their 1950s predecessors.

Before launching into ethnographic accounts of schooling and activism, I will explore this convergence, in particular as it manifests in Pashulok and Wentworth. If we are to understand how education can help us confront the depoliticization of sustainability that schooling often itself perpetuates, we need to start with understanding the historical origins of this depoliticization. While the history explored in this chapter is specific to the contexts of India (Pashulok) and South Africa (Wentworth), it matters for understanding what educating for the Anthropocene may entail. As I explained in the introduction, we can imagine Pashulok and Wentworth as representations of the frontier of the high Anthropocene, as spaces experiencing accelerating slow violence in ways that may allow us to forecast global trends. These histories are global as much as they are local.

Tracing the origins of depoliticization demands a historical contextualization of the Indian and South African nation-states to illuminate the forces shaping the political and cultural landscapes of schooling and activism in Pashulok and Wentworth. To do this, I apply an approach akin to Foucault's (1979) "history of the present," which "begins by identifying a present-day practice that is both taken for granted and yet, in certain respects, problematic or somehow unintelligible . . . and then seeks to trace the power struggles that produced [it]" (Garland, 2014, p. 373). The two key questions I pose in this chapter are: In what ways have the (post)colonial histories of India and the (post)colonial histories of South Africa shaped the depoliticization of particular generations of young people and environmental issues in these two states? How have they shaped the cultural and political landscapes navigated by teachers and activists in these spaces?

GASSING THE POOR, PRAISING THE (HINDU) GODS: THE SUBMERSION OF POLITICS IN INDIA

Ramachandra Guha is one of India's most influential intellectuals, someone whose acquaintance I had hoped to make ever since I read his *India after Gandhi* (2011), perhaps the most exhaustive history of India since Independence. Guha, who strikes me as a modern-day polymath, is also a noted historian of environmentalism. Researching the sociohistorical context of the construction of Tehri Dam gave me a good reason to contact him, and a few months later I interviewed Guha in his car on his way to the Bangalore airport. A slim, tall, and kind man with thick glasses, he looked a lot less intimidating than I had expected, but the passion with which he spoke did not seem to match his gentle disposition. "It's not just inadequate, it's positively inimical to environmental sustainability, both state governments and central governments," he said to me when I asked about his views on the environmental policy of Narendra Modi's government. He went on to list the numerous challenges facing India's environment: "A resources dependent population being denied access to their resources space because of development projects, unregulated industrial development, pollution control, disposal of chemical waste, somewhat misplaced agricultural policies which lead to excessive discharge of groundwater, air pollution." The list was seemingly endless. "We are, in a sense, an environmental basket case," he concluded.

Guha's diagnosis did not surprise me, though his use of such strong language underscored for me the urgency of the environmental crisis facing India and the rest of the world. What I was really curious to hear, though, was his assessment of the reasons behind the crisis. "Part of it is in the sense that we need rapid economic growth to lift our people out of poverty," he began. "Part of it is because of the deep links between industrial houses and political parties, funding of elections and all of that, and part of it is also just this ideological belief that environmentalism is a rich man's phenomenon."[4] Here, in two sentences, Guha touched on three interwoven threads of India's history that have grave implications for the natural environment globally.

The depoliticization of the environment in India is a composite affair, brought to the surface by an amalgamation of social, political, and economic currents with origins at least as far back as the beginning of British colonial rule. At the end of that rule, on August 15, 1947, according to Nehru, "at the stroke of the midnight hour, when the world sleeps, India will awake to life and freedom" (1962, p. 94). This quote comes from the famous "Tryst with Destiny" speech, whose title raises the question of what exactly was an independent India's destiny to be? Many freedom fighters would argue that it was to return to the prosperity of its pre-colonial "golden age," before, some might argue, the British came and destroyed India's chances at economic progress.[5] Gandhi's wing of the Indian National Congress (INC) was against the idea of industrialization, whereas Nehru saw it as the only path to progress.[6] The Gandhians wanted to return to tradition, as they saw it—agriculture-centered, rural, self-sufficient communities. The rest of the party saw seizing precolonial "tradition" as a tool to establish and maintain political legitimacy (indeed, arguably political hegemony, as discussed in Ayesha Jalal's [2009] work) as it pursued the kind of modernity embraced by the departing colonial rulers. During a vocal debate in the 1930s, "to Visvesvarayya's technocratic battle-cry 'Industrialize–or Perish!' Gandhi replied, "Industrialize–and Perish!'" (Khilnani, 2012, p. 73).[7] Ninety years later, in an age of anthropogenic slow violence, the conflict between the proponents and critics of continued industrial growth is still alive and more relevant than ever.

As we now know, Gandhi and his supporters lost the battle,[8] and Gandhian economics is today at best a footnote in economics textbooks.[9] According to Amitav Ghosh, "Gandhi was the very exemplar of a politics of moral sincerity. Yet, while [he] may have succeeded in dislodging the British from India, [Gandhi] failed in this other endeavor, that of steering India along a different economic path" (2016, p. 181). And so Ghosh concludes, "There is little reason to believe that a politics of this kind will succeed in relation to global warming today." While this statement may well be true—and the findings of this book presented in subsequent chapters certainly support this view—it does not seem to be a sufficient explanation for the almost complete marginalization of Gandhi's views on development at this critical juncture.

During my previous research in India in the early 2010s, I had the honor of having many conversations with Amrit Gangar, a historian and cultural critic and the curator of Mumbai's National Museum of Indian Cinema. One evening, while he walked me to the bus stop near his suburban Mumbai home, Amrit and I talked about the 1947 crossroads of history. Even though the streetlamp provided only a modicum of light, I could see the disgust in his face as he said to me, "Nehru became the first prime minister . . . and now, look around, this is the kind of country we've got." My initial surprise at this learned man's apparent but respectful questioning of Nehru, the widely beloved icon of India's freedom struggle, gave way to my wondering what he meant by "the kind of country we've got."[10] It took me years to appreciate what I think he was getting at: the environmental destruction caused by the embrace of industrial modernity, and the inequality and breakdown of social structures associated with India's embrace of global capitalism.

As tempting as it is to neatly compartmentalize the past and point to specific historical events as watershed moments, the phenomenon of depoliticization predated India's independence from Britain or the INC's decision to pursue a policy of industrialization. Some of these currents compelled Nehru and his allies to align with the proindustrialization wing of the INC and later helped turn them, perhaps unconsciously, into political disciples of the country's former colonial masters, with indescribably tragic consequences.

Some events crystallize history, making visible the flows of ideas shaping a state's fundamental ideology. The most shocking and tragic incident of India's post-Independence past, the Bhopal disaster of 1984, is one such event. It is worth discussing at length because, more than perhaps any other event, it illuminates the historical origins of the depoliticization of environment in India.[11] The disaster lies at the intersection of colonial and postcolonial, developmentalist, and capitalist forces of India's and the world's history, exposing the underbelly of Western modernity. These are the very same forces that stretch back in time, that acted on the British colonizers of the nineteenth and twentieth centuries and on the minds of Nehru and the INC elites opposing Gandhian economic thought through the 1930s and 1940s. They also extend forward in time, well past 1984 and into the present, where they help to explain the depoliticizing forces in education systems in India and beyond.

The world's deadliest industrial accident to date, the Bhopal disaster instantly killed at least thirty-eight hundred (Broughton, 2005)[12] and maimed hundreds of thousands (Kurzman, 1987).[13] More than a half-million Indians were exposed to the forty lethal tons of leaked methyl isocyanate gas from the Union Carbide India Limited (UCIL) fertilizer plant on the night of December 2, 1984. Kim Fortun, who undertook an extensive ethnography of the aftermath of the disaster, refers to the efforts at rehabilitation and compensation as the "second disaster" of Bhopal (2001, p. 17). Union Carbide, the American mother company of UCIL, settled the victims' case against it in 1989 for $470 million (Fortun, 2001, p. 17), a deal negotiated with the Indian government, which took it upon itself to represent the victims in court collectively in the capacity of *parens patriae*, despite the clear conflict of interest presented by India owning a 22 percent share in UCIL (Fortun, 2001, p. 99).[14] This figure is shockingly low by any standard: if the victims were paid at the same rate as those affected by asbestosis in the United States in the 1970s and 1980s, the settlement would exceed $10 billion—more than Union Carbide's market value at the time (Broughton, 2005).

In the workers',[15] activists', and scholars' version of events, the disaster was caused by the company's negligence; according to Union Carbide's discredited version (Fortun, 2001), the cause was sabotage by a disgruntled worker. UCIL never admitted responsibility for the first disaster, just as the Indian government and judiciary, the US government and judiciary, and Union Carbide never admitted responsibility for the second one. ".In the independence-era dreams of Jawaharlal Nehru, a pesticide plant in Bhopal would have been a temple of the new India, representing the dynamic synergism of science, industrialisation, and socialism.[16] Fifty years after the disaster, Union Carbide's Bhopal plant continues to operate as an icon, but of a different kind" (Fortun, 2001, p. 144). I imagine that, when Amrit Gangar spoke to me on a warm Mumbai night decades after the accident about the kind of country India had become, Bhopal was very much on his mind.

It is possible to view the disaster merely as an unfortunate but isolated event on India's path toward progress. But the long list of indignities the people of Bhopal have suffered neither starts nor ends with the gas leak in December 1984; on the contrary, the "second disaster" of utter bureaucratic failure is arguably even more shocking than the accident itself. The twin disasters are not blips; they are emblematic of long-standing institutions and underlying ideologies that, if unchecked, have a good chance of ending the Anthropocene (and with it, humanity) in a matter of decades.

Key among the currents of history that underlie the disasters is the twin pursuit of democracy and development. In India, the tension between the two is among "the contradictions [that] are literally constitutive of the postcolonial state. The Indian constitution is bifocal. It guarantees political democracy, not unlike the US Constitution. But it also has directive principles (Articles 36–51) that promise the pursuit of economic democracy"

(Fortun, 2001, p. 144). Economic democracy, however, is not for everyone. As Arvind Rajagopal pointed out in his article "And the Poor Get Gassed," not only did the "poor" state of Madhya Pradesh and the "poor" country of India not object to the Bhopal plant or effectively regulate it because they hoped to turn into a "promised land of industrial progress." Worse still, due to the huge redundancy of labor in India, "killing off several thousand, and maiming a few hundred thousand more, is not something [government planners and policymakers] could object to in principle, as long as the victims are appropriately selected" (2005, p. 25). While this interpretation may seem overly cynical, many examples of the government's botched and ineffective response to the disaster appear to support it. However, it is important to remember that the state and national governments were not the only ones responsible. Kim Fortun's account of activist narratives of the origins of the disaster is worth quoting at length:

> Some of the activists I worked with pushed the origins of disaster back to 1600, the year the East India Company was chartered in London, establishing how India would be related to the West—through the multinational corporate form. Some fixated on 1974, the year Union Carbide India was granted an industrial license by the government of India to manufacture as well as formulate pesticides in Bhopal—establishing the government's role in the disaster. Still others emphasized the early 1980s, when the Green Revolution in India was faltering—revealing that the promise of modern science and technology was not as straightforward as once believed. (Fortun, 2001, pp. 139–140)

Arguably, all these interpretations are true. To understand what happened in this disaster, we need to consider all these and other narratives as we trace the currents of history that enabled both the violence of Bhopal and the broader slow violence enacted in the context of a postcolonial, neoliberal state.

What converged in Bhopal were India's colonial past and its imagined prosperous and "developed" future.[17] Just as Union Carbide was projecting the United States's power and scientific superiority in India at the time of the Cold War, the Indian government was rushing toward a prosperous future anchored in a global neoliberal system of supranational capitalism. Here was a state that appeared to be dominated by forces willing to sacrifice hundreds of thousands of citizens to maintain an image of a "safe" haven for foreign investment, a state underpinned by a depoliticization of the environment (and certain categories of human life) with a double root in colonialism and transnational capitalism.[18]

The postcolonial Indian state is a heterogeneous entity, however (Mangla, 2015, 2017; Sutoris, 2016), and not all of its constitutive elements would subscribe to such a view. As I have shown elsewhere, in the realm of the state's educational vision, a degree of internal contestation and dialogue was palpable in the decades following Independence (Sutoris, 2018a), an argument that challenges the simplistic characterizations of the Indian state as an ideological monolith that can be found in policy literature (cf. Tilak, 2009).[19]

This heterogeneity was obvious to me during my stay at the Centre for Environment Education (CEE)—one of the world's key ESE research centers—in Ahmedabad during my initial research into ESE interventions in India. At one point, Kartikeya Sarabhai, the CEE's director, told me the story of CEE's participation in the 1992 Earth Summit in Rio de Janeiro, one of the seminal events in the history of the international environmental movement. "We wrote India's report, that sentence which perhaps you might have seen I think, I quote it often, which says, the challenge for developing countries like India is not how to get there but how not to, how do you avoid this strong paradigm sucking you into one type of development." Here was a government-funded agency challenging the colonial-capitalist ideology—the very nexus that brought about Bhopal—in an official government document only one year after India's economic liberalization reforms. This was rather surprising.

But CEE, too, could not escape the contradictions inherent in India's colonial matrix of power. I encountered the most striking example of the organization's subordination to the state in *Parampara* (CEE, 2015)—a coffee-table book proudly made by CEE that was India's official "gift" to the 2015 Paris climate negotiations. It sought to expound India's "culture of climate-friendly sustainable practices" and suggested that, "like many other ancient cultures, India has a lot to offer to the world" with its "climate-friendly traditions" (Modi, 2015, p. i). These words come from the foreword, credited to India's prime minister, Narendra Modi. When you turn the page, you see a photograph of Gandhi, along with his famous quote, "Earth provides enough to satisfy everyone's need, but not for anyone's greed." The contradiction could not be more jarring: a claim to Gandhi's intellectual lineage in a book introduced by Modi, a politician who unabashedly championed industrial development during his time as the chief minister of Gujarat and later as India's prime minister (Komireddi, 2019). Modi joined the "family" of the ultra-right-wing Rashtriya Swayamsevak Sangh (RSS, a national volunteer organization) in his early twenties (Komireddi, 2019, p. 98);[20] this was the same RSS whose ideology led its former member Nathuram Vinayak Godse to assassinate Gandhi on January 30, 1948,[21] in the name of *Hindutva*, or Hindu nationalism.[22] If the INC killed off Gandhi's social and economic doctrine in the 1930s, Hindu nationalism physically annihilated the man in the 1940s, yet both celebrate him as a national hero and ostensibly subscribe to his legacy. This is not a mere coincidence: it is a symptom of a state where tradition is appropriated by power, where neoliberal-colonial bureaucratization seeks to ensure that the word "environment" is devoid of any traces of politics in an Arendtian sense.

I first encountered Bharatiya Janata Party (BJP)–style Hindu nationalism in an undergraduate class on South Asian history, where I saw Anand Patwardhan's classic documentary *Ram ke Naam* (*In the Name of God*). The film showed, in uncensored raw detail, the party's role in the 1990 campaign to demolish the Babri Masjid mosque in Ayodhya and build a Hindu temple dedicated to Ram on its site. The campaign succeeded: the mosque was dismantled in less than five hours—directly in breach of a Supreme Court of India order—triggering waves of communal violence. Historian and founding member of the Subaltern Studies Collective Sumit Sarkar wrote of an "Indian variety of fascism" (1993, p. 164).

By 2002 Indian fascism had entered the political mainstream in parts of the country and led to the genocidal killing of Muslims. During the Gujarat riots, which left as many as two thousand dead, Modi, the state's chief minister at the time, at a minimum turned a blind eye to the violence (Engineer, 2002).[23] His involvement resulted in the United States and a number of European countries banning his entry (Burke, 2012; Mann, 2014). And yet, Modi not only rose to the top but also earned respect from much of the world. On January 25, 2015, he famously hugged Barack Obama at the Delhi airport—the same Obama whose face appeared on hundreds of red-and-blue "HOPE" stickers adorning dorm windows on the US college campus where my history class watched Patwardhan's film on the Ayodhya mosque.[24] The affectionate gesture appears less out of place when we consider its symbolic dimension: these were not two men hugging but an embrace of the ideologies of a United States–led diffusion of neoliberalism around the world with an Indian quest for national glory in its colonial-capitalist-*Hindutva* variety.

The 2014 election in India put a lone party—Modi's RSS-affiliated BJP—in power for the first time since 1984.[25] During my field research in 2016–2017, while the BJP was pushing for a Hindu political, cultural, and spiritual hegemony, the country seemed to be in turmoil, the specter of communalism and the bloody memories of Partition haunting it once again (Palshikar, 2019). A local election took place in Uttarakhand during my research in Pashulok, and religious symbols on political posters were a constant reminder that India's secular democracy was at risk. As K. S. Komireddi wrote in *Malevolent Republic*, one of the first histories of Modi's India, "Hindu rage that once manifested itself in localised violence has metastasised into a cancer of the national body politic . . . Democratic institutions have been repurposed to abet Hindu nationalism. The military has been politicised, the judiciary plunged into the most existential threat to its independence since 1975. Kashmir has never more resembled a colonial possession" (2019, p. 205). The administration made full use of India's existing and arguably restrictive laws (Ruparelia, 2015, p. 768) and passed new ones that limited free speech, the right to assembly, freedom of movement and funding, including constraining foreign funding to nongovernmental organizations (NGOs). But perhaps even more importantly, "social vigilantism by outfits that are ideologically aligned with the BJP, and the RSS," which was "backed up by mob violence" against journalists, academics, students, or anyone else critical of the government, made itself felt with increasing frequency and magnitude (Blom Hansen, 2019, p. 19).[26]

Where does all this leave the Indian state's development ideology and its alleged commitment to sustainability? *Sustainable Development and India* (Patel & Nagar, 2018), a recent volume published by Oxford University

Press India, is instructive. With a foreword by Modi—just like CEE's *Parampara*—it spelled out a technocratic view of the future, in which technology is the only way forward. It saw the Trump administration as committed to the idea of sustainable development (Patel & Nagar, 2018, p. 5), made a point of praising Modi for touring one of Tesla's US factories to observe production of the company's solar battery Powerwall (p. 179), and asserted that "sustainability strongly revolves around intellectual property rights as an instrument of advancing innovation" (p. 5). The volume focused on protecting patents, pointing to an underlying belief that only neoliberal capitalism, private ownership, and the profit motive can resolve the existential challenges of the Anthropocene. In a nutshell, the same logic that initiated the environmental crisis is imagined as the way to end it.

Flooding the Country with Development: Tehri Dam and the Depoliticization of Environment

India's large dams are perhaps the most visible imprint of the country's post-Independence development vision. They are, just like Bhopal, symbolic of something very different from the prosperity they were meant to deliver. The country built approximately four thousand large dams between Independence and 2000 (Klingensmith, 2007, p. 212).[27] The resulting reservoirs displaced millions of Indians—one study found the average number of people displaced by a large dam to be 44,182 (Dias, 2002, p. 5)—many of them Indigenous peoples and Dalits. What exactly was their sacrifice for? Studies have shown that the Indian state's irrigation policies have been "beneficial to the privileged rich landed class" (S. Singh, 2002, p. 181), whereas poverty and agricultural volatility have increased in the regions surrounding the dams (Duflo & Pande, 2007). Meanwhile, the environmental destruction caused by these mega-projects has been immense: by 2002 large dams had submerged 1.5 million hectares of forest and other ecosystems in India (Raj, 2002, p. 64). "Nothing ages worse than images of the future," Khilnani writes. "The great dams, sluicing through forests and villages, have come to be seen as the emanations of a developmental fantasy insensitive to ecological limits and careless of turning its citizens into refugees in their own land" (Khilnani, 2012, p. 62).

Tehri Dam in the Himalayan state of Uttarakhand—which displaced villages previously inhabited by the people of Pashulok, my Indian research site—is one of India's largest dams completed in the twenty-first century. Devised in 1949, under construction in 1978, and completed in 2005 (Rawat, 2013, p. 66), this 260.5-meter high rock-fill dam, with a reservoir of twenty-five square kilometers (Bisht, 2009, p. 302), has displaced as many as one hundred thousand people (Newton, 2008), according to some estimates.

But displacement was not the only harm posed by the dam. The Uttar-kashi earthquake of October 20, 1991, brought concerns about the safety of the dam into sharp relief, given its location on a geological fault line.[28] The bursting of the Dhauliganga Dam during the Uttarakhand floods in February 2021 led to up to two hundred deaths (Shugar et al., 2021, p. 300) and became another reminder that such concerns were justified. Already at the time Tehri Dam was designed, it was feared that a similar incident could lead to the flooding of entire cities—as discussed in T. Shivaji Rao's book *Tehri Dam Is a Timebomb* (1992). These concerns contributed to a fierce opposition to the project. In 1985 the Tehri Bandh Virodhi Sangharsh Samiti (TBVSS; Tehri Dam Opposing Struggle Committee) filed a petition with the Supreme Court of India against the state of Uttar Pradesh, arguing that the dam was "technically infeasible, geologically a blunder, economically unsound and environmentally disastrous. It is not a project of development but a scheme for destruction . . . a criminal act and an unpardonable ecological sin" (Verghese, 1994, p. 82).

The people of this region, known as *paharis* (of the hills), had already been disadvantaged in several ways before the dam was built. According to Rana and colleagues (2007, p. 352), "People of Uttarakhand are combating various forms of natural calamities. Their resources are fast dwindling; exodus is common phenomena [*sic*] as survival has become exceedingly difficult. The recurrent incidences of flash floods and landslides create enormous hardship to the local people. The scarcity of biomass (fuel, wood, fodder, etc.) is being observed all over the state, water scarcity in a region becomes so alarming that people have to walk for miles for drinking water." While more than 70 percent of the population in this area is upper caste (Brahmins and Rajputs), this does not necessarily translate into wealth.[29] According to census data, the population is 82 percent rural and, compared to the plains of Uttar Pradesh, "transport and communications [are] very poor" (Mawdsley,

1999, p. 103). There are "relatively few industrial units or employment opportunities." According to Mawdsley (1999), it has been estimated that between 27 percent and 74 percent of working males are absent from these hill villages at any given time. The dominant languages are Garhwali and Kumaoni, and Hinduism is the main religion, "although it owes much to the local traditions of ghosts and spirits" (Mawdsley, 1999, p. 103).

Many would consider this an underdeveloped area.[30] In India victims of development tend to come from such regions and are often "given a very raw deal in terms of compensation for their land and livelihood by the state agencies" (S. Singh, 2002, p. 181). Tehri Dam was no exception; as Nachowitz (1988, p. 9) points out, despite the government's stated goals of relocating families and providing fair compensation for their submerged land, "researchers have found that this is not the case. Entire families have been split apart and deprived of their only means of economic support. The cultural survival of these 'backward classes,' who have lived and survived without modern technology or electricity for centuries, has been ignored."

Another group notably affected by resettlement was women. Commenting on the pre-resettlement social conditions for women, Bisht noted that "because the local topography could not support a large population at one particular place, villages were small, sparsely populated and scattered. The compact nature of each village meant that everyone knew everyone else and this provided a sense of security [for the women]" (2009, p. 307). After resettlement, this sense of security was compromised. One study of women found that as many as 54.16 percent of respondents reported that, "though they have been living in this area for the past 20–30 years, they still feel insecure," and 87.50 percent complained about the separation from their close relatives due to resettlement (Rawat, 2012, p. 148). Furthermore, since women previously had been the primary cultivators in the region, as men would migrate down to the plains for work (Asthana, 2018), they participated in decision-making and had a degree of social autonomy not seen in surrounding communities in which the *parda* (veil) system was practiced (Bisht, 2009, p. 314). Displacement meant, however, that men would take over cultivation, leaving women constrained to indoor activities, thus limiting their economic freedom and social autonomy.

The landless—*harijans* and other artisanal groups—often have had no option but to emigrate out of the resettled villages (Rawat, 2013, p. 77). Peasants who were relocated to the lowland plains "can no longer farm their most successful crops including jhangora, beans, apples, and other high altitude fruits" (Newton, 2008, p. 28). The urban population of Old Tehri was moved to a site topographically very different from their home; the now-submerged town was located 1,115 feet above sea level, while the resettlement colony of New Tehri was built at 5,085 feet (Newton, 2008, p. 23). The human costs and community impact of the resettlement have been described by Chipko movement leader Sunderlal Bahuguna as "the end of a civilization" (Newton, 2008, p. 31).[31]

To many of the people whose villages were submerged by Tehri Dam, living conditions in Pashulok were an existential threat. One interlocutor after another described to me how inhospitable the area was when they were resettled here, lacking roads, electricity, irrigation, or even plots of land suitable for building a house. The name Pashulok—composed of *pashu*, the Hindi word for "animal," and *lok*, the word for "place"—referred to the land's historical use as grazing grounds for cattle (figure 3.1).[32] As I listened to my interlocutors while remembering what I had read about India's grossly inadequate resettlement schemes, I could not help but think, rightly or wrongly, that the name was apt, as the government seemed to treat the resettled villagers with a similar degree of indifference with which it might have treated farm animals.

India's development megaprojects cause "pain of displacement [that is] is usually the culmination of years, sometimes decades of waiting, hearing rumours, receiving threats" (Raj, 2002, p. 65). This was true of people in Pashulok, who told me they had lived in fear for decades. One of my interlocutors told me there were whispers about a dam in the Tehri area as early as 1962; the official announcement came in 1965.

Whenever I asked about precise numbers or dates of displacement, all my interviewees pointed me to Abhijit, a retired school principal, poet, and scholar who seemed to be widely respected. It took me weeks to get an appointment with him. When I finally arrived at his humble white house on the edge of Pashulok, we sat in plastic chairs and drank *chiya* that tasted like pure sugar. As we sat sweating in the afternoon sun, Abhijit often scratched

Figure 3.1
A street in Pashulok.

his chin as he pondered my questions. "There were many villages that were affected, but from our village of Serai 1,162 families came here," he told me. This amounted to an approximate total of 7,000 people, of which 2,000 (170 families) were from scheduled castes. "And in that about 1.5 lakh [1,500] are people who lost everything and the rest are those who either lost their home, or their farmland."

Although he stated these numbers in a somber voice, I detected an undertone of sadness as soon as we started talking about culture change in the community. "Our festivals, now they have reduced to just sharing sweets amongst the relatives. But there [in Tehri] we had relatives coming in from far away and we used to decorate and light up the entire village. We would make a wheel out of the peels and the entire village would come together to rotate it and then we would have programs of dancing and singing." By now Abhijit was gazing into the distance, and I thought he was weeping. I remembered Pashulok's temples, which were well maintained but seemed somehow sterile, devoid of decoration, and disconnected from the kinds of rituals and practices Abhijit had spoken about. "The situation here is like having your feet in two boats: the old things are forgotten, and we are struggling to adapt to the new life . . . There we all lived like one family . . . and were aware of the happiness and sadness in each other's lives." While in Pashulok, I did not encounter any community events, and the state of the community hall—broken windows, peeling paint, layers of dirt and debris on the ground (figure 3.2)—mirrored Abhijit's comments.

Perhaps because of a lack of social support outside the family, many of the residents of Pashulok I spoke to feared for their children's future. Another interlocutor, Nakul, explained this fear to me, pointing out that, back in their now submerged villages, "even if we didn't get a job, we had the backup option of farming. But here if we don't get a good education or a job, we will be on the streets." Thus, the children's future was going to be different and not necessarily better. "Here, a child who is born in the present time, when he grows up, he will automatically be buried under worries that if I don't become successful, what will I do in the future?" Nakul told me that his greatest hope for his children was to get a government job that provided financial security. The community's backup option of farming had evolved

Figure 3.2
Shadows and light inside Pashulok's community hall.

into a desire for government employment. The irony was palpable: this was, after all, the very government that had flooded their villages with the holy water of the Ganges and took away the safety of old.

But I encountered what seemed like an even greater contradiction during my time in Pashulok. Trina, one of the women I interviewed, whose calloused hands spoke of decades of working in the field, spent almost two hours enumerating all the injustices of resettlement and reminiscing about the "old" way of life that was lost—only to then pronounce loudly as she looked directly at me, "We have sacrificed everything including our land, our homes. And in return, we haven't gotten anything, yet we are satisfied that we have done it for the country. I love my India, I love my Garhwali." Who was I to pass judgment on Tehri Dam if some of the oustees saw their sacrifice as worthwhile?

THE ORIGINS AND FUTURES OF SOUTH AFRICA'S ENVIRONMENTAL APARTHEID

The practice of ethnography has undergone fundamental changes over the last century. When Bronisław Malinowski wrote *Argonauts of the Western Pacific* (1922), he relied on detailed observations he made of the Trobriand people on Kiriwina Island while immersed in their way of life, isolated from the rest of the world. In many ways, my research in Durban was the opposite: by listening to radio news every day while driving to my research site, attending seminars and lectures as a scholar affiliated with University of KwaZulu Natal, and having long chats with journalists, academics, and artists in city cafes, I was learning as much about national politics, the contemporary art scene, and the social and cultural history of South Africa as I was about the microcosm of Wentworth. At the time of my fieldwork in 2016 to 2018, South Africa was a happening place, with something akin to a political revolution unfolding in real time. It was the country of the Rhodes Must Fall and Fees Must Fall movements, countless protests over service delivery, and increasing hostility toward its president.[33] Wentworth—unlike the peripheral town of Pashulok—was where history lived, a place whose past was shaped by the likes of Steve Biko and Nelson Mandela,[34] a city at the heart of President Zuma's support base in his home province of KwaZulu-Natal. This place was so politicized that I wondered whether living in the Balkans, "the powder keg of Europe" (Paxton, 2002), in the 1910s on the brink of World War I felt similar.[35] Yet, my fieldwork findings in Wentworth pointed to patterns of depoliticization of the environment that were similar to the Indian case. Clearly, political tension in a society is not necessarily a predictor of (de)politicization of the environment. To understand why certain issues (for instance, land ownership[36]) became politicized in the 2010s while others (such as pollution) remained—at least as far as the education system was concerned—"neutral," it is necessary to trace the historical origins of South Africa's foundational contradictions and tensions.

Such an effort inevitably involves thinking about the historical legacies of apartheid—South Africa's deliberate and systemic racial segregation that existed from 1948 to 1994. This was an era marked by the political, social, and economic discrimination of non-White South Africans, state-sponsored violence, surveillance, and widespread repression of civil liberties. While contemplating how to write about this dark page of human history, all I could think of was a quote from *Eichmann in Jerusalem*, Hannah Arendt's report on the trial of Adolf Eichmann, one of the architects of the Holocaust, that took place in Israel in 1961. Summarizing the judges' ruling in the Eichmann case, Arendt wrote that "sufferings on so gigantic a scale [as those created by the Holocaust] were 'beyond human understanding,' a matter for 'great authors and poets'" (2006, p. 193).[37] Apartheid, too, is in the category of crimes against humanity rather than "merely" against individuals. Of the extensive literature I have read on this period, four lines written by the exiled Coloured poet Arthur Nortje in 1963 speak loudest to me. They seem to echo the emptiness and oblivion at the core of anthropogenic slow violence—or perhaps the seeming unintentionality with which it is executed:

Evil assumes the guise of emptiness:
the executioner cut off from his axe-wielding hand
eyeing the gallows from behind glass barrier.
This is glassy segregation.[38]

A different kind of "glassy segregation" characterized my fieldwork. After my colleagues at the University of KwaZulu-Natal (UKZN) warned me of the violence that goes on in "Wenties," as locals call the neighborhood, I spent a great deal of time looking at Wentworth from behind the glass of car windows. Located on the fence line of Engen—the oldest South African oil refinery, built in 1954—Wentworth is notorious for drugs and gang crime. The windshield seemed to offer me a degree of protection from both the fast and slow violence, although it also put up a barrier between me and my interlocutors, who did not have the luxury of looking at the violence from behind a window.

This Coloured township in South Durban was created in the early 1960s by the apartheid government, a direct result of the Group Areas Act, which segregated "White," "Black," "Indian," and "Coloured" populations into separate areas.[39] The Group Areas Act was the culmination of centuries of racial tension and imperialism in southern Africa. In what is now the province of KwaZulu-Natal, the British took over the Zulu Kingdom in the brief Anglo-Zulu War of 1879, establishing White political, economic, and social dominance in this part of South Africa (Thompson, 2014).

In Durban, the administrative center of the province, city planning and forced removals reflected both racist ideologies and capitalist logics of successive political regimes (Bickford-Smith, 2016, p. 138). Dianne Scott, perhaps South Africa's primary scholarly authority on South Durban, told me as we spoke on an autumn afternoon in her cozy office inside an ivy-covered colonial-era building at the University of Cape Town:[40] "My understanding—and I read all the old mayors' minutes and all the documents right from the 1920s—is that the idea was to create this industrial zone in the South." To make this possible, groups of non-White people were located in the vicinity of industry to provide a "labour reservoir" (D. Scott, 2003b, p. 255) as part of fashioning a "modernist industrial landscape" (p. 235). The racist ideology originated in the colonial period and lasted through the rest of the twentieth century. "So you have got the colonial city, the segregated city and then from 1948 the apartheid city," Dianne told me. Durban's racial segregation dates back to the British Colony of Natal (1843–1910), through to the Union of South Africa (Republic of South

Africa after 1961), and through the apartheid regime. Indeed, Durban's segregation, rooted in the marriage of imperialism and racism with capitalism, became the blueprint for apartheid city planning across the country, including Johannesburg (Bickford-Smith, 2016, p. 139).[41]

These are double currents of colonialism and capitalism similar to those India encountered during and after the British rule, although there are important differences. European colonization in South Africa dates back to Dutch Afrikaner settlement of the Cape in 1652, with the British taking over the Cape Colony in 1895 to secure their trading interests in India and East Asia (Trapido, 2011, p. 67).[42] Britain's influence increased after it won the Boer War against the Afrikaner Transvaal Republic and the Orange Free State in 1902. While British propaganda at the time claimed that the British took a more sympathetic view of non-White South Africans than the Afrikaners (Thompson, 2014, p. 144), their victory in the Boer War hardly changed the lot of the country's marginalized majority; in fact it often made it worse.[43] This statement from Maurice S. Evans, a Durban-based British politician (and amateur botanist) reflects the paternalism and sense of racial superiority among the British following the war:

> I feel we have a fine race of people given into our charge, a race who, while rapidly changing, are not degenerate—a people who under right guidance are capable of much, and who, under firm, considerate and wise rule are easily governed . . . Above all, our duty is, . . . as the ruling race to think for and of this people, and lead them along the right lines of development. (Evans, 1906, p. 8)[44]

Even if the British did not openly advocate violence against the non-White populations, they saw them as decidedly inferior and in need of being "led" and "thought for." Steve Biko, the founding figure of the Black Consciousness movement,[45] who once lived in Wentworth, eloquently summarized the effects of the British-Afrikaner racial discrimination on Black South Africans in his court testimony in 1976 at the height of apartheid:[46]

> I think the Black man is subjected to two forces in this country. He is first of all oppressed by an external world through institutionalized machinery, through laws that restrict him from doing certain things, through heavy work

conditions, through poor pay, through very difficult living conditions, through poor education—these are all external to him—and secondly, and this we regard as the most important, the Black man in himself has developed a certain state of alienation. He rejects himself, precisely because he attaches the meaning White to all that is good. (Biko, 1979b, p. 19)

A year later, Biko was tortured and brutally murdered at the hands of the apartheid regime, and the situation in the country led historian R. W. Johnson (1977) to title his book *How Long Will South Africa Survive?* The answer—about seventeen years.[47]

While 1994, the year Nelson Mandela was elected the first president of a democratic South Africa, was a year of hope for many, it did not put an end to the colonial-capitalist currents of the country's politics. Although Mandela's achievement of keeping the country from sliding into civil war in the aftermath of apartheid was undeniable, his government also oversaw economic reforms underpinned by the globally dominant neoliberal paradigm and the associated idea of "trickle-down" economics, which failed to relieve the poverty of a vast majority of South Africans.[48] Historians argue about the causes: while some, notably Patrick Bond (2004) in his book *Talk Left, Walk Right*, see this as ANC hypocrisy, others, such as Hirsch (2005) in *Season of Hope*, argue that the policy was consistent with ANC's pre-1994 promises and reflected a balancing act between the need to redistribute wealth and to grow the economy.[49] Whatever the reason, the economic policies of the Mandela (1994–1999) and Mbeki (1999–2008) administrations left many dissatisfied. Just as Amrit Gangar did the "unthinkable" and criticized Nehru, University of Cape Town (UCT) students behind the Rhodes Must Fall movement questioned Mandela's legacy. As activist Rekgotsofetse Chikane wrote,

> We, as "born frees", had begun to question the role of Nelson Mandela and consider whether he was complicit in the way our country developed after the fall of apartheid. . . . Our issue was not with the man himself, but the role his legacy played in stifling tough conversations about race. A legacy that we believed was predicated on a need to sell the black majority short during the negotiations to appease the white minority in the country. (2018, p. 90)

The UCT students—and others that include many of my interlocutors in Wentworth—had a point. In the 1990s more than one million jobs (almost 20 percent of the entire workforce) were lost, leading to unprecedented levels of unemployment (Bond & Hallowes, 2002, p. 44). Out of forty thousand cases of land restitution, fewer than thirty were solved under the Mandela administration (Bond & Hallowes, 2002, p. 40).[50] Social assistance programs, education, health, labor laws, and regulation of the business environment "all show marked continuities between the late apartheid and the post-apartheid eras, as did environmental management practices.[51] Public policies were reformed more than transformed" (Seekings & Nattrass, 2015, pp. 257–258). At the same time, the distribution of water, a scarce resource in South Africa, across the country's population "is even more unequal, measured in class, race and gender terms, than the distribution of income" (Bond & Hallowes, 2002, p. 35). In 1999 the Truth and Reconciliation Commission (TRC) urged the government to "accelerate the closing of the intolerable gap between the advantaged and disadvantaged by, among other things, giving even more urgent attention to the transformation of education . . . The recognition and protection of socio-economic rights are crucial to the development and the sustaining of a culture of respect for human rights" (Boraine, 2000, p. 357). Arguably, in their efforts to build a new South Africa, the Mandela and Mbeki administrations failed to challenge the long-standing currents of colonial-capitalist "development" by keeping key elements of the colonial matrix of power intact.

This continuation of (neo)colonial dynamics was palpable during my time in Durban. Jacob Zuma was president, and even children in the second and third grades of Durban South Primary would talk about him, usually in negative terms. In March 2017, just as my film workshop with children in Wentworth was picking up steam, a large march against Zuma took place in Durban, drawing thousands and marking a symbolic "enough is enough" from the people of KwaZulu-Natal, Zuma's main bastion of support. Later that month, Ahmed Kathrada, one of the last surviving leaders of Mandela's generation of freedom fighters, passed away, and his family insisted that they did not want Zuma at the funeral. The country was clearly turning against the president. I could not help but wonder, given his unpopularity, how he got elected in the first place.

The answer dates back to December 2007 when, in Polokwane, a provincial town north of Johannesburg, the ANC's 52nd National Conference took place. Here, Thabo Mbeki failed to win a third term as the party's president,[52] was subsequently recalled as president, and was replaced by Zuma, who went on to win popular support in the 2009 elections. As Chipkin and Swilling (2018, p. 4) point out, "The Polokwane revolt in the ANC was informed by a conviction that economic transformation as pursued during the Mandela and Mbeki eras had produced an anomaly, if not a perversion: a small black elite beholden to white corporate elites, a vulnerable and over-indebted black middle class and a large African majority condemned to unemployment and dependent on welfare handouts to survive." As a result, widespread calls for radical economic transformation and Black economic empowerment could be heard across the ANC and countrywide, with Zuma chosen to implement these reforms.

But the pursuit of Black economic empowerment ran into trouble: elements of the government (notably the national treasury) refused to cooperate when government contracts were awarded to Black-owned companies without regard to cost, as they did not see this as providing "fair value for the fiscus and for citizens" (Chipkin & Swilling, 2018, p. 5). As a result, the Zuma administration turned into "an orgy of power" in which "there is little time to contemplate accountability to the public who had put the party in power" and a criminal "shadow state" emerged (Booysen, 2015, p. 28). Soon everyone in South Africa seemed to be talking about "state capture"—the idea that rather than being accountable to the citizens, the state had become "captured" by a narrow elite (Renwick, 2018). While many simply saw Zuma as a corrupt leader motivated by self-interest, state capture, in reality, was a more far-reaching political project.[53] Chipkin and Swilling (2018, p. 2) contend that the Zuma administration sought to "repurpose state institutions to suit a constellation of rent-seeking networks that have been constructed and now span the symbiotic relationship between the constitutional and shadow state. This is akin to a silent coup."[54] State capture had its roots deep in history, long before the 2007 Polokwane revolt. "There is a clear and direct line of sight from the origins of the State in the Cape Colony, when it was 'captured' by the Dutch East India Company, through to the era of Cecil Rhodes and 'Milner's Kindergarten'[55] . . . in post-Boer War South Africa" (Chipkin & Swilling, 2018, p. 1). Simply put, the political visions that underpinned the colonization of Southern Africa remained at work in the present-day republic.

By the time I returned to Wentworth to share my findings in February 2018, South Africa had a new president, Cyril Ramaphosa, a long-standing trade union leader and freedom fighter. He had been elected president of the ANC at the 54th National Conference in December 2017, defeating Nkosazana Dlamini-Zuma, the wife of the former president who was widely seen as advancing the agenda of state capture. Ramaphosa led the ANC to victory in elections in May 2019, albeit by the smallest margin in democratic history—apparently reflecting the South African population's disillusion with the party that brought the country democracy.[56] It remains to be seen how successful Ramaphosa's administration and his successors may be at reversing the state capture orchestrated by his predecessor.

Where does this history leave the environment? One clue can be found in the macroeconomic growth, employment, and redistribution policy of the first postapartheid government that continues to shape today's policy. This document contains just a single tokenistic mention of "environmental sustainability," and even that is in the context of attracting foreign investment rather than reversing any of apartheid's structural legacies (Bond & Hallowes, 2002, p. 44). Bond and Hallowes (2002, p. 25) write, "Restoring the eco-socio-economic balance was one of the most challenging of all the enormous responsibilities the first democratic South African government faced in 1994, just as the painful exercise of identifying capitalism's environmental self-destructiveness occupied global elites in Stockholm in 1972 and Rio de Janeiro in 1992. Locally and globally, however, elites were not up to the challenge of adopting potential solutions." And so, just as the colonial-capitalist-*Hindutva* ideology acts to depoliticize the environment in India, state capture, along with a legacy of colonial-capitalist currents of history, has a similar effect in South Africa.

Waiting for Social Justice in "Wenties"

When I entered Wentworth for the first time, as I looked around at houses surrounded by fences with cars parked in front and saw the views of smokestacks from the township's streets, I thought to myself, "It's not so bad." But as I got deeper inside the neighborhood, I saw flats that I had heard were infamous for hosting drug gangs, children playing football in front of an oil refinery that was literally killing them (figure 3.3), piles of trash around the commons, older adults rolling on broken wheelchairs, car wrecks that served as playgrounds for children, and malnourished street dogs. And soon the smell hit me, a strong chemical odor that made me question if it was safe to inhale the air. I was, after all, smack in the middle of the South Durban Industrial Basin. The refinery smokestacks filled the horizon and provided a backdrop to the scene I was observing.

Wentworth was fashioned in the 1960s out of "a stock of 'farmland,' military housing, railway workers' housing, a former concentration camp for Boer prisoners, and a swampy informal settlement next to the refinery site called Happy Valley" (Chari, 2006a, p. 123). A vivid description of

Figure 3.3
Children playing football in Wentworth.

Wentworth in the 1970s can be found in Rostron (1991, pp. 24–25, quoted in Desai, 2017, pp. 86–87):

> Hemmed in on one side by an industrial estate and on the other by the Mobil Oil refinery [today's Engen], it sprawled over several lilliputian hills. Wentworth was eleven kilometres from Durban city centre, just off the freeway on the route to exotic South Coast holiday resorts like Amanzimtoti and Umtentweni. There was nothing exotic about Wentworth. The main approach was up Quality Street, past the gloomy Girassol Café and at the crest of the hill the dour, decaying Palm Springs Hotel. The sandy roads were rutted and uneven, often strewn with building rubble and household rubbish, and after a sudden tropical downpour the craters in the road would form small lakes. Packs of dogs roamed the dusty streets and children played in the open storm drains . . . At night the Mobil Oil refinery glowed with a thousand pinpricks of light in the velvety dark, and its slender, fifty-foot chimneys belched out vivid flames like some vast starship from outer space. The refinery was heavily fortified with tall barbed-wire fences, concrete walls and commanding watchtowers with spy-holes. It had once been attacked, in one of the few military actions in that area, by an African National Congress unit armed with rocket launchers, but the police soon winkled the unit out of their strategic position on the hill and gave chase to the guerrillas right through Wentworth, finally pinning them down in a paint factory in Hime Street, where all four insurgents were shot dead.

Short of the attack on the refinery, this description could easily be written about Wentworth in the 2010s.

The township was a direct result of the apartheid government's 1950 Group Areas Act, which led to the eviction of Indians living in Durban (many of whom were moved to the neighboring area of Merebank) and with them the Coloured people who often lived in backyard tenancies.[57] Those evicted were moved to former military housing in Austerville, today the heart of Wentworth, where they met other Coloured people forcibly moved from Cato Manor, Mayville, and as far away as the Eastern Cape. As Sharad Chari's research has shown, by the 1970s, a period of crisis for the apartheid regime and the country's economy, "subaltern Coloureds in Wentworth had few effective mediators . . . [and] turned inward, to churches,[58] soccer, gangs and a bittersweet valorization of locality" (Chari, 2009, p. 524).[59] What followed,

Chari argues, was ghettoization "in the analytical sense proposed by Wacquant[60] as a process involving stigma, constraint, spatial confinement and institutional containment" (Chari, 2006b, p. 427).[61]

Angela, one of my informants in Wentworth, expressed a similar sentiment in her narrative of resettlement. Angela was moved to Wentworth from Mayville in the 1970s and at the time of my research worked in Durban South Primary's canteen, giving out lunches to children eligible for government-sponsored meals. Back in Melville, she remembered, "it was a different scenario because there we lived with all different nations. And we were hand in hand with one another, we spoke to one another, we played with other races and all that." But in Wentworth, even though the community is also very diverse, relations between different groups are nowhere as cordial. "You find you have Indians, you have Africans in our area and they have a race issue now. It's a racial issue that goes on. So, like you [are] not free to be with these people. So, it's like awkward to live like that." What Angela seemed to be getting at was, as a result of arbitrary resettlement, Wentworth residents had lost the mutual respect and the bonds that had developed organically in Melville (and in Cato Manor,[62] District Six in Cape Town and other multiracial communities dismantled by the apartheid regime). Her comments reflected the continuity of a hierarchy of racial classification that originated in South Africa's colonial past (Klausen, 2018). They also resonated with the narrative of "not Black enough, not White enough" that I heard many times over in Wentworth—the idea that the racial position of Coloured people prevented them from reaping benefits of the postapartheid dispensation, which fueled racial tensions.

The lack of job opportunities in Wentworth was another factor adding to community friction. The luckiest among the men "have been shaped into the pre-eminent semi-skilled industrial migrants of South Africa" in the capacity of "pipe-fitters, boilermakers, fitters and turners" (Chari, 2006b, p. 428) who work seasonally across South Africa's refineries. But not all of them were so "fortunate," as drugs and gang violence proliferated in the township from the 1970s.

Unemployment statistics in Wentworth are indeed alarming. Out of approximately thirty thousand residents, at least one-third between ages fifteen and sixty-five are unemployed, a large number of people cannot work as a result of disability or illness (often caused by air pollution), "an equally sizeable group either chooses not to work or could not find work; and a significant group is comprised of currently unemployed seasonal workers" (Chari, 2006b, p. 429).[63] This last group's lot has become considerably worse since a wave of major strikes in the 1980s, when Engen started outsourcing and using labor brokers, many of whom were in fact ex-gangsters. In the words of Chari's informant Lenny, "gang leaders actually became labour brokers. It was a mob thing. It's not been broken" (Chari, 2006b, p. 430). Another strike in 2001 led to Engen's model of partial shutdowns "planned at short notice in order to lower the risk of strike activity" (Chari, 2006b, p. 431), exacerbating what was already a precarious livelihood for the seasonal workers from Wentworth. The lack of job opportunities forces residents to seek at least some of their income through drugs, theft, and sex work (p. 430).

The Wentworth residents' struggles and their strategies for negotiating around them became clear to me when I spoke to Grace, the mother of a boy in the filmmaking workshop. We sat in a classroom belonging to the notoriously naughty class 7A, surrounded by textbooks and exam papers, with stationery and all kinds of rubbish strewn around the floor and chairs randomly tossed around the room. The state of the classroom seemed to perfectly match the world outside its walls, and the subject of our conversation. A tall woman with a booming voice and upright posture, Grace cut an unusual figure in Wentworth. "She's tough," I had been warned by another teacher, but I sensed a certain softness behind Grace's loud words, a dignity rooted in her Christian faith, and a sense of purpose in her work.

A single mother of four—two older girls and two school-age boys— Grace shared a flat with her mother. She served as a youth worker in the community, going school to school to spread awareness about HIV/AIDS, teenage pregnancy, and drugs. She also worked at a shelter for women who were victims of domestic violence and/or addicted to drugs. "Life in Wentworth is hard . . . it's hard for the mere fact that the people have the perception of . . . it's Coloured mentality. We don't have to finish schools because there are shuts," referring to the shutdowns in the oil refineries during which local men get seasonal work. Grace continued, "[They want] big money, fast. They don't want to go through the whole struggle of small money, long-term jobs." But there is another way to get big money. "They'd rather go for the quick way out which is drugs. So therefore I get the drugs, I get the earrings. I get the girls. I get the fast cars. I get the takkie."[64] And this was still better than living in "Wenties" in the recent past. Thinking back to when her children were little, Grace recalled life being worse. "You know we lived in time where, when it reached a certain time in the evening, we'd sit flat on the floor and watch TV. Who lives like that?" When I asked her why she chose Durban South Primary for her son, Grace did not hesitate: "I chose [it] because of their high discipline. Discipline for me is very important."

Pollution has affected Grace's family. One of her daughters developed asthma when she was eight years old. "I thought my child was dying because I didn't know what was wrong with her because she just couldn't breathe," Grace remembered, getting visibly agitated for the first time in our conversation. Both her daughters had gotten out of Wentworth because of the violence and the pollution. "If I had my way, my sons wouldn't grow up in Wentworth."

These struggles were echoed by all of my informants in Wentworth. The need to work multiple jobs and live in intergenerational households to make ends meet was common; in fact, many of the children were looked after by a grandparent or other relative and did not live with either parent, as many were migrant laborers working away from Durban or had died from gang violence, HIV, leukemia, or other pollution-induced illnesses. The ways violence and pollution affected Grace and her family were common among my informants, and many residents seeking to lead a respectable life seemed almost to be tiptoeing around the violence in the community.[65] The emphasis on discipline in choosing a school was echoed by many parents I interviewed; it was considered the quality needed to overcome the temptations of drugs and gangs.

As reflected in Grace's struggles, Wentworth is a liminal space where the colonial-capitalist legacies of South Africa meet the harsh realities of a postapartheid Coloured township. These historical forces are behind the lack of work opportunities, inadequate education and health care, the environmental racism of largely unchecked industrial pollution in South Durban, and the continued discrimination against Coloured people. They also create a situation in which fast violence eclipses slow violence, making it very difficult to talk of or act on the "political" in the environment.[66]

And yet, Grace has not left. According to Chari, "even in the flats of Woodville Road, which housing activist Jane Glover calls 'the ghetto within the ghetto,' locals refuse to forget how cool it can be to sit at the front-door step and see the whole world go by" (Chari, 2006b, p. 435). Indeed, as much as places like Wentworth and Pashulok may seem dystopian, they are not devoid of hope. Prior to my fieldwork, several South African scholars told me the community is full of "characters," and this indeed was my experience: just as repression the world over has given rise to songs, poetry, and art, so did the tough life in Wentworth instill in its residents a unique collective sense of humor and, at least on the surface, an attitude of unbending resilience.

In *Pollution Kills*—a film students made here while taking my observational filmmaking workshop (which I discuss in the following chapter)—we find a scene that speaks to why the locals continue to live here. A woman is shown sitting on a chair in the golden early morning light wearing a robe. When the students ask her how smoking makes her feel, she replies, "Relaxed. It cools my nerves." One student who worked on the film told me why they included this scene: "[We wanted to] tell people to not smoke, like build a centre for people to make them stop and have a meeting of people that are smoking and try to convince them to stop smoking."[67] But I believe the scene—which drew laughter during screenings at the school—also was a symbolic invitation to viewers to recognize the woman's self-respect, connection to place, and pride in a culture of resilience. In this book, I join the students of Pashulok and Wentworth in their effort to capture this buoyancy of the human spirit in liminal spaces of environmental injustice and depoliticizing states. As the next chapter shows, however, the kind of schooling these children receive is often more of an impediment to than an enabler of such political imaginations.

4 READING THE CULTURAL LANDSCAPES OF SCHOOLING: DEPOLITICIZATION AND HOPE

As educators, our role is to always create the belief that there is hope.
—Mahesh, principal of a primary school in South Durban

It was a Saturday afternoon in February 2017. Pranay, a math teacher at Seema Primary in Pashulok—a school "temporarily" (for more than ten years) squatting inside a shopping complex (as seen in figure 1.7 in the introduction)—had just helped me select a group of pupils to participate in my observational filmmaking workshop. We sat in a dimly lit classroom (the electricity supply was off, as usual), with Pranay and I facing the students as we discussed their ideas for film subjects. One by one, the students stood up to explain their ideas, as if they felt I was there to interrogate them. The session reflected a dynamic that accompanied me throughout my field research: in contrast to the students' expectations, the purpose of the video project was to elicit responses from children that adults may not access verbally, generating insights into how students interpreted and understood the environment.

Here I do not mean the environment in the forms often taught through schooling. I was seeking to access the students' phenomenologies of meaning making (Dillabough et al., 2005) about the term "environment" as a starting point for understanding the symbolic worlds and social landscapes of their lives—that is, its translation into a moving image or picture. Were they aware of the slow violence affecting their communities and, if so, how did they visualize it? I wondered whether their potential knowledge (acquired through schooling or otherwise) regarding the Tehri Dam, the development megaproject that had displaced their families, would give me a glimpse into how they made sense of the dislocation and pain endured by their elders.

While the process was designed to allow students maximum freedom in choosing their film subjects, I felt the need to steer them in a direction that would be helpful for my research—a tension echoing my deeper concerns about who benefits from this kind of ethnography, how to avoid falling into the trap of extractive research, and, above all, how to ensure that I would not impose my views on the students and turn the film into a neocolonial project dictated by a foreign researcher. None of these latter "colonial proximities" (Mawani, 2010) were my aim, but the reality of fieldwork is that there is no genuine way to erase the unevenness of power from research spaces.

As such thoughts ran through my head, the scene unfolding before me in the classroom was a reminder that power dynamics partially inherited from centuries of colonialism played themselves out every day through India's education system. My fieldnotes from this day were revealing:

> Students unprepared; asked to state their subjects, which were echoing examples given by me in previous sessions (the life of the street dog, cow grazing in the field, air pollution, etc.)
>
> Teacher visibly upset; made a scene in front of the students, telling me in English that they have not done their work, and then in Hindi shaming the students (saying things like "you represent the students of India," etc.)
>
> Mood in the room visibly dropped, with the students staring into the ground and the teacher continuing in English, explaining that these are the brightest students at the school so "imagine what the rest is like" and that "Peter is taking pains, I am taking pains, this is not part of my job" and, turning to me, that "all your work has gone to waste because they did not do their part."

It felt disconcerting that the students simply repeated the possible film topics I had shared with them rather than coming up with ideas independently, something I initially interpreted as a reflection of the rote learning and lack of critical thought that I had observed in government schools during my previous research in this part of the world.[1] But Pranay's teaching style, which seemed to encourage this kind of learning (and which appeared to be the culturally dominant pedagogy used by all teachers in this school), was the bigger issue. This scene not only posed a challenge to my methodology—shaming and pressure are not conducive to creativity and the kind of freedom of thought I was hoping to encourage through the film project. It also alerted me to the (neo)colonial undertones of schooling in Pashulok (and in India at large[2]) as a legacy of the past, of that intangible but proximal temporal arc Ricœur described and its surplus effects in the space they call the field. But was it fair to relegate what was unfolding in Pashulok to a simple colonial-postcolonial continuity of ideology? I was reminded of Connell's (2007, p. 215) assertion that "metropolitan social theory comfortably talks about the constitution of society, about the building blocks of social processes, and about the reproduction of social structures. It has been much less keen—and perhaps lacks the concepts—to talk about the destruction of social relations, about discontinuity and dispossession, about the bloodshed and suffering involved in creating the world in which we currently live."

Pashulok was, if anything, a site of rupture, dispossession, and discontinuous time, a place escaping the neat currents of history and whose messiness had much to do with the disproportionate burden it bore for India's "development." A deafening quiet, interrupted only by teachers' voices (often shouting), echoed inside classrooms and through the walls, emanating into the school courtyard, a patch of grass covered with litter and lined by students' rusty bicycles. The silence was mirrored by a choreography of discipline: on my first visit, students were taking their exams in an outdoor corridor in unbearable heat (at least for me), sitting in neat rows on thin, dirty mats on sweltering concrete. All wore school uniforms, some of which were badly torn and soiled; some tops were substituted with white T-shirts masquerading as shirts, and some feet lacked shoes. With their heads bent and their faces invisible, none of the students looked up at me, even though, in the months to come, I would receive many curious looks from them whenever they were not under the spell of order. This was a place where formal education was all about social and cultural reproduction—not of intergenerational knowledge but of patterns of exclusion enacted by a state determined to keep the oustees "in their place."

My second research site, Durban South Primary in Wentworth, was, despite the very different context, similar in important ways, and the two schools testify to the potential of schooling to get in the way of a "radical" sustainability agenda. While Durban South did not squat inside a shopping complex, its campus consisted of more than four-decades-old "temporary" prefabricated classrooms that had far outlived their expected lifespan. "You can hardly hang a clock because you can't drill a hole or you break the wall," Mr. Naidoo, the tall, balding, and always cheerful principal whose eyes nevertheless seemed sorrowful, told me.

The "temporary" nature of the structures housing both schools mirrored the institutional liminality of formal education; just as the schools were waiting *in perpetuum* for a permanent facility, so too were the students caught in a limbo between promises of prosperity and the realities of life in a dam resettlement site or a township. The similarities ran even further: although I did not see any mats in Durban South, in what seemed like orchestrated rigidity, the learners here were shepherded through the school complex by teachers forming neat chains of bodies. It was as if both schools tried to make up with discipline for what they lacked in the world of imagination and physical infrastructure, or as if harsh treatment could address the underlying reasons the learners would "misbehave." Schooling in both places was giving off a distinctive odor—one Goffman (1961) aptly labeled over a half-century ago the "total institution."[3]

I wondered where Arendt's view on administrative massacre may fit in such a vision of (post)colonial schooling. Her idea—that the more bureaucratic a state and its institutions are the more violent they are likely to be— seemed particularly appropriate. This insight, derived from tracing the causes of the fast violence of twentieth-century concentration camps and gulags, seemed to apply to the twenty-first-century slow violence leveled against the planet and its "marginal" peoples. According to Arendt (1970, p. 81), "in a fully developed bureaucracy there is nobody left with whom one can argue, to whom one can present grievances, on whom the pressures of power can be exerted. Bureaucracy is the form of government in which everybody is deprived of political freedom, of the power to act; for the rule by Nobody is not no-rule, and where all are equally powerless, we have a tyranny without a tyrant." The focus on order, discipline, and power in Pashulok and Wentworth pointed in the direction of such tyranny. In these schools, the utopian idea underpinning the SDGs that the world can school itself out of the mess of a multitude of planetary-scale anthropogenic environmental crises by teaching young people about "sustainability" ran into the reality of a transgenerational transmission of bureaucratization. This was accomplished by the very medium of schooling, with its associated testing regimes and apolitical socialization.[4] Was bureaucracy to blame for this slow violence, and how was schooling, as an institution of liminality, playing its part in this violence? In what ways does the administrative machinery of procedural learning intervene in intergenerational knowledge transfer about the environment? In what ways, if at all, does historical responsibility shape the process of schooling and who mediates this learning? In what ways might schools act as sites of (de)politicization of environmental issues? How do young people make sense of slow violence?

The answers to these questions were more complicated than I expected, as I learned early on in the observational filmmaking workshop I conducted at Durban South Primary. While the students here found it easier than their peers in Pashulok to come up with ideas for subjects for their films, security concerns made it difficult to film in the community. Given the high crime rate, students were scared they might get attacked and have the cameras stolen from them. Together with the English teacher Aruna, my key informant at the school, I organized an evening session for the parents, at which we discussed the project. Aruna knew all the families personally, and I sensed she had already decided whose parents were responsible enough to be trusted with the cameras. But, she later told me, the meeting did not go as she had imagined. One of the families she believed should be assigned a camera did not come. Keen to move the workshop along, I pushed for the camera to be given to a different parent from the same group, something Aruna disapproved of and tried to communicate to me, but I missed her signals. Afterward, she told me it was dangerous to give the camera to the parent who took it. "I know that woman. Her husband is an abusive drunkard and she's like a little mouse who cannot stand up to him. He'll steal the camera and sell it to pay for his drinking," she told me. I was stunned. "What should we do now?" I asked her. It seemed the only reasonable course of action was to enter the thick, unlit darkness of a Wentworth night and retrieve the camera from the parent before it was too late. Given that Durban academics had advised me never to enter Wentworth at night, let alone walk the streets on foot, this prospect did not appeal to me. "Don't worry, they know me here and won't do anything if you're with me," she said, referring to the local gangs that allegedly dominated and controlled the informal economies of Wentworth. While we managed to get the camera back and later allocated it to a different family, this episode brought home just how much the context of fast violence in Wentworth shaped not only the lives of the children but also their experience of formal education.

In this chapter, I argue that both schooling systems, while performing bureaucratic functions and practices that disrupt intergenerational knowledge transfer, also reflect elements of hope. This was most powerfully reflected in the imaginations of environmental futures of learners at both sites who, despite the impact of schooling, often attained an understanding of the environment rooted more in Arendtian than in postcolonial and post-totalitarian understanding of politics. I encountered many students whose thinking seemed oriented toward hope rather than despair—a clear rebuff of the notion that structural "educating for inequality" defines learners' identities or takes away their agency.

SQUEEZING THE ENVIRONMENT OUT OF INDIA'S EDUCATION FOR DEVELOPMENT

Searching for environmental education in Pashulok was a tall order. Rakesh, my translator and one of my key informants,[5] helped me secure access to Seema Primary, but it soon became clear that environmental studies was not a priority there. When I first approached the principal about getting permission to undertake research at the school, I was turned down. This decision was later reversed at the insistence of Pranay, one of the teachers, who saw value in my offer to teach students the basics of documentary filmmaking. Later in my fieldwork, I learned that the reason for the original denial was the school's anxiety that my research would focus on environmental education. The subject was not regularly taught here, and the school did not want this to become publicly known. This forced me to rethink my narrow definition of ESE and, instead of seeing it as a subject, a curriculum, or a pedagogy, I began to understand that the forces shaping students' political imaginations and sense of historical responsibility had their origins in the intergenerational cultural landscapes and ideologies underpinning schooling in Pashulok across (and between) school subjects.[6]

My interactions with Pranay and Arvind, the English teacher at Seema Primary, provided insight into the ideology of schooling and how it contrasts with the oustees' lived experiences. These two teachers were the only two staff members who spoke English, and my communication with everyone else depended on translators, who were not always available. I saw less of Arvind than I did of Pranay because the observational filmmaking workshop took place in Pranay's classroom, and because he often talked to me before and after each daily session. If Pranay figures larger than life in my account of schooling at Seema Primary, it is because he figured larger than life during my time in Pashulok. Arvind's perspectives, however, helped me gain a more nuanced picture of the cultural forces at play in schooling there. Always smiling behind his mustache, he often expressed himself in flowery, colorful language while making broad gestures with his hands. Arvind was not from Uttarakhand and had moved to Pashulok in 2005 to teach. He was one of only two teachers who had been at Seema Primary from the beginning; the other was Pranay. Arvind was from the plains in the south, and he was a keen observer of what was happening in other states across India. I was particularly struck by the contrast between my expectation (and prior experience) of Indian schooling as a tool to advance the agenda of modernization and Arvind's take on the education system's shortcomings: "I feel that in the drive for development we are losing out on our moral and traditional values," he told me as we sat in the teachers' common room, surrounded by an almost perfect silence as students worked independently in their classrooms. "This is the land of Swami Vivekananda,[7] Ramkrishna Paramahansa,[8] Gautam Buddha[9] and Guru Nanak.[10] So many disciplined people took birth here. Instead of focusing so much on scientific development, we must pay attention toward moral and environmental education." Apart from the stress on discipline, Arvind's statement was notable for the list of people he saw as role models—two Hindu, one Buddhist, and one Sikh religious figure.[11] This reflected his perspective that India's culture and history were products of mysticism, an echo of the *Hindutva* state Narendra Modi was busy building in Delhi as we spoke.

Arvind, Pranay, and almost all their colleagues[12] in Pashulok were high-caste Hindus, and the ideology of casteism was indeed palpable at Seema Primary. One day during my fieldwork my usual translator could not come, and on a friend's recommendation, I asked a local college student to accompany me. He was from a lower caste, and his skin was visibly darker than that of the teachers at the school. At midday, when we were invited to the teachers' common room for lunch, my translator was the only person at the table not offered any food—something I did not notice. When he brought it up with me later, much to my horror, I remembered Pranay asking me earlier that day how much I was paying the translator and suggesting that I was wasting my money. It was then that I realized that perhaps I had been naïve in assuming that Pranay and his colleagues saw the student (and parent) population they served as equals.[13]

I noticed early on in my fieldwork that the teachers were broadly supportive of Tehri Dam, but their sweepingly dismissive view of the oustees surprised me. It came up most powerfully in a conversation with Pranay about the early days of Seema Primary:

> Initially I think for the first . . . two or three years you can compare the students which we get inside the school . . . to some you can say tribal people, some beast-like people . . . They don't have etiquettes how to sit, how to come in the school with proper uniform, to get early from the bed, take the bag, come to school, not even the, we even made them how to wash the faces. We have done many, many things, I think the people will not consider, not count them as the important factor but we think those are the factors that converted this school to the form in which it is at the present.

This stunned me; it was as if I was listening to a British colonial officer talking about India's Indigenous populations a century earlier (Seth, 2007), in an era of colonial education (S. C. Ghosh, 2012; Topdar, 2015).[14] While I could see that Pranay was bragging about how far the school had come and that some of his word choices ("beast-like," for example) could be attributed to

English not being his mother tongue, the underlying sentiment was clear—seeing the oustees as subjects to be reformed who had learned virtually nothing valuable from their elders. In an undisguised echo of the British Raj (Armitage, 2000), Pranay saw himself as an agent of the state, and the state equaled civilization, development, and progress. Along with his colleagues (as we shall see in the next section), Pranay's views and behavior seemed to be regulated by a culture of casteist exclusion.

I was troubled by this culture and had to remind myself constantly that individual teachers were only partially responsible for it, since the historical, social, and economic context of 2017 Pashulok played a big part, too. Moreover, I sought to suspend judgment because I depended on these teachers for access to my research site—Pranay in particular. One of the longest-serving and most active teachers at the school, he was not just my key informant but someone who carried himself with a gravitas that often made me wonder whether he was really the *de facto* principal of the school. When he walked the corridors in his upright posture, hands behind his back, fingers interlocked, students would slow down, look at the ground, and quietly mumble a greeting, signaling their respect and—I suspected—fear. The moment he pulled his motorbike through the school gate in the morning, something shifted in the school's atmosphere; the noise level dropped and students would stop running up and down the stairs of the shopping center where the school was located. Given his influence, I thought it lucky that Pranay became my ally and saw my project as an opportunity to enrich students' lives. But even as I owed him a debt of gratitude for vouching for me to the principal, and even as I witnessed his commitment to his students and his unorthodox methods, it was difficult to ignore that he appeared to be part of a culture of coercion and paternalism.

But Pranay was not the problem, nor was Arvind, nor their colleagues. As I try to make sense of their situation , I am reminded of the three Tanaka brothers in Seth Holmes' (2013) ethnography of Mexican migrant farmworkers in the United States. Holmes' account is full of horrors arguably greater than what I saw in Pashulok, from the exhausting, dangerous border crossing to the permanent disabilities migrants suffered as a result of unsafe working conditions. Yet Holmes argues that the Tanakas, who owned and ran the strawberry farm where his fieldwork took place, meant well and even consciously tried, within a space constrained by neoliberal capitalism and corporate competition, to improve the lot of the workers. Pranay, too, tried hard to improve the lot of his students. I soon realized that his willingness to vouch for me because he believed my project would benefit the children was part of a pattern; he worked hard to secure every such opportunity. He was almost invariably the last teacher to leave the school at the end of the day and he had built a "mathematics lab" at the school, a highly unusual interactive learning space without desks or chairs that contained lots of models, toys, and drawings designed to give the children hands-on mathematics lessons. The lab became my headquarters during my time in Pashulok, and it was where I met with the students who participated in my filmmaking workshop. Seema Primary was not simply a product of a culture of depoliticization; it was shaped by individuals and subjectivities far more complex than any particular ideology.

When it came to environmental themes at the school, the individual-ization of responsibility and depoliticization of sustainability appeared to be the norm. During one of our lunchbreak conversations in the common room, I asked Arvind how he imagined a successful environmentalist. He first gave a broad answer, but soon zeroed in on an example. "Most of us are only concerned about ourselves and in order to keep our homes clean, we throw waste outside the house, or on the road," he said, gesticulating with his hands in all directions, as if waste was all around us. "Many people burn plastic, which produces many harmful gases like carbon monoxide, which is damaging for the entire human race. It is a cosmopolitan view that these are dangerous things, and the nature lover will take care of these things." I was not sure whether the reference to cosmopolitanism was yet another way to set himself apart from the apparently not-so-cosmopolitan oustees, but it seemed clear that Arvind saw environmentalism similarly to the educators in Indian and South African schools I visited early on in my fieldwork who were practicing de-politicized forms of ESE. Perhaps unsurprisingly, the conversa-tion turned to planting trees, a common ESE project. To my surprise, Arvind was critical. "People in Delhi, Goa, you and me are planting trees. Kerala, Tamil Nadu all are planting . . . Then why is the earth still so barren? . . . Then why are we still so anxious about the weak environment? Why is it still in danger?" These were all good questions, I thought. Arvind continued: "If organizations are planting so many trees, perhaps what is happening is that we are planting trees and doing a photo session around the event, but we never look back at the tree to see if it is surviving or not." I found this critique of the commodification of environmentalism interesting and relevant, but it did not seem to negate the individualization of responsibility for the environment that Arvind seemed to have embraced earlier in our conversation—unless, by seeing if the tree is surviving, he meant tackling systemic issues that kill trees, like climate change or groundwater depletion. But by now I had heard enough from my various interlocutors about the meaning of environmentalism at Seema Primary not to give Arvind the benefit of the doubt, and I concluded that what he had in mind was more along the lines of watering the saplings.

The idea of constraining the learners' imagined agency (now and in the future) to deal with issues that could be tackled by an individual and eschewing systemic issues requiring political action came across even more powerfully in my conversations with Pranay. One day, we were sitting over lunch in the teacher's dining room—an empty classroom with a bare concrete floor, a table, and a few broken plastic chairs. Pranay told me, as he was mixing his *dhal* with the vegetable curry prepared by the school's cook, "When these students came to us in class VI, they even don't know how to write their names, but I'm sure you will be the witness, most of these students will pass with good marks."[15] I wondered if what I was really witnessing was the manifestation of systemic repression of cultures and knowledges seen by the state as not conducive to "development." Pranay continued: "And what I can say, I can claim those marks as the result of my hard work, not that of their own. The good thing that these students are having is that they at least surrender to our efforts, if I make them sit here for three hours or six hours, they don't protest against us, *ki nahi sir* [but no sir], we are not going to sit here." Though my face must have betrayed the state of my discomfort by now—after all, I still considered Pranay an "enlightened" teacher who challenged his students with innovative methods—he continued as he took another bite of the curry. "They at least realize that if their teacher is ordering them something or suggesting them something, that is going to be beneficial for them in the long run."[16] Seema Primary, it seemed to me, was affording its students little agency in shaping their own education trajectories.

If this were the case, how did schooling here seek to shape the learners' understanding of the Tehri Dam and the collective trauma of their parents and grandparents caused by forced resettlement? As time went by, I broached the difficult subject of relocation and compensation with both teachers. Arvind's take was that they were "not displaced out of their country, they are in the same state of Uttarakhand, very close to Tehri" and, while adult oustees were "very attached to Tehri," the new generation was already "settled" in Pashulok. Arvind did not seem to think much of displacement; in fact, I got a sense in my conversations with all the teachers that they were confused as to why I would choose Pashulok as my research site, as the oustee presence did not seem an important factor from their point of view. Pranay, too—while recognizing that Tehri Dam had unwelcome environmental impacts—did not express any concerns about forced resettlement of the submerged villages:

> In my opinion, the first generation is not happy just because of the nostalgic factor, otherwise . . . they've got a big amount of compensation as compared to their individual losses . . . For the new generation, they've got a big opportunity to transform their life, from a comparative backward scenario to the normal scenario regarding the education, regarding the social structure of equality and standard of life.

I believed that Pranay's experience of the oustees' attitudes (toward education, money, the Indian state) rendered their grievances illegitimate in his eyes, but his remarks were consistent with his dismissal of the oustees' cultural knowledge as worthless and therefore seemed to me an act of symbolic violence. In his mind, the oustees' financial compensation fully offset any losses; a way of life that had evolved over centuries in close contact with the natural environment became commodified and ultimately dismissed.

Over the course of my field research, I came to believe the imagination of the "normal scenario" Pranay referred to consisted of a combination of Hindu and nationalist ideas. Vasavi's (2015, p. 44) description of the culture of Indian government elementary schools is highly applicable to my experience of Seema Primary:

While everyday interactions are marked by hierarchy of age, gender and caste relations, the culture of special occasions or "function days" (as they are called) is fused with the specific culture of the local society. Independence and Republic Days, as also Gandhi Jayanti and Children's Day, are celebrated not so much for their social and political significance but as days of reverence for historical leaders represented as deities . . . The result is a combination of both banal nationalism and banal Hinduism. Such religious (mostly Hindu-derived) ritualisation combines with dense nationalism embedded in the texts . . . These ideologies predominantly legitimise the dominance of Hindu society and its practices, emphasise a culture of subservience and obedience, and promote Hindu majoritarianism.

Even though I did not have a chance to observe the celebration of any civic holidays during my fieldwork, all the teachers expressed to me at one point or another—sometimes in interviews, sometimes in informal chats in the lounge or in passing remarks—their reverence for Modi, their pride in India, and their belief that the students lacked "cleanliness" (which I interpreted to refer both to hygiene and purity in a religious sense).[17] Over time, I started seeing these remarks as a cultural practice that helped maintain the social hierarchies regulating the teachers' behavior and their perception of their students' abilities and needs.

At the same time, I was aware that the school achieved remarkable academic results by the standard of government schools in this geographical area, and that this provided a way out of poverty for at least some students. I also recognized that the social issues in the community, including the breakdown of traditional social structures, petty crime, and alcoholism, influenced some students' behavior and created challenges for the teachers. But this did not seem a justification for Seema Primary's dismissiveness of the oustees' trauma, which delegitimized and eroded their intergenerational cultural knowledge and practices and favored the infinite-growth developmentalist narrative in education. There was little space for Arendtian politics here, whether among the learners (who were not invited to interpret the history or discuss the development trajectory of their community and country) or between the learners and other generations, the debt to whom was rendered invisible.

"An Opportunity to Relax": Passing Time in Environmental Studies in Pashulok

One manifestation of the depoliticization of environmental themes at Seema Primary was the virtual nonexistence of environmental studies at the school.[18] I often encountered resistance when trying to talk to teachers about the subject. Radhika, one of the educators teaching the class, eventually admitted to me that there were no permanent teachers for the subject, which was partly the result of the unavailability of teacher training for environmental studies.[19] "Anyone can teach environment," she told me. "I teach 6th and 8th grade. The drawing teacher takes the 7th grade . . . We teach them according to the textbook and make them [the pupils] learn the answers mentioned. Sometimes we get the students to plant trees . . . we tell them about watering the plants and the manure." She speculated that the subject is taught by the drawing and physical education teachers "because we don't have a lot of workload. In my previous school they would give this subject to mathematics teachers to give them a break from their hectic schedule." The notion that no specific expertise is required to teach the subject, that teaching it constitutes a "break" for teachers, implies that environmental studies is, in the words of another educator at the school, "not taken seriously."[20] These ideas also suggest that little or no critical thinking, political imagination, or intergenerational knowledge transfer is involved in teaching children about the environment, reducing the subject to schematic, routinized, individualized actions such as taking care of plants. Indeed, as the physical education teacher concluded in our interview, "this subject gives an opportunity to relax, we get to go to the field, and even in context of the textbook teaching, it is easy. Everyone knows about plants and environment, so perhaps because of that."

India has instituted compulsory environmental studies classes across all grades in primary school. Considering the many limitations of India's education system, however, it is not surprising that the subject receives little support. According to the government's own report on the "infusion" of environmental education into India's primary school education, "there appears to be still very inadequate exposure of the students to their 'habitat'; there is little active learning from the natural and social worlds around them.

The prescribed activities may simply be routinely taught as a set material to be memorized through teaching in the classroom instead of being pursued by students on their own with an open mind" (National Council of Educational Research and Training [NCERT], 2005, p. 2). Teacher training for environmental studies is not provided, which means it is taught by teachers with various specializations; the subject also is not examined, which, in the context of India's culture of grades and credentials, diminishes the motivation of students and teachers alike to pay attention to it.

Whenever I asked the educators responsible for teaching this subject about the content of what they taught, they would ask a student to show me a copy of the textbook. The prevalence of the textbook culture and rote learning in Indian schools is well recognized (Kumar, 1988, 2005),[21] and Seema Primary was no exception. The apolitical nature of these textbooks is reflected both in their shying away from controversial topics and in the way environment-related subjects are dealt with when they enter the discussion. For example, in *Looking Around* (NCERT, 2008), the government-designed textbook for fifth-grade environmental studies, only one chapter out of twenty-two deals with fossil fuels; most discuss basic concepts of natural science and focus on observation of the environment.[22] Chapter 12, "What if It Finishes . . . ?" considers the finite nature of fossil fuels but makes no mention of climate change, or of any environmental consequences of the world's dependence on fossil fuels. It therefore would be unfair to hold the teachers at Seema Primary responsible for the kind of environmental studies the school offers. Ultimately, deemphasizing environmental studies reflects the lack of political will to turn schooling into a force critical of the government's unsustainable policies—a dynamic that arguably shapes environmental education globally.

During my time in Pashulok, I was not allowed to observe any environmental studies lessons. The reason first given to me was that the teacher was self-conscious about being observed; later it became apparent that, even though the subject was allocated slots in the school's timetable, they were usually filled with other activities such as reviewing for exams in subjects perceived as more important. Given this, Seema Primary offered to run one or two "demonstration" lessons for me to observe—an offer I refused, as it was clear these would be lessons for show rather than a representation of the nature of schooling for oustee children in Pashulok.[23] As my fieldwork overlapped with the exam preparation period, there were no genuine environmental studies lessons taking place, and I was therefore unable to examine the content of these occasional lessons.

A picture started to emerge, however, after reviewing the textbook and talking to teachers about which of its themes they focus on in lessons. In Radhika's words, "school just tells the children to keep the city clean, not emit carbon, make minimum use of cars, and travel by cycle or walk, which will help the environment and their health . . . The schools encourage the children to plant trees and we have tree-planting days." These comments reflect an understanding of action as a predefined pattern of behavior rather than the outcome of pluralistic politics (echoing the slogan on the school wall, "SAVE TREES, SAVE ENVIRONMENT, SAVE THE EARTH").

Radhika observed that grades for environmental studies were not included in students' final results, which was one of the reasons they were uninspired to participate in the subject. "When we know we aren't going to gain anything from it, then why will we study such a subject? We will only study it if we have self-interest. Children will study it if they know it is compulsory and there is importance of the subject and they are going to get jobs." The environment here was perceived as a form of instrumentality, something not to be taken seriously since, according to this version of the myth of meritocracy, it had no impact on the children's futures.[24]

This is consistent with the view that formal education is a path to economic development on an individual and a societal level that has been identified in the literature about schooling in India (Kumar, 2005; Sriprakash, 2016). Indeed, since the economic reforms of the early 1990s, India has experienced unprecedented (K. Basu, 2004; Panagariya, 2005) if uneven (Datt & Ravallion, 2002; Kohli, 2006) economic growth, and the entrenchment of a highly advanced neoliberal regime (Harvey, 2007; Patnaik, 2007; Walker, 2008) that promotes a cultural imagination of the society firmly rooted in West-centric, consumerism-driven modernity (Ganguly-Scrase & Scrase, 2008). As Sriprakash argues, this has profound consequences for education, especially in rural areas: "Where does this leave the poor rural child?

She is largely absent from cultural narratives of India's economic growth in terms of her linguistic, class and caste locations. The seeming irrelevance of her rural livelihood to the advancement of the nation's knowledge economy further underscores her marginality" (Sriprakash, 2016, pp. 153–154). Since rural children from poor families are generally constrained to public education and unable to access private schools, Sriprakash continues, "she also fails to live out the fervent aspiration for upward social mobility to which stories of both individual and national progress are attributed . . . Being placed so firmly outside normative citizen-subjecthood, the 'poor child' is positioned as a governable subject in need of reform." Underpinning the myth of mobility and the postcolonial logic of governance is the ideology of depoliticization, the current of history that turns aspiration into a commodity and schooling into a homogenizing tool for social engineering. This ideology owes much of its strength to a rule of nobody (Arendt, 1970) in which bureaucratization turns us into passive agents of slow violence.

The history of India's education system offers further clues to the origins of these cultural and political trends. The Indian state failed to fulfill the constitutional promise of education for all children after Independence and, despite many initiatives over the decades, continues to fail to the present day. By making environmental studies compulsory, India ostensibly decided to tackle, on a mass scale, perhaps the hardest task ever to face a schooling system anywhere: educating for the Anthropocene.[25] Yet, much of the education discourse in India revolves around more "fundamental" aims—bringing children into school and boosting literacy and numeracy rates. Given this context, it is perhaps not surprising that the subject of environmental studies operates as a state lie, a deception at the cost of the future, a practice that envisions children as merely following in predefined blueprints of thought and behavior, contributing to the "death of politics" in an Arendtian sense (Kateb, 1977, p. 156).[26]

If the environment is low on the agenda, and if schooling promotes the individualization of environmental responsibility, what messages do students receive about development? As the idea of development is dealt with in a number of school subjects (lessons I was not allowed to observe),[27] no clear answer emerged from my field research, but interviews with teachers suggested an adherence to what may be called the mainstream narrative of development in post-Independence India. In Pranay's words, "They [students] learn about the development of India, about what the country has made in the era after Independence but they don't treat environment as an issue, they [the government] glorify the development in the textbooks." Tehri Dam is consequently "the symbol of development, not a symbol of environmental hazard." My experience in the field pointed to the centrality of this narrative in the culture of schooling at Seema Primary. An uncritical admiration of the state's project of development, in which supposedly inclusive economic growth blends with nationalism, permeated my interactions with students and teachers alike. As Arvind told me, "quick and fast" development necessitates building dams, since they help with electricity generation and irrigation. "The state benefits financially from it. We can't oppose the dam because they [*sic*] are the pillars of development."

While these views seemed to represent a consensus among the educators at the school, I encountered at least one teacher who was conflicted about spreading this vision of development.[28] She shared her doubts about the benefits of Tehri Dam and her belief that the oustees had genuinely suffered as a result of resettlement, something she believed should have been taught as part of the curriculum. When asked whether she shared these views with the students, however, she admitted that as a government-paid teacher, she did not feel comfortable doing so.[29] Schooling here, it seemed to me, suppressed environmental knowledge and promoted a kind of practiced ignorance (Arendt, 2006) about the environmental and human costs of the dam.

"We Are Not Products of a Total Institution"

Despite these findings, the school's depoliticizing tendencies did not uniformly manifest in learners' perspectives on the environment. Through a variety of visual methods—primarily in films produced in the workshops I taught at Seema Primary but also in mind-mapping exercises and drawings of imagined past and future worlds—the learners' work reflected ideas about the environment that pointed to underlying political imaginaries unseen in the pedagogic processes. If these films and drawings could speak on behalf of their authors, they often would say, "We are not products of a total institution."

The process of making observational films with children helped me grasp the idea that in doing ethnographic research my aim was not to be an impartial observer engaged in "writing culture" as expressed through the words and actions of my interlocutors (cf. Rabinow, 2007). The process of making films, perhaps more than any other element of my fieldwork, drove home my understanding of research as life in and of itself. This became evident during the process of choosing the subjects of observational films the children were making. As the learners were aware that my research was broadly focusing on the environment, they tried to come up with topics that would be helpful to my work. I was not encouraging them to move in any particular direction and gave them a free hand in their choice of topics, as long as they came up with subjects that could be filmed. Rather than seeing the influence of my research agenda on the study participants as skewing the data, I realized that it was actually a strength of the methodology. The children were interpreting the concept of the environment in ways that differed from my definitions (e.g., linking it to the concept of purity and its religious connotations, as we shall see).[30] Apart from learning filmmaking skills (figures 4.1 to 4.3), we were engaged in a process of translation. The learners were relying on knowledge resources available to them both in and out of school to interpret what they perceived to be my agenda, which exposed me to these resources and to the ways students accessed them (figure 4.4). Schooling, it became clear, represented only one of a number of learning spaces for these young people. As a result, they were often engaged in a dialogue with the high-Anthropocene ideologies prevalent in the school curriculum rather than passively absorbing them.

The filmmaking workshop revealed the importance to the young people of intergenerational knowledge transfer outside the confines of the school. In *Ganga, the Life-Giver*, the film produced in the workshop, many of the people filmed were considerably older than the students. When I asked the young filmmakers why they focused on older people rather than filming their peers, one student replied, "Because this gave us a different perspective and knowledge about other people. We have information about our family and their daily routine, but we didn't know about the outside world." This was, however, not merely a question of curiosity; they deliberately attempted

Figure 4.1
Students brainstorming topics during an observational filmmaking workshop.[31]

Figure 4.2
Student and research assistant acting out a scene for a videography exercise.

Figure 4.3

Students practicing framing a shot during a workshop session.

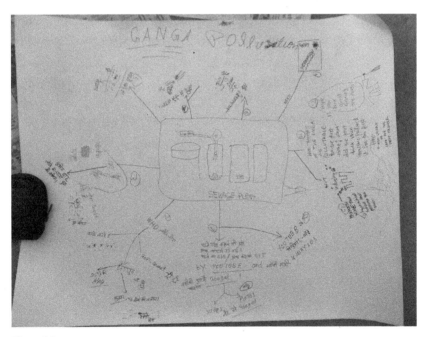

Figure 4.4

A group mind-map made in an effort to come up with a film subject in Pashulok.

119 *Reading the Cultural Landscapes of Schooling*

to turn the film into an opportunity to connect with other generations—without any conscious encouragement from me.[32]

One of the best examples of this was a scene in *Ganga* in which the students filmed a group of older men who were sitting on the riverbank, having a conversation about how pollution changed over time (figure 4.5). Here, the children were instinctively linking memory of the past state of the river with the present and the future through the medium of film. In another scene, one of the students is shown talking to older men walking along the river and asking them, "What was it [the Ganges] like when you were younger and how has it changed since then?" (figure 4.6).

Here, too, the children connected the present with the past in an attempt to reshape the future, which made the film a medium of intergenerational knowledge transfer.

Another important element of the film—a visual exploration of religious rituals performed on the riverbanks—also reflected an interest in learning how adults, rather than the children's peers, related to their environment. Apart from scenes depicting *aarti*, worship rituals performed on the riverbanks, the students filmed two adult men feeding *atta* (dough) to the fish. After observing the men through the camera, one student enters the frame

Figure 4.5
Older adults in Pashulok discussing the pollution of the Ganges.

Figure 4.6
A student asking elders in the community about environmental change.

and joins them as they explain to her how to feed the fish—a moment of intergenerational learning captured on camera.

Like the scenes previously discussed, the religious rituals were not merely spectacles or opportunities for the students to learn; they were intended to bridge the past with the future through the medium of the film. Ashawl, a student involved in making the film, explained to me: "We wanted to show what happens with Ganges from morning to night. In the morning people throw all kinds of things in the river and then in the evening they offer prayer to the river. We want to tell that only after you clean the river will there be any benefit of praying to it." This explanation reflects the students' recognition of the complexities and contradictions of prayer and pollution. The juxtaposition in the film of shots of sewage pipes and trash floating in the water and religious rituals was to serve a pedagogic purpose and contribute to solving what the students saw as the problem of the sacred river becoming polluted. But the students went beyond critique and holistically explored the contradiction between worship of the Ganges and the instrumental value attached to the river by some of the local residents. For example, in one scene an older man interviewed by the students thought back to times before the dam was built, noting that the water level in the Ganges had dropped significantly since the construction of Tehri Dam. These perspectives contrasted sharply with the developmentalist narrative taught to these children at their school in Pashulok. But the inclusion of these perspectives in the film pointed to the children's thirst for a different kind of learning rooted in intergenerational knowledge transfer, which enabled them to shape the future based on their understanding of the past.

It was not just in the context of observational filmmaking that children at Seema Primary expressed views about their environment that reflected a high degree of understanding of slow violence. In focus groups, the children drew pictures of how they imagined the environment one hundred years earlier and one hundred years later. We then gathered in small groups to talk about what they drew and why they believed this was how the environment may have looked in the past and may look in the future. These focus groups suggested that many of the students believed the past generations were better stewards of nature than the current and probably future generations, as reflected in the state of the environment. Drawings of imagined past worlds were often full of trees (figure 4.7), whereas those of the future lacked vegetation. Humans were present in the drawings of the past but their activities took up little space; the natural landscape dominated human-made landscapes. In the drawings of the future, however, few natural elements could be seen. Blocks of flats, factories, roads, vehicles and planes took over as the predominant features of the drawings, with natural environs reduced to clouds and the sun. It was as if the children instinctively understood the sheer scale of the Anthropocene and were anticipating a future in which only the celestial bodies remained beyond human control, with the Earth itself completely subjugated. Violence and the breakdown of social structures were also visible in the drawings, with one child even writing "gang" into the drawing to indicate the anticipated rise of crime in a future dystopian world.

There was poetry in these visual expressions, marked by foresight and an almost instinctive need to communicate across time and space with people the children would never know. A temporality of empathy, the fodder for building temporal arcs linking our present with the past and the future, presented itself in the film and the drawings, encompassing nonhuman entities in its imaginative powers. These children were demonstrating their

Figure 4.7
Pashulok 100 years ago, as imagined by a local student.

engagement in the cultivation of political imaginations, despite the effort to bring them into the fold of mainstream life in a "developed" India by the state's education system.

ECLIPSING SLOW VIOLENCE IN A SOUTH AFRICAN SCHOOL

Just as Pranay was crucial to my understanding of the cultural landscape of schooling in Pashulok, Aruna became my key informant in Wentworth. I met Aruna, an Indian-origin English teacher and head of the social sciences department, through an informal network of self-described environmental educators in Durban.[33] Her school was adjacent to Engen (figure 4.8), the largest oil refinery in South Durban. She indicated that the school was active in environmental education and would be open to hosting me. At our first meeting, I had a sense that Aruna was not originally from South Durban,

Figure 4.8
Wentworth school's basketball court blends into South Durban's industrial vista.

and it turned out she had moved to Durban from a farmland area in the foothills of the Drakensberg mountains. "I think the first thing I noticed when I walked into this place was the sky. There was no sky, it was just a thick layer of smoke. I was quite shocked," she told me, remembering her first days in Wentworth. It perhaps was due to her multiple frames of reference that Aruna saw the local children as full of potential compared to children from more privileged areas.[34]

In one conversation between lessons, as we were sitting in the teachers' lounge and listening to the sound of children queuing up for their government-sponsored lunches in the adjacent canteen, she told me that "the affluent child's interest is academic . . . The kids here, they are not so academically inclined again because I think the local community also speaks more—they are more politically inclined, they're watching TV politics, they're talking about what is happening in the country, they talk about drugs." As a result, children from impoverished areas like Wentworth are more politically and socially aware. "Affluent children read about drugs, but this child here has experienced it, they have seen it, they have felt it, they know what it is. So I admire these children, I really admire them," Aruna told me. It was rare to hear such praise for the students. The only other teacher who shared a similar viewpoint with me was Megan, on the morning we talked about Johny's drawings (as discussed in dilemma 2). Most educators I spoke to during my research focused on the challenges children faced and what they perceived as a lack of motivation or an inability to learn. As with Pranay, I initially thought of Aruna as an "enlightened" teacher, an outlier in a system that appeared to crush hope and human potential. That is perhaps why I was surprised when I observed her in the classroom. Just like Pranay, children seemed to treat her with both respect and fear; they often kept their eyes down and stuck to the opposite side of the corridor when passing her. This was, I thought, surely at least in part a manifestation of a wider structural landscape, the harsh environment in which students here lived, the many long-standing deprivations (in family support, in food and clothes, in safety), and the culture of deference to teachers. Observing Aruna in the classroom gave me further cues: frequently raising her voice, shaming students (she would call them "dizzy," which I construed to mean mentally disturbed), and often sending pupils out of the classroom. She seemed to maintain her authority through fear. But this too appeared to be structural, for it was not clear what the alternative was in this environment; like Pashulok, it seemed that the realities of a township school compelled teachers, even those who genuinely cared about their students, to resort to extreme measures to maintain "discipline," which they saw as a precondition of education.

Wentworth's parallels with Pashulok ran further, suggesting that here, too, education meant obfuscating and tacitly encouraging continued enactment of slow violence. Many of the themes visible in Pashulok—economic starvation of schools catering to the underprivileged, the deprioritization of environmental concerns in the schooling process despite ambitious policy goals set by the government, a prodevelopment curriculum, the individualization of responsibility for the environment, and a preoccupation with discipline—were also prevalent in Wentworth, as was the bureaucratization of teachers and the entire schooling process.

However, I also encountered glimmers of hope in South Durban in the form of outlier teachers who brought activist agendas into their classrooms. In some cases, entire schools participated in demonstrations, such as against the demolition of the Clairwood Racecourse, which took place shortly before the beginning of my fieldwork. "There were public gatherings which we attended. I delivered an address at one of the public gatherings and then we stood with placards—a placard demonstration, outside the racecourse," the headmaster of one South Durban primary school told me, conjuring up images of fifth- or sixth-graders quietly holding banners outside an industrial construction site. I found it hard to imagine that the community was so desperate to preserve the racecourse that an entire school would participate in a protest, yet it sounded like an impressive feat of courage for the administrators, teachers, and pupils to organize such a demonstration.

Despite these glimmers of hope, I observed many similarities between Seema Primary and Durban South when it came to the gloomy reality of the imprints on schooling of exclusion, inequality, neglect, and elitist policies. This seemed to have much to do with the similarities in the schools' contexts. The gap between aspiration and delivery in the South African school system mirrors that in India. Although the former is much more generously funded,[35] the political economy of postapartheid South Africa has led to a grossly unequal distribution of funding across the education system (Badat & Sayed, 2014; Engelbrecht et al., 2016). As a result, a disproportionate share of the resources ends up at the former "Model-C" schools that served White South Africans before 1994 and currently serve the privileged classes.

The government has tried to tackle this educational crisis through a series of education reforms and changing curricula since the mid-1990s, including Curriculum 2005 (based on the idea of outcomes-based education) and the current Curriculum and Assessment Policy Statement of 2011 (CAPS) (Kanjee & Sayed, 2013). These curricula have been widely criticized (Cross et al., 2002; Ramatlapana & Makonye, 2012). CAPS is seen as an educational program reinforcing existing power relations and disempowering both teachers and students (Palmer & de Klerk, 2012), a course of study in need of decolonization (C. J. Smith, 2018) and a policy initiative lacking appropriate initiatives for teacher training that would allow teachers to transition effectively to the new curriculum (Gudyanga & Jita, 2018; Phasha et al., 2016). The government not only fails to provide the children with a quality education but also obfuscates this failure through artificially inflated pass rates that do not enable children to get a job and escape poverty. This is reflected in the country's sky-high youth graduate unemployment rate of 55.2 percent as of the first quarter of 2019 (Statistics South Africa, 2019), which undoubtedly has risen further as a result of the COVID-19 pandemic that hit South Africa particularly hard. The picture that emerges is one of a school system that treats different socioeconomic groups very differently, subjecting the underprivileged ones to routinized, punitive schooling.

Given these realities, it is not surprising that Durban South Primary— like several schools in South Durban—looks good on paper. The teachers claim that virtually no students drop out and almost all proceed to secondary school, making the school attractive to pupils from areas as far south as Umlazi and Lamontville, who at the time of my research made up approximately 40 percent of the student body (a figure that had risen steadily in previous years).[36] Up close, the picture is more complex. To start with the most obvious, the school occupies a temporary structure built in 1972 (the school's founding year) that has long outlived its expected lifespan and parts of which are not considered safe to use anymore. Situated near the Engen oil refinery, many students suffer from the polluted air. According to Mr. Naidoo, the school principal, more than half the students carry inhalers and teachers keep spares for the multiple medical emergencies that transpire each year.

Despite the South African government's significant investment in education, Durban South Primary is one of many schools facing a precarious financial position. According to Mr. Naidoo, department of education funding covers only teachers' salaries for the school year and less than one month's operating expense; the rest must be raised from parents or donors. Fees are collected from parents, but compliance is typically low, with only one-fifth paying the full amount. Much of the school administrators' time is therefore spent on securing financing, leaving little space to deal with other aspects of education.

Another factor that constrains the school's ability to incorporate environmental themes into the curriculum is what Mark Hunter, a scholar of education in Durban, described to me in an interview as "the death of the local school." In the aftermath of apartheid, schools that formerly served only certain racial groups, such as the Coloureds in Wentworth, became open to all, in theory. In reality, the racial mixing of students depended on parents' financial ability to send their children to schools outside their communities. In South Durban, through a sophisticated system of buses, taxis, and other shared vehicles (M. Hunter, 2010), Black students from nearby townships (Umlazi in particular) have become increasingly able to commute to schools formerly unavailable to them. During my fieldwork, I came across schools whose student bodies comprised more than 99 percent Black students, while only 25 years earlier the student population would have been 100 percent Indian or Coloured. Mrs. Pillay, the Durban South vice principal, told me, "[Our school] is the most fortunate in that if you look at total percentage of community, Black versus Coloured, I would say we are 60–40. If you go to the other schools, I would say they're 90–10."

I came to appreciate how much Durban South had suffered as a result of these demographic changes only after spending enough time with educators who felt comfortable opening up to me about their yearning for the past and their sense of lost opportunities. "We used to have concerts, we used to have sports, we were top of the range, we beat every school," Jane, a teacher who had taught at Durban South for over three decades, remarked in a focus group. When the school exclusively served the local community, she recalled, a great variety of extracurricular activities took place on campus in the afternoon. This was no longer possible, as a large number of students got on a bus or taxi minutes after the last lesson of the day. I experienced this myself when I realized that half of the school would not be able to participate in my filmmaking workshop because the children could not stay on campus after school.

While it may appear that attending a school in Wentworth was a positive consequence of the end of apartheid for Black children, I realized that the situation was far more complex. Even as the state formally desegregated schools and opened up new opportunities for Black students, it allowed the quality of education in schools taking on Black children to deteriorate.[37] The death of the local school meant that many schools were no longer embedded in a community, which separated social and political struggles from the lives of the learners. South Durban became, perhaps more than ever before, a site of institutional liminality that promised upward mobility and an opportunity to obtain a superior education, even if it came at the cost of asthma or thyroid cancer. It was as if the cloud of toxic air hovering above the school was drawing people in because it represented economic prosperity, rather than repulsing them because it represented death.

Given this backdrop, it was not surprising that the school did not aspire to bring up generations of activists or that perhaps it was, in Appadurai's (2013, p. 179) words, beyond the school's collective "capacity to aspire" to set such a goal. Rather, what I frequently encountered in my interactions with educators was a particular conception of childhood in which politicization would happen further downstream in children's education trajectories. The children were considered too young to understand politics; thus, it was not the place of a primary school to educate them about environmental justice or historical responsibility. In Aruna's words, "I think maybe primary schools are not involved a lot in these political and environmental issues because the kids are far too young to even understand what an activist is." The reality of the South African education system is that many children never make it past primary school (Branson et al., 2014). Those who do are unlikely to focus on environmental justice in their secondary schooling, where it is often not covered by the curriculum.[38] The primary school remains the key institution through which the state can cultivate (or constrain) the political imaginations of future adults, but my findings from Wentworth suggest that, in the South African education context, it is set up to fail at this task.

The Spectacles of Fast Violence

What could make a twelve-year-old child imagine a dystopian future like that depicted in figure 4.9? Social breakdown and fragmentation appear all-encompassing, with the only verbal clue the word "destroy," and the only natural element a tree being torn down. This picture, produced by Declan, one of the students at Durban South during a focus group session about imagined past and future worlds, seems to express a fate this

Figure 4.9
Wentworth in the year 2117, as imagined by a seventh-grade student.

boy saw for his future environment. The drawing was representative of the children's concern with fast violence in the community, a concern also reflected in the student film *Pollution Kills*. As discussed in chapter 3, Wentworth suffers from major social issues, including poverty and unemployment, drug abuse on a mass scale, both petty and organized crime, gang warfare, a high prevalence of prostitution, alcoholism, domestic and gender-based violence, a breakdown of family structures, and high HIV rates. Wentworth is, in other words, a site of fast violence whose spectacles can easily overshadow the slow violence of environmental injustice and racism affecting the children and their families. When I asked Collin, one of the students who made *Pollution Kills*, to tell me about his life in Wentworth, his response revealed a powerful sense of spatial containment and fear: "My life living [*sic*] in Wentworth has been fine but at the same time it's been dangerous because of the gang violence here in Wentworth. There was been [*sic*] two gangs. It's where I stay and just up the road from where I stay, those two groups were fighting so like every time when you want to go to the shop it's not like you can even go because the shop is above. So, like when you walk up the road you don't know when you're going to get shot. So, it's very dangerous."

Collin also shared with me his experience of one of the physical spaces in Wentworth:

> I got to learn that with where I stay, I need to protect myself. I need to have a good education, I need to grow up and be something. I mustn't just be like the boys that sit on the corner where I stay. And also, as I was growing up I also learnt that where I stay there's another part of where I stay it's call[ed] Ogle Road, it's a pool there. It's a very dangerous pool because a lot of people have died in that pool. So, I went to that pool once and after that when I came back about a few days afterwards my friend came back and told me that his father's friend died in that pool. And after that I've never ever went [*sic*] to a pool.

The sense of danger is a central theme in *Pollution Kills*. In one scene, for example, a boy takes a quick break from playing soccer to talk to the film crew about violence in Wentworth. He casually talks about murders, drug use, and violence among children without breaking his smile, indicating that this is "normal" here. When I asked Mrs. Pillay how much importance young people, in her experience, attach to their health, she told me, "I think just doing today, basic needs become a more important struggle. A struggle to survive is more important."

This has profound implications for schooling in Wentworth. The teachers cited spectacles of fast violence again and again as the main obstacles to education and key challenges for students and teachers alike. In Megan's words, "You stand in front of them [pupils] and you try and teach them four times two plus six minus one, and they are still in shock over the fact that my father beat my mother up . . . I think our teachers are counselors more than anything else." My observations of school lessons were consistent with this comment. Some of the lessons I observed, in particular in the life orientation (LO) classes, almost felt like group counseling sessions in which the teacher was trying to give students advice about how to deal with the harsh realities of living in Wentworth. In other classes, teachers struggled to keep control of the students and were often ignored. These teachers' frustration was palpable. Megan further reflected on my questions about environmental themes in the education offered by the school:

> To be honest with you, I said to a teacher at school—I said I wonder what this guy [she was referring to me] is thinking, I wonder if he looks across the road and he sees the litter and the houses that have paint that is peeling and the state of the Wentworth area and he must think these people are uncultured and they are uncivilized and they are such pigs. But they literally don't see it. Because the struggle is so intense that nobody is interested in keeping the grass short or why's there so much of erosion on that bank and we need to plant grass. No . . . I'm saying that people are not there yet. Life is complicated far beyond environmental issues.

Megan's defense of the community and explanation for why environmental issues are given low priority is striking, as is her definition of these issues. Environment here is connected with aesthetics, as reflected in the "NO LIT-TERING" signs throughout the school that students captured in *Pollution Kills*.

While the aggregate impact of slow violence on the lives of people in Wentworth may be as great as that of fast violence, it is not necessarily seen. In many ways, this is the quintessential story of the high Anthropocene: the fast violence obscuring the slow violence and creating collective blind spots that are often perpetuated by the very education systems designed to make us open our eyes.

Teaching environmental education in the context of spectacular fast violence was a tall order. While teachers in Wentworth did not refer to environmental education as an "opportunity to relax" (as was the case in Pashulok), it was clear that it was deemphasized and taught in ways that individualized responsibility and eschewed the wider social implications of sustainability. Within CAPS, environmental education is seen as a cross-cutting issue and does not have an allocated subject, as it is meant to permeate the whole curriculum (Schudel, 2017). The subject with the most environment-related content is life orientation, although its focus on environmental issues is limited, as one LO teacher at Durban South told me. "There's a section on environmental awareness, but even there it's maybe three weeks just on environment. You teach them on soil degradation and all that comes up is the issue of environment." According to the teacher, this is insufficient. "What does the child do with that? Write an assignment. You cannot go back and talk to them about it and it's over and forgotten. It's done with." When I asked one of the Wentworth LO teachers to tell me about the environmental content taught at the school, his response was, "I think there is something that deals with the environment there, respecting the environment, caring for the environment . . . When I say respecting it, for example, if you go to a picnic and making sure that the place is clean, using products that would not harm the environment." This response was particularly astounding, given that we were looking at smokestacks releasing toxic substances into the air as we were talking. It reminded me of a shot from *Pollution Kills* in which the school gardener is seen wielding a bin full of trash with smokestacks rising above him, as if humans were powerless to challenge industry, their agency limited to "beautifying" the microenvironment of the school (figure 4.10).

This was consistent with what I had observed at the school—a preoccupation with cleanliness. The first thing virtually everyone mentioned when I asked about the school's environmental education was the student litter monitor program, which combined individualized responsibility for the environment with a focus on discipline and surveillance. When I asked

Figure 4.10
Trash and smokestacks in Wentworth, as captured in *Pollution Kills*.

a social science teacher whether the subject of polluted air ever came up in her lessons, she replied,

> I haven't found a situation where we really truly just sat down and discussed how the refinery affects the air around us . . . Like, what would you as a school do—there are people who are provided jobs there, who live in the area so if you are saying the refinery must move, it must move where? And who's going to work and what happens to all these people who are employed there who are breadwinners for their families . . . It's a vast and quite an intricate thing to just even think about how do you even begin to tackle that.

This complexity was afforded no space in the curriculum, which meant that teachers were not discussing it in their classes. One school principal in South Durban called the curriculum "straitjacketed" and noted that "environmental justice is not part of it." Any attempt to bring the "radical" agenda of sustainability into the schooling process would be considered subversive.

Just as in India, the South African educators made it clear that the curriculum, or at least the way they interpreted it, emphasized development over the environment. Aruna, my key informant in Wentworth, said to me, "If I look at all the subjects, like I said it is all about money. How much of money can we get. What can we sell, what can we buy." The school appeared to be aligned with an informal economy of township entrepreneurialism that shaped young people's imagination of the future. "Obviously, if you tell the child we need the trees and plants to give us food, then the child will say in order to get the food, we need money to buy the food. So again, it's industry development over nature." This commodification of the environment mirrors Seema Primary teachers' view of the dam as a pathway to development, suggesting an underlying extractivist assumption in both curricula that the natural environment is to be exploited for its economic benefits in the name of development.

Another ideological similarity between schooling in the two places was the narrative of the self as capable of rising up against all the odds. While in Pashulok this could be supposedly accomplished by submitting to the teachers' efforts, educators in Wentworth talked about the need to make the right moral choices. Perhaps the best example of this tendency came up in my interview with Mrs. Pillay, who told me that, to inspire students, she uses herself as an example. "We lived in a room where half the divider was the lounge and that was the bedroom, two bunks, four children." Mrs. Pillay has since "made it" in Wentworth, which she attributes to making the right life choices. "All they just see is [Mrs. Pillay] driving this Mercedes, living on Treasure Beach,[39] having these children that also have their own cars." That's why the students are often surprised when they learn of her background. "It's hard work, it's sacrifice, and it's having a strong will that has brought me to where I am . . . You can get out of this, you can."

While Mrs. Pillay undoubtedly meant well, and it is very possible that her personal example was an inspiration to many students at Durban South, this narrative also plays into the landscapes of depoliticization at the school and in South Africa more broadly. It individualizes the dreams attached to a failing constitution and eschews the state's and the education system's inability to deliver on their promises of equal opportunity and environmental justice. Such a vision, which was echoed in many of my interactions with teachers and administrators in Wentworth, takes the collective element out of politics and leaves behind a depoliticized theory of action devoid of historical responsibility.

At both the Indian and South African sites, the culture of schooling was contributing to commodifying and depoliticizing spaces of freedom. It sought to cultivate children's aspirations to an abstract notion of national development and a personal goal of winning the race for a "good life."[40] The rituals of discipline and the symbolism of schooling for development sought to mold political narratives of selfhood into homogeneous, shapeless forms. They were doing this by suppressing political imaginations, eschewing historical responsibility, undermining civic equality, and advancing a high-Anthropocene myopia of slow violence. The borders of learning in these communities were designed to be firm and impermeable, to prevent the emergence of agonistic pluralism and undermine the transfer of intergenerational knowledge, and thus to hinder action or the start of anything anew (Arendt, 1998). These spaces of institutionalized liminality painted state-sponsored lies of meritocracy disconnected from past and present as the destiny of educated citizens. Such falsehoods contributed to bureaucratization and made taking action in response to the environmental challenges of the Anthropocene less likely. However, this culture did not fully negate the individual agency of educators who, despite the systemic headwinds they faced, sometimes espoused a different kind of politics.

A Politics of Hope

Perhaps because of my longer immersion in the Wentworth site, as time went by I started seeing the teachers there as more rounded, more complex, more closely tuned into the experience of slow violence than those at the Indian site.[41] While spectacles of fast violence and other factors that contributed to the individualization of responsibility at the school were front and center in my fieldwork, I also started noticing departures from these dominant trends. These originated with what I came to call outlier teachers, educators who sought to inject themes of environmental justice and historical responsibility into their teaching despite the limitations of the curriculum. I started noticing that the direct exposure of both learners and educators to pollution and its health effects led to an experiential awareness, and a tacit critique, of the high Anthropocene which echoed the notion that "we are not products of a total institution."

In some cases the critique was explicit. One headmaster in the area told me, "We talked about the threat of nuclear [power] in this school. We've talked about the Clairwood Racecourse and the traffic that it's bringing in and the kind of effect it will have in the community." While such examples were not common, and teachers often reported that schools failed to take part in protests because of industries' greenwashing efforts, this points to the possibility of synergies between spaces of schooling and spaces of activism. Individual educators also engaged in similar "transgressions." Ella, a teacher, told me that she went well beyond the CAPS curriculum in her teaching and incorporated what she called "hidden education," which mostly revolved around ethics and building up the children's self-confidence. "Where I can, I will teach my child and create my child to be confident, to have that self-confidence in yourself that you can stand up for yourself. That is not in our syllabus. So I teach that in the class because I want my learner tomorrow to be an activist, you know whether it is politically, whether it is . . . being an environmentally friendly activist or being in parliament . . . so that tomorrow they can stand up for what is right and they have a voice."

Ella's approach contrasts starkly with the apparently dominant narrative of "the good life" in Wentworth. This particular teacher taught second-grade students. She shared with me her worries that the principle of standing up for what is right that she sought to instill in her students may be eroded because of the focus on discipline of more conventional teachers in higher grades. I shared her concern, based on my observation of what went on in these classes. But there were exceptions. Lee, a seventh-grade history teacher, once shared with me that he tied the history of South Durban into his lessons. "We looked at the political situation then where they just stuck this [factory] here and they didn't care because it didn't affect the Whites at that stage." This teacher was, in effect, taking the experiential learning of the students living in Wentworth and applying it to a historical narrative stressing the environmental injustice caused by decades of apartheid.

It was clear that the students were relying on such narratives in their understanding of their community's social predicament and in their imagining of the future. This became apparent in the filmmaking workshop I conducted with children here. Having reflected on the methodology of the workshop in Pashulok, I slightly modified my approach once I started working with children in Wentworth. I started the workshop with a series of sessions in which we collectively brainstormed and drew mind maps on the blackboard to depict what was unique about Wentworth and how this uniqueness could be captured visually. The children initially came up with ideas that showcased their community in a mostly negative light and reflected the dominance of fast violence in the lives of local residents. But they also mentioned themes of slow violence, historical injustice, and hope. Some students were critical of Wentworth's predicament and pointed to local civic groups and individuals whom they saw as working to alleviate the suffering of local residents. This double approach manifested itself in the films the students produced—*Pollution Kills* about the impact of the Engen refinery on the health of Wentworth residents and *Wentworth Changing to Progress*, a cinematic tapestry of individuals and organizations working to improve the community.

Many scenes in the films showcased individuals, both alive and deceased, who left a significant mark on the community. In the opening of *Wentworth Changing to Progress*, for example, the children filmed Uncle Lala, a local retiree who spends his afternoons directing traffic outside the school (figure 4.11). They asked him why he does this and captured his response on video. He said that he, too, has children and therefore cares about the pupils' safety.

In the film the children also incorporated footage of Dance Movement, "an organization that children from Wentworth can go to so that they have something else to do like dance [figure 1.4 in the introduction] so that they're not sitting at home and becoming gangsters and doing drugs and stuff like that," in the words of Cheryl, one of the student filmmakers. Another group captured in the film was the Keith "Skido" Joseph Foundation,[42] a civic organization dedicated to the memory of an activist and MK [*uMkhonto we Sizwe*, the armed wing of ANC] fighter from Wentworth.[43] As Cheryl explained, "It's a foundation that helps people get jobs and does a lot of things like to prevent corruption and stuff." Zooming in on the foundation's slogan, "The legacy lives on," the children connected the debt to the dead to a hopeful future—a temporal arc built over a gloomy presence that nevertheless expressed the hopefulness of pluralistic politics.

Figure 4.11
Uncle Lala controlling traffic in front of the school in Wentworth.

The students working on *Pollution Kills* included not only shots of smokestacks in Wentworth and interviews with local residents suffering from pollution-related health issues but also their interactions with environmental activists. The students met Desmond D'Sa, the leader of the South Durban Community Environmental Alliance (SDCEA), whom they filmed demonstrating various techniques for measuring air quality (figure 4.12). At one point in the film, as Desmond explains that factories must meet pollution levels set by the government, the student behind the camera asks what happens if the industries "don't listen." Desmond responds that, in such a situation, the student should let him know and SDCEA would take up the issue. While on camera, Des reassured students that activists have the power to bring the industry to task, but his frankness in one of our conversations betrayed a more nuanced answer to the student's question: "From the once striving country with the most progressive constitution in the world, the most progressive environmental laws and the best equipment . . . used to give them [municipal officials] the evidence [of pollution], . . . is now been [*sic*] destroyed. It tells you a lot from [*sic*] where we come from and what the vision was of our forefathers and the people that came after them." This differentiation between the forefathers—who symbolize the promise of a

Figure 4.12
Desmond demonstrating how air quality is measured.

different kind of politics—and the country's contemporary leaders points to an intergenerational liminality of action, a collective paralysis that meant that SDCEA could keep trying to revive the politics of old but the odds were stacked against it.[44] Perhaps it was this liminality that the student instinctively recognized when he asked what happens if the industries "don't listen."

By exposing these dynamics, the film paints a layered picture of a troubled community that is not without hope and that rallies around air pollution as a shared enemy. Put differently, the students' film captured much of the complexity of the activist struggle and the community-activist relationship that took months for me to grasp during my field research. The film reflected a degree of awareness and engagement with environmental justice that went well beyond the school curriculum, as well as an openness to learning about the state, justice, race, and environment through a collaborative "agonism" over assembling a short film.[45] Ultimately, the film had a political agenda, as Collin shared with me on my last day at Durban South Primary: "Our goal with the film was to like show them that pollution is killing us. It's not just the pollution is here and the pollution is going to go. It's like to show them that the pollution is destroying our community that we're living in."

When we showed both films to Mr. Naidoo, the school's principal, and several teachers on my last day at Durban South, I could not help but feel after the screening that some among the school staff questioned their beliefs about these students. Rather than representing walking bundles of social problems, potential troublemakers, or clean slates to be filled with state-sanctioned knowledge, these young people showed both motivation and an aptitude for articulating counternarratives to what they were taught in school. They quickly engaged with and mastered a medium of storytelling and expressed a pluralistic vision of their community. They saw and understood slow violence and avoided the trap of fatalism in their narrative, suggesting that they were confronting slow violence in real time.

It was not only the student filmmakers who were educating themselves for the Anthropocene. The drawings made in focus group sessions, which depict how pupils imagined Wentworth one hundred years ago and one hundred years into the future, also demonstrate a political imagination that far surpasses the visions of past and future taught in the South African curriculum. For example, seventh-grader Luke came up with a schematic depiction of the future consisting of "deforestation, starvation, dry land, dry puddle, climate change" (figure 4.13).[46] In Luke's words, "In the past I drew like . . . they used to go fetch water in the river. Like it was an ordinary life, no technology and everything. And then in the future there's like climate change, there's starvation, dry land and dry and all the deforestation thingies." When I asked him why he thought these environmental crises would occur, he responded in a way that suggested he was connecting his experience of living in Wentworth to systemic patterns of human behavior:

> **Luke:** Like land pollution, we always educated people on littering but it doesn't have an impact on them on what's going on in the environment. They're still going to litter. They're still going to do their own things in the environment and they know that and they still do it.
> **Peter:** Why do you think they keep doing it?
> **Luke:** I don't know why they do it, I don't know, hey.

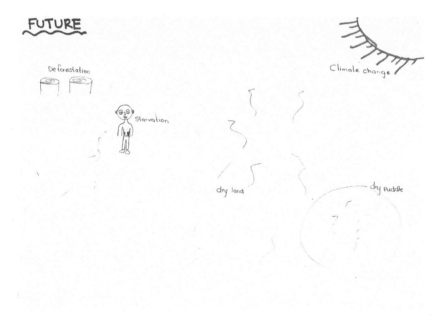

Figure 4.13
A dystopian future, as imagined by Luke.

But Luke seemed to know more. His drawings not only demonstrate an acute awareness of environmental challenges central to the high Anthropocene moment but also extrapolate from these and point to a dystopian future in which human agency is diminished, where the future becomes a slave of the past. His imagined depiction of Wentworth one hundred years ago (figure 4.14) is considerably more idyllic, with a more realist portrayal of a natural environment in which people are able to live without destroying the resources on which their existence depends. The schematic depiction of the future and the realist depiction of the past mirror the limitations of what is knowable: whereas memory and history teach us about a past that existed and allow us to imagine it in concrete terms and to have a dialogue with it, visualizing a future that has not yet come to be relies on an awareness and extrapolation of our perception of the current reality. Luke stripped this extrapolation down to a few concepts and selected traits of a future world that were the most directly related to human agency in the present. These

Figure 4.14
Luke's imagination of an idyllic past.

drawings suggest that their author has been, to some extent, educated for the Anthropocene despite not being schooled for it.

Another student, Denira, drew an imagined past (figure 4.15) that suggested a similarly romanticized view of life one hundred years ago. Her depiction reflects harmony between nature and humanity, with abundant trees, clean water, dispersed houses, and the people's palpable happiness. Denira's drawing becomes even more significant when compared to her portrayal of the future—except that she appears to have misunderstood the task and wrote "Future (What's now)" on the top of the drawing (figure 4.16). The present is portrayed here as optimistically as the past. There are fewer trees and no mountains and the houses have turned into multistory buildings, but the picture shows no evidence of violence, slow or fast. People's smiling faces are all over this picture as they engage in enjoyable activities, from listening to music in a cabriolet to soaring in a balloon to flying kites. The image stands in stark contrast to the verbal descriptions of Wentworth I

Figure 4.15
Denira's imagination of life in the past.

Figure 4.16
The future as the desire present, according to Denira.

heard during my fieldwork from both adults and children, which focused predominantly on fast violence, the lack of a future, and the desire to leave. The drawings contradicting these perceptions, of which there were many during the focus groups, suggest that the children not only imagine different futures for themselves, their families, and their peers but also reimagine the present, almost as an act of resistance to the schooling's oppressiveness and its institutionalization of liminality.

While "hope" in this context may not take the form of Arendtian action and may operate instead as emotion within the structures of feeling (R. Williams, 1977), it still has the potential to challenge the practiced ignorance (Arendt, 2006) advanced by the school system. The sources of the students' radical reimaginations and symbolic acts of resistance echo visions of a more environmentally just world held by activists in both India and South Africa, to whom we turn in chapter 5.

III   WHAT IS THE ALTERNATIVE?

Chains black and white, Cape Town, 2017.

DILEMMA 3   THE MYTH OF IMPARTIALITY, OR HOW I (ALMOST) BECAME AN ACTIVIST

Rakesh was an associate of Sunderlal Bahuguna, the renowned environmentalist behind the Chipko movement, and had worked with one of my filmmaker friends in India. I was looking for an "in" into the activist world of Uttarakhand, and the mutual friend introduced us. Our first meeting, in a bustling café near Delhi's Connaught Place, is etched in my memory. A tall, gregarious, gray-haired, kurta-wearing man with thick glasses, Rakesh reminded me of many of the intellectuals I had met during my years living in South Asia. But there was also something different, something very non-middle-class about him. "He's a Gandhian," my friend told me before the meeting. His self-discipline was palpable, and the way he talked and moved betrayed a spartan lifestyle. Yet, I soon realized he also had a strong desire for recognition. Unlike Medha Patkar or his mentor Sunderlal Bahuguna, who were revered by Western journalists and academics, Rakesh's obscurity beyond Indian activist circles was clearly a sore point. Of Kailash Satyarthi, the anti-child-labor activist who had shared the 2014 Nobel Peace Prize with Malala, he said, "If he got the prize, I should get it, too."

A week later, we were sitting in the principal's office of a school in Pashu-lok. Rakesh had related the history of recent local protests and sold me on the idea that this was the most suitable site for my research. Two days into my fieldwork he was effectively making key decisions on my behalf, and I felt deeply vulnerable. My ethnography was not supposed to be a treatise on Rakesh's worldview, but I felt it was sliding in that direction. Nevertheless, his rhetorical abilities and his charm were massive assets in gaining access to hard-to-reach spaces. The school principal had firmly said "no" to us at first, but Rakesh convinced one of the teachers, Pranay, whom he had never met before, to vouch for me and sign a letter taking full responsibility for whatever happened. I was impressed, even more so after learning that this teacher was in fact a supporter of the Tehri Dam and did not share Rakesh's views at all. But there was something about Rakesh—my friend refers to him as a moral compass—that enables him to bend others to his will. I was glad to have him on my side.

Whose side was he really on, though? I have no doubt that, in his mind, he was on the side of "the truth," which became a point of contention between us. I was not so much interested in a singular truth as I was curious about the subjective experiences of those ousted by the dam project, the many individual truths forming the painful mosaic of displacement. Rakesh kept asking me why I needed to interview individuals rather than groups of oustees and why the interviews needed to be so long and personal. When translating, he often altered both my questions and the participants' answers, something I noticed even with my very basic Hindi, and at times we argued about this in the middle of interviews. In the end, due to Rakesh's "translations," I had to hire professional translators to go over all the interview recordings and identify discrepancies. Rather than phenomenology and hermeneutics, Rakesh was concerned with justice, which, it seemed to me, was a black-and-white affair to him. The whole process felt like a performance in which I was to play the judge, Rakesh the prosecutor of the corrupt Indian state, and the Pashulok oustees the witnesses he called to testify in support of his case.

From the beginning, I was aware of the performativity (cf. M. Z. Rosaldo, 1982) shaping our interactions. I could see that Rakesh wanted to impress me. I suspected this had something to do with my gender, the color of my skin, the fluency of my English, and the Cambridge University logo on my business card, and this made me uncomfortable. Rakesh felt the tension, too. I remember sitting in his rented room in Rishikesh on a cold February evening, debriefing after a long day of interviews, when he offered me his hat. When I declined, he said, "You don't want it because you think my head is dirty." I could sense the discomfort in his voice.

And then there was the money. I was paying Rakesh a daily wage for his assistance with the project. This made for a power dynamic even more fraught with inequality, and it motivated Rakesh to show "results" for his work. For example, he aimed to conclude the process of finding a school willing to have me within hours, or at most days, while I was open to a longer exploration in an effort to get the site selection "right" (even though I was not sure exactly what that meant). Matters got further complicated after Rakesh asked me to tell him how much my doctoral degree had cost; when I told him, he took it as evidence that I was wealthy, despite my attempts to explain that my degree was paid for by a scholarship. This prompted him to ask me to pay him more, even though the request was not framed as such: rather, my payment was to be a contribution to the "cause" he was fighting. There was no escaping it: by choosing Rakesh as my key informant and translator, I entered a highly polarized field. In his eyes (and gradually in mine, too) I entered it more as a fellow activist than a researcher.

Rakesh left after a week, as we had agreed, because of his busy schedule, and for the rest of my fieldwork I worked with local translators. It soon became clear that the people he introduced me to, who all shared his views about the dam, the Indian state, and development, were far from representing the only voice in Pashulok. I later encountered people who applauded the dam and whom I suspect Rakesh would not have wanted me to meet, and people with other opinions he likely did not know about (cf. Drew, 2017). But that first week with Rakesh left a lasting legacy on my understanding of the conflict and on the way the local community perceived me. It also planted a dilemma in my mind: Should I take sides in this conflict to potentially gain depth at the expense of breadth, as some people would likely open up to me while others would refuse to talk to me? Or do I try to stay neutral? Given that I was seen to be associated with Rakesh, did I even have a choice? And what about the ethics beyond research ethics: if I believed the treatment of the oustees was not just, was I not obligated to do what was in my power to help?

Working with Rakesh was simultaneously fascinating, rewarding, and frustrating. It took away any pretense of my being an impartial observer and forced me to confront my own politics and the politics of the field. His fast research felt anti-ethnographic while simultaneously being one of the most significant ethnographic encounters of my fieldwork that gave me a window into the politics and psychology of activism in 2017 India. For all the ways Rakesh's presence complicated my research, he increased the "available light" (Geertz, 2001) in the room.

5 ENVIRONMENTAL ACTIVISM: AN ANSWER TO EDUCATING FOR THE ANTHROPOCENE?

When I was there talking to the parents, I was actually crying. I spoke to them and I said: "I want to tell you as parents, I am making a vow. The scales are removed off my eyes, I'm going to fight on, I'm going to fight on with the industry with all the energy I have within my body." This year, that child died, she never saw high school. I have seen this happen once too often in my journey, in my walk, in my talking with parents and children.
—Desmond D'Sa, activist, South Durban

We were in a car driving southward from Phoenix, Durban's biggest township. Desmond D'Sa, sitting in the front seat, sounded tired as he assessed the community event we had attended. The turnout was good, he said, but there was less tension than usual because only activists and community members came, with representatives of the petrochemical industry notably absent. He was not happy to see a group of people who showed up wearing blue Democratic Alliance[1] T-shirts. They claimed they had come straight from a rally and did not have time to change. He suggested that they tried to hijack the environmental agenda, despite the fact that there was "no political party" in South Africa actually targeting environmental issues in its program. The event we had just attended was the last in a series of community gatherings organized by the South Durban Community Environmental Alliance (SDCEA), which Des chaired. The gatherings had been held around the city in the aftermath of a large fire in a candle wax factory in South Durban on March 24, 2017, that had attracted national attention; it took firefighters more than three days to extinguish it (S. Hunter, 2017). While sitting in a café in Cape Town, I saw images on the television of firemen fighting thick clouds of black smoke in South Durban. I was speaking by phone with a Durban academic studying social movements, who ironically had just told me, "It's been a bit quiet in South Durban in recent years." When I arrived in South Durban a few days later, it was anything but quiet.

The meeting with Des in Phoenix in many ways encapsulated what SDCEA came to represent for me during my time in South Africa. The group was active all over the city in the aftermath of the fire. In the eyes of city residents, South Durban was no longer just a geographical area but a symbol for resistance to environmental racism, industrial pollution, and the unfulfilled promises of the country's postapartheid dispensation. Several people spoke in Phoenix, where, on this somber occasion, Des was not in the spotlight—this was clearly a coalition rather than a one-man show. The alliance was a broad church that included scientists, renter associations, labor unions, and religious groups. While Des was a charismatic leader who was deeply passionate about social and environmental justice, he was not a scientist or a policymaker, two professions crucial to SDCEA's mission.[2]

Des reminded the people in attendance of their constitutional right to a clean environment and encouraged them to file claims for compensation if their property had been damaged by the cloud of smoke that hovered above the city for days after the fire. In conversations with interlocutors in South Africa, I heard SDCEA being referred to as radical or antidevelopment, but in Phoenix those labels did not ring true; this was simply a civic group encouraging citizens to claim their rights. Perhaps this is what my colleague meant when she said that things had been quiet in South Durban. But on that evening, Des's voice echoed loudly across the Phoenix Community Centre.

Encountering SDCEA was a stimulating experience. Here was an organized activist group advocating for a future without the slow violence of environmental destruction. Moreover, it was not only imagining this future but taking action to achieve it. The tension between wanting to espouse the practices of the activists I encountered during my research and needing to keep a distance when studying the ideology underlying their efforts was with me throughout my field research.[3] It was tempting to take SDCEA at face value without engaging with it ethnographically.

After all, action—the fostering of which I earlier argued is crucial to educating for the Anthropocene—is at the heart of activism. Yet I had to remind myself that the history of environmental activism does not uniformly reflect the Arendtian vision of action as an outgrowth of agonistic pluralism. Some environmental movements opted instead for radicalism (Cianchi, 2015; Pellow, 2014; Taylor, 2008)[4] aimed at advancing various alternative ideologies, ranging from eco-anarchism (Hall, 2011) to deep ecology (Katz et al., 2000) to eco-socialism (Baer, 2018) and other aggressive utopias or "ecotopias" (Pepper, 2005).[5] Environmental activists are confined to the margins of political life in many societies, and even in countries where environmentalism has entered mainstream politics, it has not led to a "fundamental transformation in the attitudes of policymakers" (Carter, 2018, p. 2). It is thus not surprising that formal education systems—often among society's most conservative elements—have a troubled relationship with activism.

Despite the sometimes thorny history of environmental movements, it would be tempting to suggest that educating for the Anthropocene simply means replacing formal schooling with activist education. Activists say they care about social justice, human and animal rights, conservation, Indigenous knowledge—in other words, many of the agendas that can help us confront slow violence. Previous research shows that place-based activist movements often have local knowledge valuable to social action and generate alternatives to globalized, neoliberal development (Escobar, 2008). But such a substitution may risk simply replacing one ideology with another, swapping a narrative for a counternarrative. Understanding the implications of activism for education in the age of the Anthropocene therefore requires exposing the cultural and ideological landscapes of activism, as shaped by the contextual forces of space and time.

The submersion of villages, forests, fields, and hills caused by the Tehri Dam is a testament to the totality of the Anthropocene and a reminder of the resultant need for education to reinvent itself. Rotting trees and other organic matter accumulated beneath the dam's surface, which released carbon dioxide and methane, which contribute to climate change, into the atmosphere (Fearnside, 1995, 2005; Gunkel, 2009; Hertwich, 2013). This is one of the many ways an act of fast violence against a Himalayan valley gave rise to decades of slow violence against the planet. Meanwhile, the polluted air in South Durban slowly poisons the people living in the city. From a hill above the industrial basin, people can seem like gladiators in a Roman coliseum, leading a futile fight for their lives against forces greater than themselves—except that these contemporary gladiators are not forced to fight one another and can instead engage in agonistic pluralism, giving rise to actions that battle the slow violence of industrial pollution.

These inter- and intragenerational agonisms shaped the historical trajectory of both the antidam activists in Pashulok and antipollution activists in Wentworth. Their agendas converged on a number of issues, particularly recognizing planetary boundaries and the impact globalizing neoliberal regimes have had on the environment. While these movements appeared to be more in sync with the challenges of our times than the schooling systems in their respective countries, they did not articulate an alternative educational philosophy nor seek to change the fundamental features of schooling. At my research sites, the worlds of activism and formal education, for the most part, remained disconnected.

Although all the interlocutors mentioned in this chapter[6] self-identify as activists, they are a diverse group. Some are national-level figures I interviewed in the capitals and elsewhere in both countries.[7] In Pashulok, they are community members with a history of involvement in marches, fasts, and demonstrations. In South Durban, my principal informants were professional activists working full time for SDCEA. While in Durban it is possible to speak of an organized movement, the activist presence in Pashulok is dispersed. These differences are due to the histories of these two spaces and account for the differential implications of educating for the Anthropocene explored in this chapter.

In the course of my research in India and South Africa, I identified two modalities of agonistic pluralism—that crucial prerequisite to Arendtian politics—which underpin the evolution of both movements. In what I came to call vertical or intergenerational agonistic pluralism, activists "think with the dead" about ways to envision what future development may look like for the unborn. Lifestyles of past generations enter the conversation about future lifestyles in a temporal arc that links memory of the predevelopment past with imaginaries of future progress. In contrast, horizontal or intragenerational agonistic pluralism brings together groups with different identities that cut across race, class, ethnicity, age, language, and gender as they seek solutions to common foes that indiscriminately affect them all, such as air pollution or involuntary relocation.[8]

These two manifestations of agonistic pluralism resemble the geological strata composing the Earth's crust. Just as layers of rock reveal stories of bygone eras that enable humanity to engage in a kind of unilateral dialogue with the deep past, an imagining of worlds long gone, vertical agonistic pluralism cuts across layers of sedimented memory and fuels an imagining of deceased others. Relics of these imagined others give life to a dialogic rendering of the past and enable the living to speak across generations and agonize over the future with the (imagined) dead. The uppermost layer of sediment—the "now" taking place atop the Earth's geological strata—becomes a "theatre of memory" (Samuel, 1994), where intergenerational dialogue gives rise to action. The cultural, political, and social landscapes of the now are also sculpted by horizontal agonistic pluralism, which connects the outgrowths of different sediments, and their different interpretations, to a web of subjectivities and allows action "in concert with others" (Arendt, 2018, p. 232). Where vertical agonistic pluralism builds bridges across layered time, horizontal agonistic pluralism moves through spaces of difference, tightening the social fabric. The vertical shapes a shared sense of culturally embedded horizons of the possible (and the related horizons of the ethical) by tracing the temporality of culture. The horizontal facilitates dialogue with socially and culturally distant others, enabling action in unison with those we initially disagree with but whose humanity we share. Both modalities are crucial not only to agonizing about what is to be done but to carrying out the chosen course of action. Put differently, the vertical and the horizontal do not constitute a binary; they represent the logics behind manifestations of agonistic pluralism, logics that are complementary and provide the ingredients needed to act with others, the living and the dead. In practice, the two modalities operate hand in hand, as I show in my ethnographic accounts of activism in Pashulok and Wentworth in this chapter.

Their joint action is what I refer to as vertical-horizontal agonism.[9] Such "all-embracing" agonism—one that does not agree with everyone but engages in a dialogue with anyone—is the enemy of totalitarianism (cf. Arendt, 1962) and, as I argue in this book, the slow violence of the (high) Anthropocene.

Understanding this logic and synergistic action enabled me to examine the ways activist spaces in Pashulok and South Durban might fill the void left by the depoliticized, bureaucratized formal education provided by the state, as discussed in chapter 4. The questions I explore through this analysis include the following: What are the actions, rituals, and symbols shaping activist movements in Pashulok and Wentworth? In what ways may activism be positioned as a form of education? What are the roles of agonistic pluralism, historical responsibility, and intergenerational knowledge transfer in molding the cultural landscapes of these activist movements? The multisited nature of my research greatly enriched my exploration of these questions. Even though Pashulok directed me to vertical and Wentworth to horizontal agonistic pluralism, together they illuminate the dualistic character of agonism, which may prove to be an important ingredient in educating for the Anthropocene.

THE BURDEN OF THE PAST: SEDIMENTS OF MEMORY AND THE STRUGGLE AGAINST THE TEHRI DAM

Antidam activism has a long history in India. Mulshi *satyagraha*, the first documented large-scale antidam movement during the country's colonial era, started as early as 1920 (Vora, 2009). As discussed in chapter 3, the postcolonial Indian state conceived of large dams as the pinnacle of its development efforts (Khilnani, 2012), which greatly increased the human and environmental costs of these megaprojects. It was not until the 1970s, however, that the *Narmada Bachao Andolan* (The Save the Narmada Movement) led by Medha Patkar put the negative effects of dams into the national and international spotlight (Patkar & Kothari, 2017; Jagadeesan, 2015; Nilsen, 2010; Routledge, 2003; Wood, 1993). Yet, despite the efforts of internationally known activists and artists, including novelist Arundhati Roy (Jefferess, 2009; A. Roy, 1999) and filmmaker Anand Patwardhan (2016), the Indian state continues to build large dams. The Tehri Dam is one of the largest and most controversial of such projects. It displaced more than one hundred thousand people and generated apocalyptic scenarios in the minds of many because of its location on a geological fault line prone to earthquakes (Rana et al., 2007; Sharma, 2009). It is also the site of recent antidam struggles. The protest was once led by Sunderlal Bahuguna, a key figure behind the Chipko movement (Rangan, 2000),[10] and garnered national attention (Drew, 2017). However, many consider the protest a failure because it did not prevent the dam from being built.

My own encounter with India's megadams started on celluloid. Researching the history of the Indian state's development, as reflected in documentary films the government produced in the first two decades of Independence (Sutoris, 2016, 2018a), I realized that large dams were part of the "new" India's genetic makeup. Combining technological mastery, (post)colonial notions of development (India's first large dams were built by the British colonial government), a "multi-virtuousness" (simultaneously providing electricity, irrigation, and flood control) and the sheer visual spectacle of their vastness, large dams were the ideal symbol the postcolonial government could use to rally Indians around a new, nationalist brand of progress. As reflected in the films' low-angle shots of dam walls, the victorious soundtrack music, and the grandiose language used in voiceovers, large dams symbolized not only material progress but also the Indian nation's ability to master nature and reflected the high modernist (J. C. Scott, 2008) essence of the governments' development ideology.

It is therefore not surprising that large dams also became a symbol of resistance to the successive Indian governments' development policies. The "video revolution" of the 1970s and 1980s saw a democratization of access to filmmaking technology, and dams emerged as a prime target of the activist genre of documentary that ensued. Anand Patwardhan's 1995 classic, *A Narmada Diary*, helped establish the *Narmada Bachao Andolan* in the international popular imagination as a defining movement of late twentieth-century environmentalism. The movement's counternarrative saw dams as the ultimate symbol of inequality, in which the already privileged benefited while the poor paid the human and environmental costs. It also pointed to the government's disregard for the rights of India's rural and often Indigenous people who lived in the areas most affected by dams. The government's narrative of development and denial of slow violence could hardly be farther from the activists' counternarrative of social and environmental injustice.

I do not judge which of these perspectives has more merit. Certainly, my experience in the field and my understanding of the situation based on published accounts (Asthana, 2018; Bisht, 2009; Nachowitz, 1988; Newton, 2008; Rawat, 2013; Sharma, 2009) made me sympathetic to the views of antidam activists.[11] A great irony was that frequent power cuts in the area made it difficult to charge cameras at Seema Primary when making films with schoolchildren even while the Tehri Dam was generating a thousand megawatts of electricity, most of which went to distant urban areas. More than a decade after resettlement, the school attended by displaced children was still squatting in a shopping complex because the government had failed to build a new one. However, I did not seek to establish whether the oustees' grievances were legitimate. Rather, what was significant about the oustees' narratives for my analysis was the underlying logic that saw the dam's construction and their resettlement and compensation not as mere economic transactions but as events that affected the local population and the environment in ways that cannot be measured. Put differently, money cannot replace land-with-history. The activist narrative recognizes losses far beyond the material, such as the disruption of cultural identities and intergenerational bonds[12]—the kind of loss that no amount of "development" can ever make up for. Forced relocation, which disconnects culture from its material environment, disrupts a people's awareness of and ability to honor their debt to the dead by preserving a way of life and their debt to the unborn by ensuring environmental sustainability. In short, relocation sites do not offer a lifestyle that can sustain a population across generations. It is in the painful awareness of the multilayered, irreversible nature of loss that the "counter" in the activist, oustee-centered counternarrative of India's development lies.

Even though the clash of the state and activist perspectives was at the root of the protests against the Tehri Dam, the movement differed significantly from the more widely publicized *Narmada Bachao Andolan* in both aims and outcomes. During a short break from my fieldwork in Pashulok,

I took a train to Delhi to speak to activists who remember both movements and could shed light on their differences. In Delhi electricity from Tehri powers air conditioners and air purifiers, while drinking water from the dam finds its way into taps that are dangerous to drink from. The city's corridors of power, enveloped in a cloud of toxic smog, have become the battlefields of justice and sustainability for many veterans of India's antidam movements. Walking into the office of one of them, Arnab, I was met with a mixture of kindness and suspicion. While many scholars have generated research broadly supportive of the activist position, some have questioned the involvement of middle-class urban "outsiders" like Arnab in grassroots protest movements. When I asked about his motivations, Arnab told me such questions were "mischievous" and encouraged me to consider to "which side" my research would contribute. This interaction was a reminder of the tension between participation and observation inherent in the ethnographic gaze: Could I produce a "thick description" (Geertz, 1973) of the activist narrative without becoming an activist myself? If not, would this not make it impossible for me to access competing narratives while trying to paint a fuller picture of the cultural and political landscapes navigated by young people trying to make sense of India's dams, sustainability, and development?

Opening our conversation, Arnab flatly noted that the movement against the Tehri Dam did not succeed because it did not mobilize enough people. "The other thing is that Tehri raised much more technical issues, actually," he noted, pointing to the dam's location on top of a geological fault and concerns about safety because of earthquakes. He maintained that these issues were not acknowledged by the government. Looking out the window, as if he were focused on a distant object, he said, "They will set up a committee and if this committee says that this is not safe then they will set up another committee, then they will set up a third committee and so on." The decision to proceed with the project was based on the benefits to interest groups rather than to the country at large. Arnab recalled that, in the late 1970s, Indira Gandhi, then India's prime minister, "actually wrote on the file of Tehri that this project will only benefit the contractors. I haven't seen that in writing but a planning commission member, Arun Ghosh, told us that he has seen it—and he would have seen it if [he said] he has seen it." I heard this anecdote many times during my fieldwork. In the activists' imagination of the past, Indira Gandhi—whom many remember as an authoritarian figure responsible for the Emergency of 1975–1977—has become a symbol of the benevolent state. But if Indira Gandhi disapproved of the project, why did she not stop it?

By the end of my fieldwork, I understood that, in the activist consciousness, the Tehri Dam symbolizes a corruption of the state in which the well-being of many (alive and unborn) is sacrificed for the financial profits of the few. For Sunderlal Bahuguna, for example, "the erection of Tehri Dam presented an ecological, social, and religious challenge. He argue[d] that when the Ganges flows in its natural course, it benefits all, irrespective of caste, . creed, color, or economic circumstances. When it is dammed, it becomes the possession of the privileged and powerful who dispense its blessings on a partisan basis" (James, 2013, pp. 172–173). Yet the state responsible for the damming was not the enemy. Representing the laudable, hefty ideals of Indian Independence, including the constitutional right to a clean environment, the state was simultaneously the bearer of hope rooted in the histories (and mythologies) of the Independence struggle and a perpetrator of atrocities against India's natural environment and its most vulnerable peoples. The history of the state contradicted the activists' memory of its actions and, despite the state-sponsored violence of many types captured in these collective memories—slow, fast, symbolic, literal—history still won. The activists were not anarchists advocating to dismantle the state; they saw themselves as being truer than politicians and bureaucrats to the ideals of the constitution the state was supposedly built on. Theirs was a politics of hope that reflected a symbolic world order in which ideas of the past had the potential to transform the co-option of governance by nondemocratic forces into the humane state freedom fighters once pictured as India's glorious future. For many of these activists, Gandhi and his contemporary incarnations such as Sunderlal Bahuguna were a metaphor for this not-yet-realized, overdue future they felt was worth fighting for. Indira Gandhi, by association with her father Jawaharlal Nehru, retained a degree of impunity in this imagining of history as future; thus she could be exempt from blame for the Tehri Dam despite being the prime minister overseeing the project. But the spatial dimensions of this imagination were uneven, and the localized activist consciousness in spaces like Pashulok was more concerned with the dead (Tehri residents and their natural environment) than the Dead (freedom fighters and their ideas about India's political future). Both the dead and the Dead belonged to a world that was simultaneously beyond and within reach, that blended an imagined past with horizons of the possible, where hope met despair. This fusion is at the core of the activists' intergenerational (vertical-horizontal) agonistic pluralism. To understand why a dialogue with other generations is key to their struggle, we must first understand the trauma that gave rise to the oustees' activism in the first place.

The Cultural Trauma of Dispossession in a Himalayan Valley

It was not every day that I saw oustees in Pashulok get emotional. Whether it was true that these *pahadis* were the "tough people" of the mountains, as the stereotype in India goes, or that the language barrier made it hard to build trust between us, I saw a lot of stoic faces during my conversations with older people in Pashulok. But this was not the case with Rahul, a man in his sixties with a wrinkly face, a spattering of gray hair and a gentle, soft voice that did not seem to match his strong frame. A veteran of grassroots activism, he could recall events from the earliest days of the antidam struggle, but he seemed to wish to leave much of this history behind. Yet some memories could not easily be forgotten. When I asked Rahul to elaborate on his comment that the activist history was a painful one, he told me a story that took place in the early 1990s:

> Against the building of Tehri Dam and around the issues of our resettlement, we had done a protest in Tehri. Sunderlal Bahuguna was leading us. So to scare the government we had gone where they were building the road. There was a guy amongst us, Chimnu Bhai (from the musician caste), so that the government listens to our demands and does proper settlement. The armed police over there started hitting us with their sticks. Chimnu Bhai was injured on the head and all his instruments broke. Some women were also with us, and they were about to fall down the Bhagirathi valley. There was a slab under the tunnel. If that slab was not there, they would have fallen down. So that is a very scary memory. We were only asking for our rights, but what did we get. We could have died that day, but we got saved.

In such anecdotes, the slow violence of dispossession and displacement and the decades of uncertainty and anxiety that preceded it turned into the fast violence of clashes between activists and police, each representing a different narrative of development and citizenship. The trauma of displacement was compounded by the trauma of state violence. Ultimately, some protests brought concessions from the government, but these were short lived. Rahul told me that, following the initial protests, the government increased each family's compensation from 2.5 to 5 lakh (₹250,000 to ₹500,000); however, they did not offer any land. "Our situation was that of nomads," he said, eyes staring into the distance. Government promises, Rahul explained, included a government job for at least one person from each resettled family, free electricity, and subsidized water—none of which was fulfilled. "When we came here, we realized that the situation was completely opposite of the promises made to us. There was no provision for living, food, nothing. This place was like a jungle; there was just marking of the size of the land (2.5 bigha)[13] . . . We are still fighting for land rights."

The predicament of India's dam oustees was worse than the government claimed. It was often so grim that the appalling treatment of the Bhopal casualties, discussed in chapter 3, seems less shocking when put in the context of the plight of the oustees and other victims of "development." The memories of activists in Pashulok strongly suggested that Tehri was no exception.[14] According to a report of the activist organization *Matu Jansangthan* (2002), the inadequate policies were highlighted by a government committee set up in 1998 under the leadership of Hanumatha Rao, but the recommendations for redressing the situation were ignored. The critique expressed by Rakesh, my activist-guide and translator, was even more scathing: he called the rehabilitation process a "land scam" because in the name of resettlement the "forest land" at Pashulok was rezoned as a residential area.[15] Since many oustees ended up selling their land (informants' estimates ranged from 40 percent to 60 percent, but no official statistic is available), Pashulok effectively became less of a rehabilitation site and more of a new urban development (figure 5.1) where, in Rakesh's words, "everyone is a property dealer." This signaled an almost total breakdown of communities—the very outcome activists opposing the dam had feared for decades.

Figure 5.1
The "property dealership" of Pashulok.

For my interlocutors, activism was about stopping the dam and, when this failed, about holding the government accountable for its own promised compensation for the oustees.[16] Stories of marches, fasts-unto-death, and violent confrontations with state authorities were still alive in the minds of local activists during my field research in 2016 and 2017.[17] However, as more than a decade had passed since the dam's completion and the large-scale population relocation, the intensity of the protest movement had declined, and only those involved in the struggle for land rights still considered themselves activists. These Pashulok residents established a nongovernmental organization (NGO), *Visthapit Samanvye Vikas Samiti* (Rehabilitation Coordination Development Committee), to represent their rights with government authorities and conducted fasts and marches to highlight the injustice of not being given formal rights to the plots of land on which they built their houses. According to Dinesh, one of my informants who was involved in setting up this organization,

Our people held a meeting and we discussed that our children's future was in danger. So, everyone in the village got together and started a demonstration. When we tried to reach out to the government for our land rights, but it fell on deaf ears, we had no choice but to protest. People from 16 villages, people from different valleys, who were from different backgrounds but had been resettled in the nearby areas, got together to protest. Women, old people, young people, everyone supported us and we started a movement called *Tehsil Gherao* [surround the Tehsil or administrative house] and did it 2–3 times. We were continuously going to our secretary and were passing on the message to our representatives through the media and other forms. Women also played an important role in this; they did candle marches, sat for hunger strikes, contributed in the Tehsil movement, and so on.

My interlocutors, however, noted that this movement had only been active in the six months before my fieldwork; before then there had been no major protests for years.[18]

My account of activism in Pashulok so far implies that the enduring legacy of the antidam struggle is the oustees' effort to get fair compensation. This is consistent with the views of Pranay and other teachers at Seema Primary, discussed in chapter 4, who stated that the goal of the activist agenda was to secure more land and money for oustees. However, after immersing myself in the site, I came to understand that this is a distortion of both the activist agenda and the underlying motivations. The ability to mobilize after years of inactivity suggests a generative space of sedimented memory that enabled collective action. Even during quiet times, activists retained their political socialization rooted in the intergenerational trauma of displacement, a recognition of the debt to the dead and to the unborn, and an acute awareness of both the material and ethereal losses caused by resettlement. This is analogous to what Checker (2005, p. 116) referred to as "'quiescent politics,' that is, the retention of political awareness, leadership, and organizational skills in practical consciousness during seemingly dormant periods," which she observed in her ethnography of environmental activism in Hyde Park in Augusta, Georgia (United States). Such "quiescent politics" is possible thanks, in part, to an ongoing conversation with the dead in negotiating the future for the youth (and the unborn), which I explore in the next section.

Histories Lost and Found: Thinking with Past Generations about the Future of Progress

The past throws a long shadow over the lives of those in Pashulok who are old enough to remember life before resettlement. While activist efforts are aimed at receiving what they see as just compensation from authorities, at the root of their criticism of the Tehri Dam is the failure to recognize the history that, in their minds, has been submerged along with the villages of Tehri. The grief for lost histories came into sharp relief for me when I visited the town of New Tehri[19] to interview local activists. Sitting in a room crammed full of children, mattresses, cooking utensils, and the heaviness of memory, I listened to Arjun, an activist his comrades described to me as a scholar and historian. We were sitting in his two-room house that appeared to provide shelter to a dozen family members, with the Tehri Dam below us on the slopes of the valley. Rakesh and I climbed many stairs up to Arjun's house from where our driver dropped us off and, despite my relative youth and being used to climbing steep slopes, I found myself catching my breath at the top of the stairs. "A city of stairs," the locals came to call New Tehri, a town built by the Indian government to replace one submerged by the dam.

The place truly felt like a distorted replica, an outgrowth of the narrow visions of government technocrats rather than a town with an organic history (figure 5.2). Its Himalayan backdrop reminded me of Kathmandu, a city where I lived for several years as a development worker, but the mountains seemed to be all the two places had in common. Unlike Kathmandu, with its organic web of bustling alleyways, New Tehri felt quiet, almost deserted, as if the neat lines of planners' blueprints for the city's streets remained just that, a lifeless artifice. In a scene before me, a cow seemed to be policing the entry to a staircase, which no one in sight seemed interested in climbing. It was almost as if the cow were the guardian of the Hindu nationalist state and its development project—the development of an Anthropocenic world in which people had little desire to participate (figure 5.3).

Arjun's face showed his pain as he told me about the richness he believed was lost along with the old town of Tehri. He spoke of a civilization that had inhabited the valley for thousands of years. "This place, along with four or five other important places, is even mentioned in Kedarkhand, which is

Figure 5.2
The emptiness and artifice of New Tehri town.

Figure 5.3
A cow "policing" a stairway in New Tehri.

an ancient scripture—a part of a Skanda Purana,[20] which signifies that this society is very old and traditionally rich," he told me as his children, lying on their beds but wide awake, listened attentively. I wondered how often stories about predam times were told in this house and whether my presence had inspired their telling; the children's eyes were wide open as they hung on Arjun's every word, which made me think they had heard such stories before. "It has been here since prehistoric times," Arjun continued, "a time that is so old that it has a mention in Puranas but no mention in history books that are known to us. Before history started getting written, Tehri was inhabited by people of the Yaksha,[21] Gandharva,[22] Kinnar lok tribes." But this was not Arjun's main point. He was building up to a conceptual challenge to the state's notion of rehabilitation, which eschewed this richness. His references to cultural loss—folklore, music, rivers—represented the activists' palpably emotive narratives and ritualistic retelling of loss and rupture:

> That's why it is said that it isn't just the people who are displaced from the place. When the policy was made to rehabilitate people, it mentioned figures—the number of families, the number of people, the amount of land being rehabilitated. But it cannot quantify or evaluate the cultural damage, or damage to the river, water, the banks, the wood flowing in the river, the grass and trees growing beside the river. No rehabilitation policy mentions the trees, the river, the society, the folk songs, or the history. History, culture, trees, river, community, family relations, and society relations—everything was displaced. Even the language was displaced. Now we do not use that language here anymore.

Arjun was not merely critiquing the government's reluctance to consider the numerous losses caused by its megaproject. He suggested that the disruption of culture caused by the dam rendered futile any attempts to "rehabilitate" history, because this history had been displaced, disconnected from space forever.

Arjun's register of the various losses, those obliterated by the dam, and those made invisible by the state's compensation scheme may seem reminiscent of the romanticizing and essentializing of the past found in much early anthropological writing about Indigenous populations (Pels, 2008; Said, 1979). It is certainly true that activists I talked to in the field often spoke of the predam past in uncritical terms. I wondered to what extent the violence of forced resettlement was overshadowing caste inequalities and other forms of social tension of the predisplacement past. But, even if the activists' imagination of the past was overly optimistic, their grief was fueled by more than mere nostalgia. Back in Pashulok, Dinesh, an uncle of a student involved in the filmmaking workshop, reminisced about what life was like before resettlement, recalling the love and care residents showed one another in old Tehri. "Now here we are brothers but we aren't even able to sit together. There the villagers would gather and chit-chat," he recalled. Remembering his childhood, he noted that "we would see our elders in groups of 5–10 sitting together. Now if we ask someone to sit, they will probably say we don't have time. Even I will have the same response. At that time, people had time and figured out things together." This idea of no longer having time did not appear linked to an accelerated pace of life as it may be in the postindustrial societies of the "Global North" (cf. Thomashow, 2020) but to a spatial reconfiguration of the community that was disconnected from the space that had evolved organically over generations to facilitate a culture of sharing, exchange, and care for the commons.[23]

The yearning for a lost sense of community was at the heart of most of my informants' concerns in Pashulok; they invariably spoke of community in the past tense.[24] Submerged villages and extended families were not resettled together, resulting in the geographical separation of relatives and neighbors who often ended up in rehabilitation sites dozens of kilometers apart. All my informants described the sense of alienation this created in Pashulok and the difficulty of keeping in contact with their relatives and friends. Most poignant were the comments about what this fragmentation meant for intergenerational knowledge transfer. When I asked Rahul what he learned from his elders in his youth, he told me:

> It was a value that whatever state one is in at the moment, one should make sure that the next generation is in the same state. To maintain stability, which will give the next generation the same freedom that my ancestors gave me. The same culture, the traditions should be maintained . . . But our ancestors were foresighted and they had planned in such a way that if we were in dire need we could depend on the land we had. We could stretch ourselves to meet some

emergency needs. But here we have nothing . . . Progress was not individualistic; it was for the whole society. But that does not exist now.

Many informants remembered their past society as one of sustainability based on nonindividualistic progress and solidarity, and they were determined to pass this on to the next generation. Rahul pointed out that the new generation embraced different aspirations. "Because the young blood can drift anywhere, so our ancestors told us that before making any big decision, one must be careful not to destroy everything one already has. That in your imaginary leap, don't end up losing your present." Indeed, the "imaginary leap" of Tehri Dam, the expectation that it would bring about development, cost the people of the submerged villages and towns their preresettlement present. It also endangered the conversations with the dead that had helped maintain a social equilibrium of environmental sustainability for centuries.

What is striking in these narratives is a recognition of the activists' ongoing challenge to the government's view of development as equated with progress. For activists, the state's notion of progress was a narrative of deceit. They opted to think about the future with the dead.[25] Thinking about what enabled their predecessors to sustain their lifestyles in the now submerged areas of Tehri for centuries is an important part of the puzzle of sustainability for these activists. The trauma of resettlement makes it difficult for them to pass on to their children the values and knowledge they received from their elders. This is in part because the activists had to undergo a major transition and still are struggling to adjust more than a decade after arriving in Pashulok. Rahul repeatedly stressed to me the richness of flora and fauna in the village he was displaced from.[26] He also pointed out that in Pashulok the oustees could not cut down any trees because of strict laws, whereas back in his village the community did its own safeguarding of natural resources and allowed each family to cut down one or two trees annually, at the same time ensuring that new trees were planted every year. Perhaps even more importantly, social resources were also in short supply in Pashulok. "We could look up [our friends in nearby villages] for support in case of need. Now we are in an opposite situation, that if I even need to go there for help, first I need to make sure I have the money to go there. Those connections are far off now."

Aside from their impact on the oustees' quality of life, these changes made it difficult for the older generation to sustain transgenerational knowledge transfer and engage their children in vertical agonistic pluralism.

The task is further complicated by the breakdown of religious and cultural traditions and rituals. Rahul recalled *pandav* dance performances held at night in the village temple for which the whole community would come together. "It did not rain in the mountain, so for irrigating our crops we would worship our deity *narsingh*. So these traditions stopped there, now we can't practice them. We are modernizing now and forgetting our old customs." The activists seem to be the ones in this community who try to keep the intergenerational dialogue alive—despite a social climate, an education system, and a state not conducive to such an effort.

The activists, who "speak for the dead" in this dialogic exchange, seek to carry forward the values they believe were enabled by the dead's ways of life, such as solidarity and care for the commons. They hope that, as future generations move along the path of development, young people will find ways to integrate these values, as the activists see them, into their new lifestyles. What this dialogue transmits, therefore, is not a literal meaning of memory (which would risk passing on a nostalgic or romanticized picture of agriculture-driven village life) but its surplus meaning: the hidden values, beliefs, and insights into the human condition, as identified by activists living in the present,[27] which the dead possessed without necessarily being conscious of them.[28] This is where government thinking about development is at odds with the activists' perspectives, as the state's idea of development relies on literal meanings gleaned from the "developed" "Global North"— economic growth, factories, power lines, and dams—rather than the surplus meanings found in the intellectual, social, and economic history of development as viewed through the prism of temporal distance. Surplus meaning may include notions such as welfare, prosperity, or happiness—timeless ideas that need to be reinvented constantly, an effort that lies at the root of activist consciousness in Pashulok.

Many forces, however, act against the young's ability and willingness to be receptive to their elders' efforts to build intergenerational bridges through tradition. As chapter 4 demonstrated, the schooling the young people are receiving in Pashulok is one obstacle but there are other forces at play. According to Rakesh,

[I]t's not because of Tehri Dam, it is because . . . see, these people are not living in some corner, they're living in this world, and this world is for development, for so-called progress and progress doesn't mean fresh water, progress doesn't mean fresh air, progress doesn't mean free-flowing river, progress doesn't mean beautiful scene, plain hills, open hills. Development means big infrastructure projects, development means big dams, natural resources are resources to use, natural resources are not just to, if you're allowing a river free, it means you're wasting water, this is their mindset and this is what our education system teaches them.

Beyond referring to sedimented memories of a preresettlement past, the images of fresh water, fresh air, and a free-flowing river have symbolic meaning. By pitting these images against the government's dominant notion of progress, Rakesh suggests that India's development is not only incompatible with stewardship of the natural environment but also, by disconnecting memory from the "theatre" in which it was shaped, an obstacle to intergenerational dialogue. To Rakesh, the locus of the definition of development is shifted outside the local community, and the community is no longer in charge of shaping its own development trajectory.

Prashant, another antidam activist I talked to in nearby Dehradun, sees this transformation as a reflection of a larger trend. He points to the urbanization of India and China as contributing to the disconnect of people from nature. This means that, while the generation with direct memories of preresettlement life may feel a sense of loss and therefore can be critical of the government's dominant development paradigm, the next generation is simply not feeling that, or perhaps is feeling it as a disembodied form of nostalgia. This pessimism is echoed by Rahul, whose view on the future of his community in Pashulok is very bleak:

Peter: What kind of future do you think is possible in this place?
Rahul: We hope to make this place good.
Translator [Rakesh, who translates and adds]: But in reality, what is possible?
Rahul: It is very difficult. Imagine this is a big garbage dumping ground and we are asked to clean it.

The idea of a "big garbage dumping ground" not only refers to the physical state of the environment in Pashulok, as perceived by Rahul, but also symbolizes the uphill battle the activists are fighting against the forces undermining intergenerational dialogue. While it may seem their efforts are doomed, the very presence of activists in the community suggests otherwise. The trauma of displacement highlighted the importance of talking with the dead about the future of progress and teaching the youth about the importance of such vertical agonistic pluralism. It is too early to tell what this may lead to and whether it may help to clean up the "big garbage dumping ground" of destruction and short-sighted ideologies at the heart of the high Anthropocene moment.

It became clear to me by the end of my fieldwork that these activists walked a fine line between nostalgia for the past and vertical agonistic pluralism. They were not simply clinging to tradition but engaging in what Ricœur calls the hermeneutic imagination (Kearney, 2004). To engage in such radical imagination "inside tradition" means "to be simultaneously outside it. This is one of Ricœur's most compelling insights: to imagine ourselves as we truly are is to imagine ourselves otherwise" (Kearney, 2004, p. 73). Activism in Pashulok is underpinned precisely by an imagination whose temporality extends across layers of sedimented memory into a conversation with the dead, and this conversation, in turn, informs the coalition-building needed for effective activism. This is one way to "imagine ourselves otherwise." Activists in South Africa, too—while cutting across sediments of their own, many of them (dis)colored by the legacy of apartheid—thought of the dead while speaking across social divides to the alive who were, in a certain sense, radically different from them. The horizontality of "imagining otherwise" was particularly pronounced in South Durban; this is where I turn next in this exploration of the interface between activism, education, and the Anthropocene.

THE COMMON ENEMY: CHALLENGING ENVIRONMENTAL RACISM IN SOUTH DURBAN

"Why would a guy from Cambridge come to a place like Wentworth?" asked one of my interlocutors in South Durban, a scientist with a doctorate.

I believe his question was motivated in part by curiosity about how I found my research site, but I also sensed him wondering what I could possibly discover here. A few months later, I titled a conference paper summarizing my preliminary findings "From Intervention to Inspiration: Shifting Imagination of Sustainable Development to the 'Margins.'" In the immediate aftermath of my fieldwork, it seemed to me that such a shift—corresponding to disproving my interlocutor's apparent assumption that little could be learned in Wentworth—was precisely the underlying political goal of my project. I believed that, rather than being in need of outside intervention, spaces like Wentworth in fact had the potential to inspire ideas, approaches, and policies that could shape the landscape of education across the "Global North"/"Global South" divide. Reflecting on this idea with more temporal distance, I argue that outside intervention and inspiration are not mutually exclusive and that the title of my paper expressed more the hypothesis with which I entered the field than the ethnographic realities I experienced during my field research. While it is true that communities living on the fence line of industries (or communities displaced by dams) may be more politicized around environmental threats than much of the rest of the world, the demands of activists often are precisely *for* outside intervention because the collective agency of these groups is simply not sufficient to enact change at the scale and pace needed to resolve the underlying causes of the environmental issues. Put differently, it is not necessary to choose between seeing a space as troubled and in need of help (which can easily slip into a [neo]colonial paternalism and condescension) or viewing it as having qualities that cannot be found elsewhere (an approach that can result in a romanticizing of often-harsh realities). If my field research in South Durban taught me anything, it was that this is a false dichotomy; a place can simultaneously be a source of inspiration and in need of assistance. Wentworth is one such place.

While the politicization of the local community resulting from decades of environmental racism is understandable, the emergence of organized grassroots activism in South Durban is slightly more surprising. Unlike antidam activism in India, much of which is an example of "environmentalism of the poor" (Alier, 2002; Guha & Martinez-Alier, 1997; Nixon, 2011), the South African environmental movement has a distinct history of "environmentalism of the rich" (Dauvergne, 2016) which "lov[ed] wild animals much more than black babies" (Prozesky, 2009, p. 300). Apartheid-era environmentalism represented a largely White middle-class phenomenon focused on conservation and preservation of the "inherent value of nature," often at the expense of South Africans of color and the so-called "brown" environmental issues such as pollution, sanitation, and equitable access to natural resources (Leonard, 2013; Steyn, 2002, 2005).[29] But the movement has moved toward a more holistic approach (Khan, 2000), and South Africa now has a diverse, internationally acclaimed environmental movement that sees sociopolitical conflicts as integral to environmentalism. SDCEA is one of its notable components (Barnett & Scott, 2007a; Freund, 2001; Leonard & Pelling, 2010; D. Scott & Barnett, 2009).[30] Desmond D'Sa, SDCEA's leader, is the 2014 recipient of the Goldman Environmental Prize (also known as the "Green Nobel Prize") for the African region—an honor that was extended to Medha Patkar for her antidam activism in India in 1992. Spending time with both these figures during my fieldwork, I realized that, despite the different contexts from which they emerged and the different proximate objects of their respective struggles, Medha Patkar and Desmond D'Sa represent movements that have a lot in common. Perhaps the most important similarity is their sustained opposition to the mainstream development paradigm of industrial modernization that, in their eyes, makes a mockery of the rhetoric of human and environmental rights that allegedly represent the bedrock of the Indian and South African states.

Yet their different histories led to different conversations at the heart of these movements.[31] Both have been shaped by intergenerational (vertical) and intragenerational (horizontal) agonistic pluralism. The Indian activists' response to the disruption of intergenerational dialogue and cultural identity alerted me to the vertical aspect. In South Africa, I saw the horizontal reflected in apartheid's legacy of dialogues across formerly uncrossable lines of race, ethnicity, gender, and class, which inevitably also linked this dialogue to the horizontal/intergenerational aspect. In a country that continues to be marked by stark inequalities, the horizontal agonistic pluralism at the core of present-day South African environmentalism is a countercultural[32] force that challenges not only the ideologies of the state (and the transnational ideologies of neoliberal capitalism and [post]industrial modernity in which the state is embedded) but also the binary logic of apartheid that continues to shape South Africa's society and economy. The common enemy of environmentalists in South Durban is not merely the mainstream development paradigm but the demon of apartheid history. This is where history meets the present through the imperial matrix of capital accumulation.

It did not take long for me to realize that this history is still very much alive, in South Durban and across South Africa. During the early stages of my fieldwork in the spring of 2016, I was already shocked at the disparities between the haves and the have-nots, a divide that seemed to correspond with the historical racial polarization between Whites and non-Whites but was also increasingly about class (M. Hunter, 2010; Seekings & Nattrass, 2005) and the phenomenon of state capture (Bond, 2014) by corrupt economic elites associated with the rule of Jacob Zuma (Booysen, 2015). Before engaging in research in South Africa, I considered this country a success story on a continent troubled by illness, endemic poverty, and the economic domination of foreign superpowers (Somerville, 2016), but the realities I encountered here—along with the scholarship of South African scholars (e.g., Bloch, 2009; Bond, 2000, 2014; D. Scott, 2003a, 2003b; Seekings & Nattrass, 2005; Steyn, 2005)—convinced me otherwise.[33] Like many foreigners, I fell in love with the vistas of Cape Town while scouting for my research site. But by the time I boarded a train to Johannesburg, my next destination, I felt there was something soul-crushing about the divide between the wealthy and still predominantly White parts of the city and the "flats" and townships surrounding these guarded spaces of apparent prosperity. It was possible to live for years in a place like Greenpoint (an affluent Cape Town neighborhood) without encountering poverty, crime, and the gross injustices shaping the country's society. "Apartheid never ended," I wrote into my ethnographic diary as I reflected on my time in Cape Town during my long, slow train ride to Johannesburg.

For environmental activists, continued segregation means they are dealing with groups of local residents who see themselves as fundamentally different from their neighbors who have a different skin color. While postapartheid laws allow a group like SDCEA to organize formally—which would have been unthinkable before 1993—the task of bringing together the various groups of people in South Durban is arguably not much simpler than it was during the totalitarian regime. It is as if the history of division is projected onto the present despite the smokescreen of a nation that supposedly has moved on.

This is where the idea of a horizontal agonistic pluralism comes into play. While activists in South Durban certainly engage in dialogues with past generations, their most visible strength seems to be in their ability to build coalitions across different racial and class groups in the face of the apartheid of the present. Air pollution is a particularly potent bonding agent, as all in South Durban are affected by it irrespective of their skin color, wealth, age, or gender. Just like the vertically rising waters of Tehri Dam that submerged sedimented layers of memory, the life-threatening chemicals of South Durban's oil refineries and factories rise up through the smokestacks and spill across the entire industrial basin. Given the history of environmental racism, these industries' economic importance to the country, and the vested interests of transnational corporations and the government in keeping the factories going with as little investment in environmental cleanup as possible, fighting this pollution is arguably what scholars of the environment call a "hard problem." This combination of the vertical-turned-horizontal industrial pollution, the economic and political order that make it extremely hard to challenge, and the apartheid-like racial divisions are a furtive ground for a pluralistic, agonistic breed of activist resistance that cuts across deeply entrenched social divides. Just like the polluted air, SDCEA's presence spreads horizontally like an expanding cloud, covering areas it previously would have been unthinkable to link together in collective political action.

This horizontal expansion is reflected in the history of local activism. During my time with activists in South Durban, I often heard references to Earthlife Africa as the predecessor of present-day environmental organizations like SDCEA and its sister organization groundWork, which operates internationally. Founded in 1988 in Johannesburg, Earthlife Africa was initially a platform for mostly left-leaning White South Africans challenging the environmental injustice of the apartheid regime. It held a national conference about sustainable development in September 1992 at the University of Natal in Pietermaritzburg,[34] which was, according to many of my informants, a pivotal moment in the history of South Durban environmentalism. Chris Albertyn, whom many in South Durban consider a key figure behind the emergence of SDCEA and groundWork, presented a paper titled "Effluent of Affluence: How I Came to See the Dirt on Adam Smith's Invisible Hand," in which he argued that unfettered free markets were responsible for much environmental destruction (Albertyn, 1993, p. 214), echoing a critique of global capitalism similar to the one advanced by Western environmental movements at the time (Guha, 2000).[35]

I interviewed Chris Albertyn in 2017 in a coffee shop in Kloof, a leafy suburb of Durban. Expecting to see a hippie, I met a soft-spoken, reflective man whose white beard and deep-set eyes reminded me of stereotypical images of ancient druids, with whom he also seemed to share the gift of wisdom. Chris had the aura of a professor, but his occasional pauses between sentences and the subtle movements of muscles in his face betrayed a past of varied experiences well outside the ivory tower, some of which were, no doubt, painful. Thinking back to the early 1990s, he recalled that the movement initially was "99 per cent White." He said that its culture was "still White middle-class academic" and that it was "very conscious about trying to make space or trying to embrace broader demographics," the result being that "the issues we took up became more embracing of issues that affected all races." When I asked him what it was about that point in time that made such a shift possible, he noted that

> it was just the condition of the time and the context that allowed us to do that. We were able to link it up with worker struggles, worker health-and-safety struggles in industrial areas and . . . [we] talk[ed] to working-class people around things that were really important to them, particularly from a factory perspective and health and safety and realizing there was a narrative of a broader set of values and a broader set of aspirations of how we would like to see the world that was shared more widely.

Chris pointed to a window of opportunity that opened up as a result of political changes in the early 1990s. A shared goal of overcoming the divisions of apartheid set the stage for a new type of pluralism in which it was not just middle-class White academics who came together to agonize over what "sustainable development" could mean in this part of the world.[36] Wider participation in the conversation meant that the previously singular debt to the unborn—to preserve the natural environment—gave way to multiple debts, including the debt of equality and historical justice and the debt of truth about the past, as reflected in South Africa's Truth and Reconciliation Commission (Boraine, 2000; Sitze, 2013). It also became clear that these debts could only be discussed through inclusive vertical-horizontal agonistic pluralism rather than the nonpluralism of apartheid. Just as environmentalism became multicolored—the "white" alongside the domestic "brown" and international "green" agendas—sustainability became multilayered, the environmental alongside the social and economic. Chris continued: "What it meant to be green in South Africa was that it was inclusionary, it was recognizing [that] multiple facets of the same problem can be looked at from different perspectives, a worker perspective." It was about finding shared narratives and a common language rather than "trying to co-opt one schematic faction to say our issue is more important, you should come and fight our issue." The goal was to look for shared interests among the various groups coming together and rally around those, he explained. Apart from the intrinsic value of diversity, the shift toward finding intersections of different agendas was a strategic move. The early 1990s were not only a time of hope when social transformation seemed within reach but also a clear opportunity for the environmental movement to have a greater say in the country's politics.

These newly found opportunities manifested in South Durban soon after the election of Nelson Mandela as South Africa's president in 1994. There is some evidence of protests against the environmental impact of petrochemical industries on local populations before the 1990s—including complaints from the White population living on the Bluff (a historically White neighborhood in South Durban less exposed to industrial pollution than Wentworth) as early as the 1960s.[37] However, the event remembered by many as pivotal was Mandela's visit to the Engen oil refinery in March 1995, when local activists staged a protest at the refinery's gates.[38]

I talked about this important episode with Patrick Mkhize, a veteran of the South African trade union movement and an SDCEA stalwart. Patrick's office was located in downtown Durban on a street I had not driven through before. Local academics told me that the city center was not safe and advised me to avoid it, so I always took care to drive around the downtown area rather than through it, until the day I met Patrick. The streets were swarming with people on that hot spring day. While the postapartheid White flight from Durban's central business district was not as significant as in Johannesburg, the downtown certainly did not feel like the "citadel of [White] privilege" that it had been under apartheid (Schensul & Heller, 2011, p. 104). The area was full of Black-run businesses and residences and—according to local academics and teachers at Durban South Primary—crime. While this change might seem symbolic of a changing world order, it masked the underlying continuity of economic disparities. Black people may have been able to move to the city center, but they still lived in poverty as the wealthy and the privileged (including me) detoured around the downtown area, further reinforcing segregation.

Patrick, a large man with a charismatic laugh and expressive face who had clearly seen much in his lifetime, sat down with me in a small conference room in the offices of the workers union, which he led. We talked about history, activism, education, and politics. When we spoke of Nelson Mandela's visit to South Durban, he became visibly animated. "So, Mandela, wherever he went, nobody could stop him. But because we managed to stop Mandela and Mandela got out of the limousine and came to us and said what is the problem? And we told him what is the problem," he said joyfully. "And we said, 'We are pleading with you Madiba, get back in your limo and go back, don't enter these premises.' He said, 'I want to meet you tomorrow.' You see? I want to meet you tomorrow." Patrick pulled out his cell phone and after a minute or two of looking through his photographs, he located a picture of a meeting between Mandela and the South Durban activists and proudly passed the phone to me across the table. In that meeting, Patrick continued, Mandela "was very emphatic that management, the business owners must listen to what the community says because there must be cooperation and coexistence between the two or otherwise the one must relocate. And we said the business must relocate, not us, you know." While Mandela was not in a position to ask the factories to move because of the political economy of the postapartheid moment and South Africa's dependence on foreign capital (A. Hirsch, 2005), his support of the activist struggle helped to generate resistance and endowed the movement with a powerful, legitimizing origin story.[39]

In contrast to present-day activism being seen as a challenge to the government, the early postapartheid moment saw a merging of the two. Many environmental activists, including Desmond D'Sa, had come from the ranks of the ANC, and South Durban played an important part in bringing the environmental agenda to the forefront at this time of political transformation (Barnett, 2003). It represented a space where the logic of apartheid was successfully challenged—a microcosm of the ideal of the rainbow nation (Mandela, 2013).[40]

I had a chance to learn about the early days of South Durban activism from Rico, one of the core staff members at groundWork. Rico was White; His name and accent betrayed his Greek origins. Bald, wearing rimless glasses, jeans, and a t-shirt, my first impression of Rico was that of a minimalist and a family man. We first met at a dinner organized by a mutual friend in Durban before I visited South Durban or met other activists. At the time, Rico was focused on making sure his children did not turn our friend's house upside down. During our discussions over the coming months, which revolved around the big picture of environmental movements in 2010s South Africa, Rico often reflected on the kind of world his children would grow up into. In one conversation, he shared with me his extensive knowledge of the historical evolution and unique nature of South Durban activism:

> The communities around South Durban uniquely cross this racial and ethnic and class barrier and manage to form an alliance in Durban and it's kind of politically endorsed. Nelson Mandela comes to South Durban. Kader Asmal, who I think was the minister of water affairs at the time, Bantu Holomisa at the time was the minister of environmental affairs. All of these politicians kind of endorse community activism around the issues they're working, whether it's wasteland for sites or air pollution or water pollution or whatever . . . And that was like the mid- to late-90s. So that was like the honeymoon period. It's the first dispensation and the strong political mandate by the people, government is strong. It's still kind of in opposition to industry because industry is generally White-owned capitalist.

While the "honeymoon period" may not have lasted beyond the 1990s as successive governments failed to deliver on the promises of the Mandela years, the meshing of activism and government left a lasting legacy in South Durban and beyond.

Air Pollution as a Social Equalizer?

SDCEA is one of the most enduring legacies of this period of hope.[41] In an interview, Desmond D'Sa described it as an "alliance of twenty groups from churches to conservation groups to civics to home hostel dwellers to unemployed people to flat dwellers." Initially focused on fighting air pollution in South Durban, SDCEA has become involved in other issues over the years, including public health, energy, livelihoods, and development.

But air pollution remains the main focus because everyone in South Durban breathes the same polluted air. Air pollution has become the common enemy, much as apartheid had united activists for decades before 1994. Unlike the brutal system of apartheid, however, polluted air is a prime example of slow violence. Toxic substances accumulate in the bodies of local residents over years or even decades before causing symptoms. This leaves the activists in South Durban with a difficult task, as Rico, whose background is in epidemiology, pointed out to me. "If we look at the global evidence-base for the global determinants of health, [air pollution is] the thing that causes most people to die around the world. Indoor air pollution and outdoor air pollution combined is at least twice as much and maybe as much as three times as much responsible than the second and third highest causes of death globally." Despite this, the slow violence air pollution causes is difficult to expose. Rico mused, "So how do you articulate that? How do you say to people there's this thing in your community that is invisible, that you can't see because it's not visible to the naked eye and in many cases, the science that helps understand how it affects you is not very well-known?"

SDCEA has employed a variety of techniques to do this. They have collaborated with scientists and scholars on studies of air pollution's impact on communities in South Durban. The most notable outcome is a 2008 epidemiological study of asthma and respiratory disease among children attending Settlers Primary School (Kistnasamy et al., 2008), which is located on the fence line of Engen oil refinery.[42] The study found that 52 percent of the children suffered from asthma; figures from other South African studies range between 0.14 percent and 15 percent (Kistnasamy et al., 2008, p. 367). During a "toxic tour"[43] of South Durban (figure 5.4), Bongani, SDCEA's air quality officer, told me this finding "actually broke the Guinness Book of Records."

Bongani, a young, energetic, smiling, slim man seemed, like Des, to have an elusive air of idealism about him. Perhaps it was his unrelenting optimism in the face of environmental destruction, the way he maintained eye contact with everyone he spoke to, or his ability to be simultaneously gentle (in his manners) and firm (in his opinions) that made him appear to me to be the "future of SDCEA"—an opinion I expressed to him one day as we sat in the cramped office. Desmond (who, I thought, would eventually retire) was out, and I was curious to see how Bongani would react to my remark in his absence. "No, bru, I can't do this forever. I have a little daughter and education is not cheap in this country," he said. This struck

Figure 5.4
Bongani during a "toxic tour" of South Durban.

me as disappointing but hardly surprising; Bongani had already spent more than five years at SDCEA. It seemed too good to be true that such a talented young man would stay in for the long haul, given the activists' low salaries and taxing lifestyles. As we kept talking, I learned that Bongani saw his activism as an important way of providing for his daughter but that eventually he would need sufficient earnings to be able to send her to a decent school. His was a "calculus of sustainabilities," I thought—he was walking a tightrope between sustaining the individual and sustaining the planet, a walk that many environmental activists are only too familiar with.

It was remarkable that SDCEA, with its small staff and limited resources, had managed to create awareness about pollution on a local, regional, national, and international scale. While alliances with researchers were helpful in drawing attention to the lethal effects of air pollution, as with the asthma study, much more needed to be done to address the issue. Desmond and Bongani explained to me that SDCEA pursued a mixed strategy of collaboration and conflict:[44] it worked with government authorities in some instances (e.g., by participating in environmental impact assessments of proposed developments in the industrial basin)[45] while simultaneously confronting the government through protests, marches, media exposure (Leonard, 2014b), and other means.[46] This approach was evident as soon as I walked into the SDCEA office, which at the time occupied a flat on the ground floor of John Dunn House.[47] On the first of my many visits, I saw a large megaphone on the floor of the entrance hall, leaning against a large cabinet. On top of the cabinet was a row of neatly arranged books and brochures published by SDCEA over the years. Next to the cabinet was a bucket with a hole in the lid, which was used by SDCEA's notorious "bucket brigade."[48] Before Desmond walked in from his "office" (a small room he shared with two colleagues and several stuffed cabinets) and gave me a hug, I made a mental note to remember this peculiar arrangement of objects in the hall, which corresponded to SDCEA's multipronged strategy of organizing (the megaphone), monitoring (the bucket), and advocacy rooted in scientific research and publishing (the cabinet and row of books).

Perhaps the most significant achievement of this strategy was the eThekwini municipality's Multi-Point Plan of 2000, which led to the creation of a network of state-of-the-art air-monitoring stations around South Durban (Aylett, 2010b), capable not only of measuring the pollutants in the air but, by triangulation of data from multiple stations, of identifying the sources of the pollution. According to Siva Chetty, former manager of the program, who was sympathetic to SDCEA's agenda and had become actively involved in its activities, "You can see it in the graphs in that period that [air pollution] dropped like by a hundred per cent and we reached compliance" with legal norms of acceptable levels of pollution. The system also enabled the municipality to correlate exposure to polluted air with health effects. But even more importantly, as Siva told me, he "was able to use the monitoring network to link who's causing that. And when I was able to show that, industries started coming in and dealing with that situation because causation was clear, you know, they couldn't use uncertainty to evade the situation, which they've used for decades." By approximately 2010, however, the municipal authorities "allowed the network to fail," as one activist put it. Data on air pollution are no longer available, leaving SDCEA no option but to capture air samples for analysis at an independent lab rather than relying on the monitoring network—a major setback. SDCEA also is dealing with the local communities' lowering participation in its protests against air pollution. As a South African academic who had studied the work of SDCEA told me prior to my fieldwork, things had quieted down in South Durban.

SDCEA's grassroots activity, rather than its work with government, was most relevant to my research. The waning participation seemed a curious phenomenon; after all, it took a lot of grassroots pressure for the Multi-Point Plan to become reality, which suggests that protests would intensify after the plan failed. In pondering this during the early days in the field, I wondered to what extent SDCEA's efforts were an outgrowth of grassroots activity rather than it being the source of this activity. Which way did the causality go? After a few weeks in the field, it became apparent that such a binary distinction was an oversimplification. The activists were raising awareness about air pollution and other environmental issues while simultaneously letting the community shape their activist efforts—these are not mutually exclusive scenarios.[49]

Understanding how air pollution is tied up with historical patterns of exclusion, inequality, and the manufactured invisibility of entire communities is key to understanding how fighting the common enemy of air pollution contributed to the emergence of horizontal agonistic pluralism in South Durban. The following narrative that Bongani shared with me sheds light on this connection:

> A resident that is residing in these communities, be it Merebank, Wentworth, Clairwood or Isipingo or the Bluff, most of these communities, they are not employed in these refineries . . . Engen was built in 1953. This area is zoned as a residential area, it is not an industrial area. And when there are people who were products of forced removal from Cato Manor and other areas who were brought close by to add on to the communities that were already residing here at the time and it was the very same people they were brought here to create cheap labour during the apartheid time . . . A person that grew up in this community, [who has] been exposed to such pollution, that person there are big chances [of] suffering from cancer, leukemia or asthma . . . So that does not put you in the position to be employed permanently . . . The very same people that made you sick, they cannot employ you permanently. Now the only way that these people are getting employment is when there are shut downs. One month shut downs, two weeks shut downs or at max, two months shut downs.

Other activists added to this narrative, drawing links between apartheid-era injustices and the present levels of HIV, alcoholism, drug addiction, domestic violence, and gender discrimination prevalent in South Durban. Where does one begin to disentangle this layered web of injustice, this entanglement of global capitalism and apartheid history?

Desmond went as far as to claim in his interview in *Beauty and the Beasts*, a documentary about industrial pollution in the area, that the local communities are now worse off than during apartheid. The film takes its name from the juxtaposition of the area's natural beauty and the destructiveness of industry, as seen from a viewpoint above South Durban (figure 5.5).[50] When I asked Desmond whether he stood by this statement, he replied:

> In some areas during the apartheid era, for example Clairwood, there was no trucking depots, there was no illegal chemical companies. There were jobs—sewing machine jobs, factory jobs. A lot of people living there but their places were all nice and done up and clean and that recreational areas and all that were there. Today, the democracy hasn't come to people despite the fact that we all

Figure 5.5
The "beauty" and the "beasts" of South Durban.

fought for this democracy . . . So whilst during the apartheid era poor people
had a say in the city, we could go and live on the beach and fish anywhere and
everywhere and there were shelters for poor people, today [there are] no shelters
in this city.

Seen through Desmond's eyes, air pollution is symptomatic of a larger
phenomenon—that of a manufactured invisibility of the people of South
Durban by the South African state, both pre- and post-1994. While air pollution eating into the lungs and thyroid glands of the local people may be
a form of slow violence, the conditions that allowed it to go on for decades
are not simply due to neglect or ignorance: they are the direct result of non-
pluralistic politics inherited from South Africa's imperialist, eugenicist, and
totalitarian past. Such slow violence would, however, often turn into fast
tragedies, such as in the case of the child who died of cancer, who Desmond
spoke about in this chapter's epigraph. During my conversations with Des, it
became clear to me that he had witnessed many such cases over the years and
that this was one source of his determination to remain steady in the activist

struggle. Reflecting on these incidents while in the field, I thought that "slow violence" was not so much an ontological fact as it was the outcome of perceiving the world from an ever-accelerating temporal frame of reference. In other words, "slow" is relative, and the pace of life in (post)industrial societies arguably alters our perception of time, lowering the visibility of fundamental environmental transformations that will, sooner or later, make themselves known through "fast tragedy" on a mass scale.

While air pollution provided the spark for activist efforts, it also fueled people's discontent about the abyss between the state's promise of human rights-driven policy in the post-1994 era and the reality of South Durban. This discontent does not always turn into support for the environmental agenda. In fact, SDCEA often has found it challenging to convince local communities to participate in its protests. In Desmond's words, "People think that somebody is going to come from somewhere and save them and help them out of their misery." He looked around the room as he told me this, visibly upset, then continued: "They don't see this need that you must take collective responsibility and stand up. You actually got to beg people, you actually got to pay people to fight for their rights." But, according to Desmond, it was not always like this: "I mean, those days when I was marching, we used to go on our own buses and take the bus and go there. Nobody paid for a bus for me to march, I marched. Today if you don't hire taxi or hire a bus, people don't march." While the declining motivation to attend marches may be symptomatic of an increasing sense of hopelessness, Desmond's comment also suggests that the local community may not be as invested in fighting against pollution as it once was. Indeed, Desmond admits that not everyone in the community agrees with SDCEA's agenda. "Out there people disagree with us on a number of issues, they just think that we should approve of things, let it go through. We are hard-nosed about development and we don't compromise, and if development is going to impact on people for generations after that, I don't think we are in a game to compromise." Such a "hard-nosed" approach, unsurprisingly, pits SDCEA against many diehard proponents of economic growth. Desmond continued: "So that's been the biggest thing where people have accused us of stopping jobs and getting rid of their jobs, but those are not sustainable jobs you know, casual jobs so we tell them too."

The accusation that environmentalists are antidevelopment is not unique to South Durban (cf. Jacques, 2009; Rowell, 1996). In contexts of high unemployment and endemic poverty, people are often likely to be more concerned with economic growth and jobs than the environment. Yet, according to Bongani, SDCEA managed to attract as many as thirty thousand people to its marches, which indicates some success in raising awareness about environmental justice and in conveying to local residents that such issues are not antithetical to development and growth. Patrick Mkhize shared with me some of the strategies SDCEA has used: "People will look at what is very close to them and other things [and] see them or regard them as very far away, whereas the actual truth is that these are the long-term dangers that they need to eliminate. Environmental degradation is the same and equal problem if not worse as the drug trafficking in our community." And yet, SDCEA feels the need to at least mention the issue of drugs and drug-related violence in each public event it organizes. According to Patrick, "[I]f in an environmental awareness meeting, you don't talk about the drugs, those who have attended will walk out of that feeling that they had actually wasted their time. You talk about environmental issues and then you talk about the drugs, that will make their day okay." In the community meetings organized by SDCEA that I attended in South Durban, I saw this strategy of weaving narratives of slow violence with condemnation of fast violence (such as drug trafficking and gang shootouts) in action. SDCEA brings people together by making air pollution visible through familiar narratives of oppression, convincing communities that environmental justice is one of the many manifestations of the state's neglect of South Durban and that it must be fought along with other forms of injustice.

It is tempting to attribute the emergence of this all-embracing agonistic pluralism to the impact of air pollution, which presents a common enemy to the different groups of people in South Durban. But other ingredients were also needed. The window of opportunity for activists of the immediate post-1994 era provided the oxygen, and air pollution affecting diverse groups of people was the spark. The fuel for the fire of activism in South Durban is the decades of oppression of the communities in the area that underlie both slow and fast violence against them.

Having explored the sources of the agonistic pluralism underpinning this activism, I now turn to the question of its impact on the younger generation.

Where Are the Young Activists?

In multisited ethnography, the order in which research is conducted at the sites matters. Having completed the bulk of my field research in India before coming to South Africa, the question of intergenerational knowledge transfer—a key concern of the Indian activists engaging in vertical agonistic pluralism—was at the forefront of my mind when I started my research in Durban. I kept looking for patterns of intergenerational and intragenerational dialogue that could illuminate the ways the youth in South Durban were being shaped by activists' efforts. I soon realized that most of the activists were, as in India, of the older generation, the young activists being notable mostly by their absence. People like Desmond and Patrick, veterans of the antiapartheid struggle, seemed indispensable to the environmental movement. The older activists soon started talking to me about their concern that young people were simply not interested in activism. In this section, I examine various narratives of generational disconnect that activists shared with me in an effort to understand the obstacles the environmental movement faces in its efforts to reach young people.

One explanation for why activism may not appeal to young people in South Durban is linked to their socioeconomic predicament in present-day South Africa. Cleo, an SDCEA-affiliated activist and a teacher at a local secondary school, illuminated this link for me during our interview. I drove to Cleo's house, which sat behind a warehouse, which was behind a factory, and I was surprised that any residential properties could be located in this heavily industrialized area. Welcoming me, Cleo asked if I had become used to the smell of chemicals in the air; I had not. Cleo, a passionate woman in her fifties, was one of the most vocal people I met in South Durban. As a teacher she was uniquely positioned to speak to the interface of education, activism, and the environment. "The socio-economic circumstances for our children very often mitigate against them seeing the environment as a priority. It's just not the first thing on the agenda simply because many of them come from child-headed homes or single-parent homes or worse with grannies who are pensioners who are supporting [a] multitude of grandchildren," she told me. These realities created a profound disconnect between the everyday lives of children and the efforts of an activist/educator like Cleo. She continued, "You can't create two situations, one where they come from a home that's really deprived and lacking everything, almost third world, and then come to school where everything is about the law, application to the law and their rights." The effects of poverty and associated fast violence, in other words, make it difficult for activists to convince people to focus on combating slow violence. This may seem a convincing answer as to why there are not more young environmental activists. The previous section has shown, however, that SDCEA and other activist groups in South Durban have been rallying the local community around a multilayered critique of inequality, of which environmental decay is just one component.

Bongani's answer to my question about the dearth of young activists in Durban revolved around cultural notions of success and associated materialism: "As a developing country in Africa, most of our kids or most of our youth have been sold the idea of looking at media, TV, looking at the developed countries, looking at actors, musicians, businesspeople flashing those nice cars, nice lifestyle and so forth." Cleo went even further: "A lot of our young people are seduced by wealth. They're going to leave school, go to university, lead a good life, work for one of these bigshot companies, own a beautiful car, a beautiful apartment . . . and basically escape the constraints of their real life. So, activism doesn't pay, not financially." This explanation is certainly part of the answer. Several students I worked with during my fieldwork admitted to me that activism was not attractive to them in part because it was not a lucrative occupation. Yet, if this narrative applied to all young people, there would be no young activists from poor backgrounds anywhere in the world, which is clearly not the case. There were more pieces to the puzzle in South Durban.

Activists also suggested that their efforts lacked appeal for the young people in the community because of apathy. Cleo noted that children "have grown up around maladministration of environmental justice for so long that many of them have accepted it." She estimated that, on days when one of the refineries flares up, ten children out of nine hundred at the school may complain "because they're asthmatic and they feel it in their chest rather than smelling in their nose. But many others just wouldn't complain, so [there's] a lot of apathy."

Chris Albertyn also used the word "apathy" when talking about the young generation's lack of involvement in activism. "We are living in a very different context," he told me. "I think people who are growing up now just don't have the context to question some of the things we might question naturally in the 80s and 90s and said why is it like that?" His understanding is that apathy is not simply about not believing in one's agency but about the lack of an identifiable "enemy" one can fight against, such as the apartheid system.

While apathy is clearly one reason for young people's lack of activism, there are others. The depoliticizing of formal education in South Durban, as discussed in chapter 4, and a postcolonial, post-totalitarian South African state fraught with paradoxes and hypocrisies, as examined in chapter 3, are important parts of the picture. And then there is greenwashing, as Cleo shared with me:

> In fact, there's a long-standing joke at school "don't tell [Cleo]" because I've always said I won't touch tainted money, it's blood money. Mondi [a paper mill in South Durban] has built a science laboratory at our school and they asked me to organize the opening ceremony. I refused because I wouldn't touch it. Sapref [along with Engen, one of the two oil refineries in South Durban] has built the life sciences laboratory at school, I won't get involved in it. I do a lot of fundraising at school but I will go to small guys and say "Oh, you have an overrun of tiles that you can't sell anymore, two meters or three meters." And we get those tiles and re-tile. We've done about fifteen toilets at school but I would never go to Sapref because I honestly believe they're buying silence . . . A child can learn without a lab but a child can't learn with a lung that's gasping for breath.

The "blood money" Cleo refers to is the income that schools in South Durban derive from an education trust set up by local industries. These payments do not come with any formal expectation that schools will not participate in activist efforts, but many of my informants—in SDCEA, the schools, and the wider community—agreed that the implicit understanding is that schools receiving money will keep quiet. Cleo pointed out that, even if this were not the case, the projects the trust is funding often advance the interests of industry. She told me about a math, science, and technology school run by Sapref. Cleo pointed out that the choice of subjects is not accidental; Sapref offers scholarships and bursaries to young people to encourage them to take up careers in the petrochemical industry. "All they're doing is they're keeping their workforce at a steady place, that's all. They don't want to start looking around for people. They'll have a ready corps of learners from which to draw," she told me. "There's always something behind it and we've got to learn to look." Cleo's skepticism about the industry's altruistic motives resonated with a number of my informants. However, other teachers and school administrators I encountered in the field believed it was possible to accept money from the industry to benefit the learners without affecting the schools' priorities and their ability to be involved in campaigns organized by activist groups in South Durban. As argued in chapter 4, however, even in the absence of greenwashing, formal education here is underpinned by development ideologies that are more closely aligned with the industries in South Durban than with activist groups. Greenwashing, then, appears to be an important but not necessarily decisive force in the depoliticization of environmental issues in the schools. It does contribute—along with apathy, cultural notions of success and materialism, poverty, and fast violence—to the struggle activists face in bringing youth into their movement.

This is a long list of answers to the question this section began with, but is the question itself valid? Because many people I interviewed felt the lack of young activists, my conversations with informants became colored by my assumption that this was the case. I became more direct in asking for the reasons behind an intergenerational disconnect, rather than first establishing whether my informants thought there was a disconnect in the first place. On my last day in Durban, Chris Albertyn called out my bias. He pointed out that a lot of my questions boiled down to, "Where are all the activists? Why aren't there more activists?" According to Chris, producing more activists was not necessarily the solution:

> Maybe it would be a good thing if there wasn't a need for activists. Maybe if everybody was sufficiently conscientised to say "that's wrong, we shouldn't be doing that" . . . This idea of an activist coming to stand up there and ring a bell

and point to somebody to say they're bad, we have to change this, is a particular activism which our history has had in South Africa because there were really bad things happening so it's a flavor of activism to say we have to have an us and them, there has to be an enemy . . . If everybody in the street thought the same that, no, what happened here is wrong and we are all going to go talk to our local counselor or person responsible for . . . that's still activism and there may be one or two leaders that emerge out of there and take a leadership role but it's within the context that they are in. You can't create an activist a-contextually.

This comment raised important questions for me. During my time in the field, my enthusiasm about the activists' work grew by the day, just as my disillusionment with the formal education system kept rising. But is the solution to the crisis of the high Anthropocene to use education systems to turn young people into activists?

If educating for the Anthropocene means educating for action in an Arendtian sense, then vertical-horizontal agonistic pluralism provides an important alternative to the depoliticizing formal education in both Wentworth and Pashulok. But agonistic pluralism and activism are two different concepts: to be an activist, after all, is often seen as a form of leadership. There is often a degree of elitism involved in the way we think about activism. The kind of society Chris talked about is indeed more likely to be shaped by action than a society polarized between activists and nonactivists. In such a society, agonistic pluralism is truly pluralistic and embraces not only those critical of the status quo but also those who support the existing state of affairs. This does not mean that activism does not have the potential to transform education. It does suggest that the goal of any such transformation should not simply be to start generating more activists but, as Chris put it, to strive for a society "in which there is no need for activists."

6 TOWARD A DIFFERENT ANTHROPOCENE POLITICS

Another world is not only possible, she is on her way. . . . On a quiet day,
I can hear her breathing.
—A. Roy, *War talk*, p. 75

The activist perspectives in chapter 5 teach us that historical responsibility has the potential to give education the edge it needs to transform the relationship between society and the environment. Shifting away from social, cultural, and political reproduction—and the associated continuation of slow violence and environmental degradation—is what is required of education as we shift further into the high Anthropocene. Indeed, paying off ESE's "debt to the unborn" and "debt to the dead" means shaping changes in global and local political and cultural systems that would help advance the wide-ranging agenda of environmental sustainability.

What can we learn from activists and educators operating on the frontier of the high Anthropocene—in this book explored through the stories of Pashulok and Wentworth—that may illustrate what education for the Anthropocene looks like? Both sets of actors offer clues to the answer. The logic of activists—agonistic pluralism with its horizontal and vertical manifestations—and of teachers, many of whom are driven by a desire to see their students rise above the socioeconomic stratum into which they were born, are both key pieces of the puzzle. The rigid, discipline-oriented culture and coloniality-fueled state ideologies of schooling in India and South Africa, with the attendant dehumanizing bureaucratization of teachers and students, can obscure the motivations of individual teachers, which often are not dissimilar from the motivations of activists.

Let us consider a simple example from my field research. In one of my conversations with Rico, an activist working with groundWork in Durban, I tried to get a more concrete sense of how activists imagine schooling to align with their agendas. One of Rico's ideas was that teachers could be role models: if they chose not to drive to school, for example, students would see that it is possible to live without a car. Only a few days later I spoke to Mrs. Pillay, vice principal of Durban South Primary, who told me that teachers are indeed role models for students (as I have explored in chapter 4). She said pupils may be inspired by the fact that she drives a Mercedes to school despite coming from a poor background. Rico's and Mrs. Pillay's views represent two very different ideas—the politics of restraint (along the lines of Gandhi's philosophy) and the narrative of an individual who "made it" in life against all the odds (just as India and South Africa aspire to "catch up" on their path toward "development"). Rico's notion of restraint focuses on his recognition of slow violence, and Mrs. Pillay's success story resonates with many who experience the fast violence of living in poverty. While it is not difficult to see why teachers often did not see activism as an educational resource, and vice versa, the two narratives are arguably not at odds with one another; rather, they are complementary, just as slow and fast violence are two sides of the same coin—both reflect the inhumanity of the "human" age.

How can research help us build a bridge between formal education and environmental activism? In this book, I have charted several ways to trace the ideology of depoliticization and capture radical historiographies of slow violence in the "here and now." I demonstrated the potential of innovative participative methods not only to identify transgenerational knowledge about the environment but also to help facilitate its transmission to new generations. Slow violence knows no borders, and this work shows the need for transnational ethnographic research to help negotiate the complexity of education in the Anthropocene. I also pointed to the ability of "old theories" to speak to "new realities," thus advancing our understanding of slow violence. While the environmental multicrisis is unprecedented in scope, the dynamics that led to it are not new. Much can be learned by thinking with twentieth-century thinkers such as Arendt and Ricœur about how we read the twenty-first-century cultural landscapes of the Anthropocene.

This book is merely an introduction to the vast potential of activism to inspire a different kind of education in the Anthropocene. Researching activist movements beyond Pashulok and Wentworth would further expand the lexicon of existing ideas and practices (of educators, activists, and others). And activism is only one among many potential education modalities that can be studied for the unique contribution they make to facilitating Arendtian politics. Spaces of spirituality and faith and the many modes of knowledge transmission among Indigenous communities are two examples of further areas of research that are needed to gain a fuller picture of humanity's collective ability to define and practice education for the Anthropocene.

In this final chapter, I discuss why the bridge between activism and education matters and put forward a number of lessons we can learn from this ethnography. I begin by summarizing the limitations of the kind of ESE I observed in schools in Pashulok and Wentworth. I then argue that, in spite of these limitations, we should not give up on schooling as an important element of educating for the Anthropocene. I locate the idea of such "blended" education (encompassing schooling, activism, and other forces) within the debate on the future of the Anthropocene and argue that, while not a panacea, striving to educate for the Anthropocene is an important component of acting on our historical responsibility vis-à-vis past and future generations. Next I identify a number of activist lessons for educators that can help inspire a different kind of schooling. I conclude by discussing what I came to see, through the research presented in this book, as the three ingredients of educating for the Anthropocene—radical imagination, agonistic pluralism, and intergenerational dialogue.

THE ENVIRONMENTAL MULTICRISIS, POLITICAL "NEUTRALITY," AND DISRUPTION

As my findings have shown, the schooling provided by Seema Primary and Durban South Primary is more likely to be an obstacle to, rather than an enabler of, educating for the Anthropocene. It could feel like the people there (learners and teachers alike) were being sold the false idea that the speed of slow violence is beyond their reach. These schools often appear to advance the sustainability of the sociopolitical status quo rather than of the planet and its natural environs. Sustainability in these systems is about shallow time, whose horizons extend no further than an individual lifespan or at most the lifespan of the current civilization, rather than about deep geological time with its associated questions of the debts to the dead and unborn, planetary stewardship, and our survival as a species (Davies, 2016).

Such schooling equates freedom with the reach of individual agency. Arendt, however, teaches us that we are only ever free in connection to others; she sees freedom as participation (Tlaba, 1987). It is arguably the lack of connection (both to humans and nonhumans) that precipitated our environmental multicrisis. The Indian writer Rabindranath Tagore saw the flaw in modernity's promise of "freedom" long ago and expressed his concern with the elegance of a poet: "An automobile does not create freedom of movement, because it is a mere machine. When I am myself free, I can use the automobile for the purposes of my freedom" (Tagore, quoted in Shrivastava & Kothari, 2012, p. 246).[1] While the car for Tagore is a means to an end, for the Anthropocenic imagination it is an end in itself because it allows humans to overcome the "limitation" of only being able to walk on foot.[2] Turning the production of material things into its own goal leads us into the mental world of *Homo Faber* ("Man the Maker"), human beings who believe it is possible to control the environment and their fate through the use of tools (Arendt, 1998). Homo Faber is preoccupied with what Arendt calls "work," a process that sees everything in the world as a means to an end. Living in such a world disconnects us not only from others but also from significant parts of our own selves.

Whose responsibility is it to challenge such Anthropocenic imagination? One could rightly argue that this should be primarily up to the parts of the world which carry the greatest portion of responsibility for the environmental multicrisis and which are better positioned to cope with the impact of environmental decay than those who have lost or will lose everything.[3] But places like Pashulok and Wentworth—the frontier of the high Anthropocene—can help inspire an imagination of alternative futures rooted in recognition of the colonial pasts and depoliticized presents enabling slow violence across the globe.

There is at least one way in which everyone is involved: we now all carry the burden of responsibility for the fate of life on Earth. Within the next few generations, or perhaps sooner, we could become the only known species that *chose* to become extinct and took many other species down with us. This moral predicament, unparalleled in human history, is universal. After all, even though the "ordinary people" in Nazi Germany often had little to do with the Holocaust, we are still left asking why they did not do anything to prevent it. In their defense, they may say they did not know about the concentration camps while they were operational.[4] Today, given the copious scientific studies and unending media reports about the impending doom, we can hardly say the same about our complicity in what may become the Anthropocene's ultimate destruction, however powerless we may feel.

Surely education must be part of the solution. Governments and international institutions recognize this, and while the currently dominant idea of sustainable development that underpins their policies is arguably an oxymoron (as shown in chapter 2), the underlying premise can hardly be disputed. Humanity's predicament calls for an active and urgent response, and education has an important role to play, not in an instrumental way but through enabling and shaping action in concert with others[5]—the cultivation of which is, as I have argued in this book, a key part of the solution to the slow violence of the Anthropocene age.[6]

For education to take the concept and consequences of the Anthropocene seriously and help prepare young people to live in a world facing planetwide existential challenges would be nothing short of a massive disruption of its dominant paradigms, cultures, and practices.[7] In the Anthropocene, education's responsibility cannot be reduced to the transmission of knowledge and skills or cultivation of specific behaviors (such as recycling) or even the advancement of critical thinking. Education in the Anthropocene must find ways to enable individual and collective reflection on our historical responsibility for the fate of the planet and of humanity that we now all carry while simultaneously facilitating action on this responsibility. The onset of the Anthropocene challenges the very definition of education and its fundamental goals and calls for research that looks outside the conventional paradigms, spaces, and practices of education for inspiration to help education fulfill its responsibilities at this unprecedented time.

One starting point is to recognize that there is no such thing as politically neutral education (Freire, 1972, 1998, 1999); however, often the discipline itself may repeat the misguided belief that it exists.[8] Not designing our education policies and systems with the goal in mind of rendering ourselves more political would mean shooting ourselves in the foot, because, whether we like it or not, education will have an impact on the politics of our society.[9] This will happen by either advancing bureaucratization (as is currently the case for many education systems around the world) or helping people see the ways they are already bureaucratized (and the ways out of this predicament). ESE cannot afford to be politically neutral in a world so polarized around environmental issues, for neutrality itself is a form of politics that normalizes the status quo.

BRIDGING SCHOOLING AND ACTIVISM IN EDUCATING FOR THE ANTHROPOCENE

This became apparent to me one day at Durban South, when two SDCEA activists—Bongani and one of his colleagues—came to the school to give a presentation to students about water scarcity. I hoped to witness an engagement between environmental activists and educators in real time and expected to hear a politicizing narrative. Even though the children seemed engaged and listened intently to what Bongani was saying (figure 6.1), the content was quite different from what I had seen at the community events SDCEA had organized for adults. There was no mention of environmental justice or the politics of environmental racism; the focus was solely on making children understand that water was a scarce resource and what they could do to help protect it—such as fixing a leaking tap in their home. It seemed that SDCEA lost its teeth when in the school environment and aligned itself with the dominant, politically neutered discourse of individualized responsibility.[10]

It was as if the ideology of depoliticization that shapes the culture, political economy, and practice of schooling in Wentworth (and Pashulok) made SDCEA less radical when operating inside a school. How can ESE operate in

Figure 6.1
Bongani talking about water at Durban South Primary.[11]

the context of a depoliticized, individualized, and bureaucratized approach to the environment, not just in the realm of education but at the level of state ideology? In such a world, what can schooling learn from activism? The propensity of activist movements in Pashulok and Wentworth to facilitate conversations among groups of people who often do not talk to one another (such as the past and future generations in India or Coloured people and Whites in South Africa) makes activism a potential vehicle for education. Schooling in spaces where activists who value agonistic pluralism are present has several options to try to get closer to the idea of educating for the Anthropocene. It can relinquish its monopoly on education and recognize the importance of alternative actors and spaces in the process of educating youth, or it can work more closely with activists by integrating more of their approaches into the curricula and their pedagogies, or even bring activists directly into the schools.

While the ethnographic accounts of the two activist spaces presented in this book provide a glimpse into the cultural and political landscapes shaping these movements, they do not directly illuminate the transmission of activist politics to the youth. This reflects the somewhat bifurcated structure of my fieldwork, which revolved around schooling and activism—two distinct phenomena that occur within the same communities but are framed by different spatial and temporal boundaries and engage different sets of actors. Since I interacted primarily with young people in the context of formal schooling at both sites, the topic of activism rarely came up. Yet, as the student films discussed in chapter 4 attest, these young people were aware of the activist lexicon associated with political socialization critical of the state. Furthermore, they put this lexicon into action by creating films that spoke to a reimagined future for their communities. This parallel between activist ideas and young people's political ideals is hardly a coincidence. It suggests that, while few of the children outwardly aimed to become full-time activists, many of them had been exposed to, and in some cases had internalized elements of activist imaginaries. While there may be few young full-time activists about, what seems to be happening in these communities is the emergence of a kind of part-time activist who does not necessarily join a movement or act on activist impulses but whose political imagination nevertheless has been shaped by the political pedagogy of activism. This imagination is a latent resource that can help individuals break out of the institutional liminality of spaces such as Durban South Primary and spark action in an enabling, pluralistic context, such as filmmaking with fellow students.

Activists' understanding of politics in both Pashulok and Wentworth converges around a number of features that seem to appeal to young people. Here I focus on three of these characteristics. The first feature is the polyvocal nature of the activist movements, which runs contrary to the popular view of activism. We often think of activists as associated with singular issues, such as anti-nuclear power, anti-oil drilling, or antidam agendas. Such labels, often espoused by activist groups themselves, portray these movements as narrowly focused on a single issue. They also obscure what such movements may be *for*. A degree of polarization may be inevitable in the context of political contestation, which leads to a very narrowly defined activist agenda, but such an approach to issues of environment and sustainability fails to grasp individuals' interrelated concerns and imagined futures for the environment. The activists in Pashulok and Wentworth embrace such diversity that fuels coalitional, polyvocal movements that incorporate a range of sociocultural and economic agendas rooted in the historical exclusion of the populations these movements represent. My observations in the field suggested that this polyvocality and openness to diversity appealed to young people, who often identified with some of the voices reflected in the movements.

A second characteristic of an activist political imagination—one grounded in a form of politics that shapes young people's visions of action—is the focus on countermemories of the state. Running contrary to official, state-sanctioned narratives of "progress" reflected in textbooks, curricula and, as chapter 4 has shown, in some teachers' personal views, counter-memories reflect localized histories more palatable to the children in these communities. The trauma of displacement, for example, is visible to all in Pashulok, whereas one must travel to a place like Delhi to experience the benefits of the dam—like the electricity supplied to the capital. The sharing of countermemories also contributes to social cohesion and intergenerational dialogue, something the young people in both sites expressed a hunger for during our interactions.

The third and perhaps most important feature is the activist effort to turn temporal distance into a generative space. Intergenerational dialogue is at the root of activists' radical imaginations of the future and can only be successful if young people engage in the dialogue. Ricœur recognized disengagement as one of the principal challenges of the contemporary era:

> This indispensable interplay between past and future is becoming increasingly threatened in our time. As our horizon of expectation becomes ever more distant, our inherited space of experience becomes more restricted. And this growing discrepancy between expectation and heritage lies at the root of our crisis of modernity. "The entire present is in crisis", writes Ricœur, "when expectancy takes refuge in utopia and tradition congeals into a dead residue". Our contemporary task is to confront this crisis and prevent the tension between expectation and tradition from further degenerating into schism. (Kearney, 2004, p. 67)

By keeping the memory of slow violence alive, activists seek to prevent the deterioration of expectancy of the future into the utopic myth of endless economic growth. At the same time, they try to ensure that tradition is reimagined and reinterpreted for the needs of the present, rather than becoming irrelevant. By shining a light on the tension between the old and the new, activists are not creating a conflict, as many would accuse them of doing, but are trying to remind their communities of the fundamental contradiction at the root of the dominant neoliberal, postcolonial model of development—the push for a future uprooted from its past.

The activists do not merely critique; they also advise. Thinking about the temporality of development leads activists at both of my research sites to emphasize intergenerational justice—the idea that we owe it to future generations not to destroy the environment. This is due in part to the fact that the battles they engage in often span decades; thus their efforts are inherently future oriented. In the words of Thando, a SDCEA activist, "It doesn't happen overnight, you know, the things that we fight for. So as much as you might think you are fighting for here and now . . . you are actually fighting for the future as well because some of them take long, some of them take time to actually get to a point where they are where you want it to be." When prompted to discuss the extent to which the idea of intergenerational justice holds currency outside the activist circles, Chris explained, "If you quite simply go to a very poor area where it's not the next generation, it's the next meal, standing up there like a missionary and trying to tell people they should be concerned about generations to follow just doesn't make sense. Not to say that it's not important but that's not what is going to turn people on in this context." This view mirrors many similar discussions I had with other activists in India and South Africa. They do not believe they have a monopoly on the idea of intergenerational justice, nor do they see themselves as preachers trying to convert others to their ideas. Rather, they sense concern for the intergenerational as integral to being human, even if other concerns that seem more pressing in the present moment may take priority. The debt to the unborn, in other words, is not something that must be taught or externally imposed.[12]

Aside from our debt to past generations for preserving the environment on our behalf or our debt to the future generations to do the same, some activists also see intergenerational justice as a question of human identity. In Rico's words, "Future generations are an extension of ourselves. It's how we live forever. If we don't care about them, then we don't care about this place that we live in. And how can we not care about them? If we say we don't care about them then it means we don't care about ourselves because it's the only way that we continue to live on. It's through them even if they are unborn, it's the way we live forever." This counternarrative is one of hope rather than a simple critique of dominant paradigms, ideologies, and policies. The activists' proposed alternative is to replace the individualism of our consumer society with a recognition of our shared humanity and the intrinsic worth of that humanity—and by extension the value of the natural environment.

These ideas of intragenerational and intergenerational justice offer an alternative to the state's definition of justice. Activists propose to subordinate the agenda of development and economic growth to what they perceive as the higher moral impulse of caring about our species—and therefore also the Earth—that they see as an intrinsic part of the human condition. They hope that, by mobilizing this instinct, the states' narratives of justice (hollow due to bureaucratic polarization and corruption), rights (upheld in rhetoric but not enacted in practice), and development (developing for the few at the expense of the many—alive and unborn alike) can be challenged.

THE THREE INGREDIENTS OF EDUCATING FOR THE ANTHROPOCENE

How can we translate these ideas into educational goals? In this book, I have explored three key antidotes to bureaucratization and depoliticization— what I have come to see as the three ingredients of "educating for the Anthropocene."

The first one is radical imagination. Being able to reimagine different worlds is the opposite of bureaucratization—it requires creativity and autonomy and relies on an internal locus of possibility. It defies predictability and planning, allowing access not just to the "here and now" but also the "there and then," the "not yet there," the "elsewhere," or the "nowhere" (Jovchelovitch et al., 2017, p. 116). The high Anthropocene moment calls for a reimagining of the world that may be unthinkable to many. Just as "critical thinking" as a "twenty-first-century skill" has been co-opted in the service of neoliberal, technocratic future-making, so has imagination become constrained to a limited set of possibilities that fail to confront slow violence. In a review of empirical research about young people's thinking about futures, Anne-Katrin Holfelder (2019, p. 948) has concluded that "what all of these studies have in common is that the future is not seen as something one acts on, but rather as something which acts upon oneself." What is needed is a *radical* imagination capable of seeing beyond the dominant paradigms of the high Anthropocene.

The second ingredient is agonistic pluralism. According to Arendt (1998), politics is not a place; it is a path. To move along the path of Arendtian politics means collectively agonizing over a question as equals to find a way forward. In Mouffe's (2000, p. 15) words, "Envisaged from the point of view of 'agonistic pluralism', the aim of democratic politics is to construct the 'them' in such a way that it is no longer perceived as an enemy to be destroyed, but an 'adversary', i.e. somebody whose ideas we combat but whose right to defend those ideas we do not put into question." This, Mouffe adds, "is the real meaning of liberal democratic tolerance, which does not entail condoning ideas that we oppose or being indifferent to standpoints that we disagree with but treating those who defend them as legitimate opponents" (2000, p. 15).

To radical imagination and agonistic pluralism, we also need to add intergenerational dialogue as an antibureaucratization force. Communicating across generations takes us out of the shallow time of bureaucratized behavior and brings us closer to the deep time of a world that predates and outlives the individual. Intergenerational dialogue is key to fostering what Paul Ricœur (1984) calls historical responsibility and the understanding of the "debt to the dead" and "debt to the unborn" (which I explained in chapter 2). It also enables politics as a form of action that demands a connection to others.[13]

What does an education that blends these three ingredients look like? One way to describe such an approach is by using four verbs—grasp, care, imagine, and communicate (figure 6.2). By grasping what is at stake in the Anthropocene—the survival of human civilization and all of its accumulated achievements in language, art, science, technology, and countless fields of

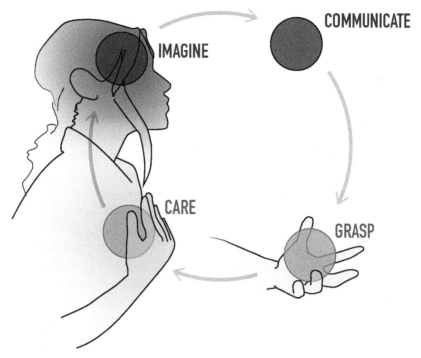

Figure 6.2
Visualizing educating for the Anthropocene. (Courtesy of Nuith Morales)

human endeavor—we are engaging in intergenerational dialogue with the dead (who are responsible for these achievements) and with the unborn (who may never experience the human civilization). This grasping is also an act of care, which fuels our radical imagination of alternative futures. As we communicate our visions of the future, we practice agonistic pluralism in trying to find common ground with the imaginations of others that can help fuel political action. The process is iterative: communication with others might make us realize that we have not fully grasped the reality in front of us, which can lead us to re-imagine the future, and agonize with others over this new vision. Of course, there are many other ways to imagine an approach to education in the Anthropocene that incorporates radical imagination, agonistic pluralism, and intergenerational dialogue; the key is to free ourselves from expectations of any particular outcomes and engage in education for the sake of education.

But while these three ingredients can be very powerful, we need to also remember that education is not a panacea. This is in part because changes in education systems can take years, if not decades, to manifest in society at large. Another reason is education's inherent limitations, as Arendt points out:

> He who seriously wants to create a new political order through education, that is, neither through force and constraint nor through persuasion, must draw the dreadful Platonic conclusion: the banishment of all older people from the state that is to be founded. But even the children one wishes to educate to be citizens of a Utopian morrow are actually denied their own future role in the body politic, for, from the standpoint of the new ones, whatever new the adult world may propose is necessarily older than they themselves. It is in the very nature of the human condition that each new generation grows into an old world, so that to prepare a new generation for a new world can only mean that one wishes to strike from the newcomers' hands their own chance at the new. (1961, p. 177)

This sobering conclusion cautions us against seeing education as an instrument of social engineering for building a new, utopian world. However, this should not stop us from determining how to align education systems with the needs of the new geological epoch we live in. Such answers are, almost by definition, partial and localized; if I learned one thing while working on this book, it is that there is no one way to educate for the Anthropocene. There is not even a singular Anthropocene to speak of (cf. Yusoff, 2018). But, there is a finite Earth threatened by humanity's thirst for infinite growth—and that is why we need to talk about educating for the Anthropocene.

As I bring this narrative to a close, two images stay with me. One is of an old advertisement for concrete in Pashulok (figure 6.3), and the other is of human handprints on a wall surrounding a factory in South Durban (figure 6.4). Both are seemingly banal scenes, yet both tell a story about educating for the Anthropocene. The slogan "Build with confidence" painted over cracking, aging concrete evokes the false promises of the Anthropocene's architects, the misplaced confidence in modernity and technological progress that underpins the myriad ways slow violence undermines our confidence in the future of the planet and of humanity. The handprints, on the other hand, appear

Figure 6.3
"Build with confidence."

Figure 6.4
Handprints in South Durban.

to scream, "We, the people who live in Wentworth, also are here!" and remind the barons of industry that fence line communities will not give up their struggles for environmental justice and, by extension, their historical responsibility to future and past generations. I believe that educating for the Anthropocene means simultaneously giving life to both of these images—the intellectual recognition of duplicity and the galvanizing of the hopefulness of action. The perspectives in this book suggest that we have the ingredients we need to bring educating for the Anthropocene into the spotlight. Now is the time to act.

Notes

DILEMMA 1

1. Helen and the names of other interlocutors in this book are pseudonyms. If an informant chose to be named, I refer to them by their full name and their affiliation. Throughout the book, I provide as much ethnographic detail as possible about people, places, and events, but in some cases the level of detail is limited by the need to protect the identity of individuals and institutions that opted not to be named in the book.

2. This episode occurred during my research into the effectiveness of "handprint," an ESE intervention that sought to empower students to "use their hands" to make tangible contributions to the sustainability of their communities, rather than focusing on the environmental "footprint." This idea originated in Bangalore, India, spread across the country after being picked up by the Ahmedabad-based Centre for Environment Education (CEE), and eventually found its way to South Africa through international networks of educators connected to CEE.

3. There was nothing in my field notes from the visit to the school to suggest the children were in any way disabled, although I am not qualified to assess this. It is possible that at least some of the children were attending this school because of their socioeconomic status and poor academic results (which could be for a number of reasons) rather than because of a disability.

4. ESD refers to educational programs and approaches promoting sustainable development, but not all programs that are concerned with the environment or environmental sustainability would fall into this category. Another group of interventions is linked to the notion of environmental education (EE), and these usually refer to programs that make use of the physical environment in which education takes place. The term ESE incorporates both ESD and EE research and practice, as well as approaches that may not fit into either the ESD or EE paradigm but are related to environmental or sustainability concerns. I use the term ESE to denote formal education interventions designed to address any aspect of the natural environment or sustainability, as these are all relevant to the concept of "educating for the Anthropocene" I develop in this book.

5. From this point onward, I use the term "education" in a broad way, referring to intentional learning processes within or outside an institutional setting. When referring to education

taking place in the context of government-run schools, I use the term "schooling" or "formal education" interchangeably. Educational programs—inside or outside the classroom—designed to address an environmental or sustainability concern are referred to as ESE. These distinctions are important: part of my argument is that "educating for the Anthropocene" is about more than schooling, an idea that contradicts much of the educational development discourse, which often effectively equates education with schooling.

6. Throughout this book, the word "imagination" refers to "all those *imaginative processes by which collective life is symbolically experienced and this experience mobilised in view of achieving political aims*" (Glăveanu & de Saint Laurent, 2015, p. 559; emphasis in original).

7. I borrow the word "multicrisis" from Karen Litfin (2016).

CHAPTER 1

1. This translation of the term assumes that *anthropos* is a compound of *anēr* and *ops* (eye, face), but this theory has not been proved, and the term is frequently translated simply as "human being" (Etymonline: Online Etymology Dictionary, n.d.).

2. It is arguably appropriate to use the term "man," given the masculinist imprints that have shaped the ideology of the Anthropocene (Grear, 2015; Grusin, 2017).

3. By "marginal peoples," I refer to groups of people left behind by modernity and development. This includes Indigenous groups (Adivasis in the Indian subcontinent), people living from subsistence agriculture in rural areas, and people on the margins of society, such as Dalits in India or people living in slums in South Africa. Large-scale development and infrastructure projects that have major environmental and human consequences tend to be built in places far from privilege and to disproportionately affect marginal peoples.

4. In the context of South Africa's diverse constituent groups, the term "Coloured" usually refers to people of mixed heritage who do not refer to themselves as "White," "Black," or "Indian." This "intermediate" group was recognized by the apartheid government as a separate racial category and suffered from racial discrimination (Adhikari, 2005).

5. In providing this description, I was inspired by Rachel Carson's (1965) *Silent Spring*, one of the defining books of the environmental movement, in which she invites the reader to envision a place that suffers from all the major environmental issues of the second half of the twentieth century in an effort to imagine what the planet's future might look like. My description of South Durban, likewise, combines the key issues, even though I have not personally experienced being in a space affected by all these issues simultaneously.

6. Neither Pashulok nor Wentworth existed in their current forms prior to the "great acceleration" (McNeill & Engelke, 2014) of the post-World War II globalizing transnational processes. Both spaces were molded by governments in response to the by-products (or "negative externalities" in the language of economics) of the consumerism-driven, infinite-growth-seeking world.

7. The belief that state-sponsored education can help bring about sustainability is reflected in a range of UNESCO's publications (e.g., Nolan, 2012) and underpinned the Decade of

Education for Sustainable Development (DESD) in 2005–2015 (for a critique of the limited reach of DESD, particularly in Africa, see Manteaw [2012]).

8. Whether economic growth can be decoupled from continued extraction of natural resources has been subject to debate. I align here with the view that such decoupling is very unlikely to happen in time to avoid catastrophic environmental decay, as argued by Parrique et al. (2019).

9. By "environmental learning" I mean processes both outside and inside institutional spaces of education. I borrow this use of the term from Thomashow (2020).

10. This type of research shares some of its goals and approaches with the kind of participatory analysis applied in the context of photovoice (Wang & Burris, 1997) and the visual methods inspired by the anthropology of childhood (G. A. Johnson et al., 2012).

11. The Holocene is the current geological epoch (as the Anthropocene has not yet been officially recognized, largely because of disagreements about its beginning), which began approximately 11,600 years ago, following the melting of glaciers at the end of the Pleistocene.

12. This brief article was followed by more elaborate analyses of the Anthropocene (Steffen et al., 2011a, 2011b; J. Williams & Crutzen, 2013), including analyses of the implications for human survival and the changes needed to avoid extinction (Costanza et al., 2007; Robin & Steffen, 2007; Rockström et al., 2009; Steffen et al., 2007).

13. For comparison, the "background," or expected rate, of natural mammalian extinction is about 0.25 per million species-years (Kolbert, 2015, pp. 15–17).

14. The discussion of a human epoch can be traced back at least to the late eighteenth century. The first identified instance of using the prefix "anthropos-" to refer to a human epoch occurred in 1854 in a series of articles by the Welsh theologian and geologist Thomas Jenkyn (Lewis & Maslin, 2018, p. 31).

15. The argument for locating the origins of the Anthropocene in ancient history is made by Ellis (2011), but this view is not among the "mainstream" proposed beginnings (Dalby, 2016). For an overview of the different arguments for and against various dates, see Smith and Zeder (2013).

16. Referring to Marshall McLuhan's article proclaiming the end of Earth-Nature and the beginning of "man-made" Earth in 1974, Bonneuil and Fressoz (2017, p. 60) argue that "the scientific imaginary of the Anthropocene inherited ideologies, knowledge and technologies from the Cold War."

17. Quoted from Crutzen and Stoermer (2000, p. 18).

18. Bonneuil and Fressoz (2017, p. 66) borrowed this analogy from Malm and Hornborg (2014, p. 67).

19. A discussion of what the *anthropos* in the Anthropocene refers to can be found in Usher (2016).

20. During the imperialist age, "an 'environmental orientalism' reserved the 'external' influences of the environment on human history to discourses on 'less advanced' societies, as

a counterpoise to an industrial society moved above all by an 'internal' logic of progress" (Bonneuil & Fressoz, 2017, p. 31). The "external" influences now often take the form of toxic byproducts of modernity (such as e-waste) exported to the Global South, which shows that "environmental orientalism" (and indeed "environmental racism") that dehumanize the non-White other are still at play.

21. See, for example, Bonneuil and Fressoz (2017), Berners-Lee (2021), McKibben (2019), and Kolbert (2015, 2021).

22. The interview with Trisha was conducted in Hindi with the help of a translator. The accuracy of the translation for all such interviews that appear in this book was checked with the help of a second, independent translator who listened to the audio recordings and verified the transcripts and their English translations.

23. "Oustee" is often used in the literature on India's dams to refer to people displaced from their land. The connotation is that state coercion and force were used to move people, rather than them relocating voluntarily.

24. See also Komljenovic & Robertson (2017) and Robertson & Komljenovic (2016).

25. For more context, see also Nambissan & Ball (2010), W. C. Smith & Joshi (2016), Tooley (2013), and Woodhead et al. (2013).

26. Throughout the book, I refer to "Global South" and "Global North" in quotation marks. These categories—while at times helpful in clarifying meaning—advance a bifurcated view of the world reminiscent of earlier binaries (such as colony and metropole). This can contribute to the homogenization and essentialization of societies.

27. Anthropology itself has colonial origins as a field that was used by colonial empires to study the colonized "other." Perhaps in part because of this history, anthropology has also engaged in decades-long conversations reflecting on this colonial heritage (Pels, 2008) and ways to decolonize the discipline and its methodologies (Allen & Jobson, 2016). In my work, I endeavor to make the most of this "reflective edge" of anthropology.

28. For the purposes of my argument, I am relying on Harvey's (2007, p. 22) definition of neo-liberalism as a "theory of political economic practices proposing that human well-being can best be advanced by the maximization of entrepreneurial freedoms within an institutional framework characterized by private property rights, individual liberty, unencumbered markets, and free trade. The role of the state is to create and preserve an institutional framework appropriate to such practices."

29. The workshop encouraged students to think carefully about their subjects, framing, and composition. This is one of the reasons why professional-grade camera equipment was used; the use of such equipment required students to go through a series of conscious choices (about white balance, sound source and volume, focal length, focus) every time they pressed the "record" button (cf. Sutoris, 2021).

30. This conception is related to Potts and Brown's (2005, p. 255) notion of "anti-oppressive research," which is characterized by "committing to social change and taking an active role in

that change." Throughout this research project, I aimed to facilitate the co-creation of knowledge through the observational films made by children that I discuss in chapter 4, in the tradition of collaborative ethnography (Lassiter, 2001). During the course of my research, I also identified with the related notion of "critical ethnography," whose aim is "to theorize social structural constraints and human agency, as well as the interrelationship between structure and agency in order to consider paths towards empowerment of the researched" (Atkinson, 2001, p. 193). An earlier, still relevant, definition of critical ethnography focuses on its being "structured in relation to our efforts to construct a mode of learning, and a conception of knowledge that may enhance the possibility of collectively constituted thought and action which seeks to transform the relations of power that constrict people's lives" (Simon & Dippo, 1986, p. 196).

31. This use of liminality is also linked to Karl Jaspers' concept of the "axial age" (Jaspers, 1953).

32. In inherited spaces of marginality, the proximal cause of marginalization may no longer be visible (or it might not even exist anymore, e.g., direct colonial rule), but its impacts are real. This too is liminality—a use of the term similar to Wacquant's (2016).

33. In this book, I avoid the use of the term "developing," as this concept is often understood to refer to a universalist notion of a single model of development toward which all countries (should) be moving. Instead, I use the term "low-income country" whenever possible. For a discussion of universalisms and particularisms in educational development, see Sutoris (2018b).

34. Citing UN statistics, Rawat has argued that "India uproots most people for progress . . . 60 to 65 million people are estimated to have been displaced in India since Independence [due to development projects], the highest number of people unsettled for such projects in the world. Of these people, 40 per cent are Tribals, 40 per cent Dalits and other rural people" (Rawat, 2013, p. 65).

35. As Bond and Hallowes (2002, p. 32) point out, the "Constitution also provided a caveat in mandating 'reasonable legislative and other measures that prevent pollution and ecological degradation, promote conservation, and secure ecologically sustainable development and use of natural resources *while promoting justifiable economic and social development* (emphasis added), quite consistent with international sustainable-development rhetoric.'"

36. I approached Engen for an interview to include their perspective on air pollution in this book, but I received no response.

37. This is how the school staff often referred to their school, which was built in the 1970s as a temporary structure made of prefabricated plywood panels. Although it was supposed to be replaced by a permanent brick-and-mortar building within years, the temporary structure was still in place at the time of my research.

38. According to Wacquant, advanced marginality is characterized by "realities of extreme poverty and social destitution, ethnoracial divisions (linked to colonial history) and public violence, and their accumulation in the same distressed urban areas" (1996, p. 123).

39. Sunderlal Bahuguna was also directly involved in struggles against Tehri Dam (James, 2013; Sharma, 2009), as discussed in more detail in chapter 3.

40. This is not an official figure, as the Indian government does not keep statistics on the number of oustees who have left the rehabilitation site. This figure was quoted by one of my interlocutors in Pashulok and independently confirmed by two other community informers.

CHAPTER 2

1. By "sculpting" I mean deliberate changes to cultural landscapes of societies, including through the medium of advertising, film, fiction writing, and other channels.

2. In selecting the examples of educational thinkers in this paragraph, I relied partly on my own knowledge of the field and the figures considered influential within it and partly on the register in the volume *Fifty Major Thinkers on Education: From Confucius to Dewey* (Cooper et al., 2001).

3. For a discussion of the potential of education to aid specifically in addressing climate change, see Bangay and Blum (2010).

4. The degrowth literature, while not (yet) prominent in the development or education literature and largely confined to a small number of niche journals and a biannual International Degrowth Conference, has generated a number of economic, political, and philosophical debates (Demmer & Hummel, 2017; Fournier, 2008; Latouche, 2010; Sekulova et al., 2013; van den Bergh, 2007) that are likely to gain more attention as the Anthropocene becomes further established as an object of research and as humanity moves further into the environmental multicrisis.

5. According to Dryzek (2016, p. 945), ecosystemic reflexivity "differs from simple reflexivity in at least two ways . . . the incorporation into human institutions of better ways to listen to ecological systems that have no voice; and an ability to re-think what core values, such as justice, mean in the context of an active and unstable Earth system."

6. Some of this literature—and arguably much public discourse—privileges technological solutions. For example, Denny (2017, pp. 131–137) lists four potential scenarios: (1) "business as usual," (2) "love, peace and granola," (3) "the technofix," and (4) "we're doomed." Of these, he argues, only (3) has the potential to prevent some of the Anthropocene's gravest potential consequences. A similar line of thinking also appears to underpin Bill Gates' (2021) influential book, *How to Avoid a Climate Disaster*.

7. As Caradonna (2014, p. 156) points out, "UN involvement in sustainability has suffered from many shortcomings and failures. The main issue is that many of the treaties, frameworks, and agreements . . . have been ineffectual and are often seen as a load of hot air. The Rio Summit was marked by bitter disagreements between the global North and the global South and between NGOs and governments. The documents produced in Rio were greatly watered down and reflected the disagreements of member states. The following UN summits in Johannesburg (2002) and Rio (2012) basically acknowledged the massive gap between where the UN would like the world to be and where it actually is."

8. The Club of Rome, founded in 1968, is a membership organization consisting mostly of scientists, academics, and (former) politicians that is concerned with potential future challenges to humanity.

9. The Charter states, "Environmental education, properly understood, should constitute a comprehensive lifelong education, one responsive to changes in a rapidly changing world. It should prepare the individual for life through an understanding of the major problems of the contemporary world, and the provision of skills and attributes needed to play a productive role towards improving life and protecting the environment with due regard given to ethical values" (United Nations Environment Programme, 1975).

10. The environmental destruction of the Soviet system is described in detail in Peterson (1993).

11. African countries were not included in the analysis because of a lack of available data.

12. These quotes from Latour and Giroux were included in a May 2019 call for articles for a special issue on *Educational Philosophy and Theory* on the topic "ESD in the 'Capitalocene': Caught up in an impasse between Critique and Transformation."

13. A similar logic has also been used to offer alternative interpretations of pro-environment "terrorist" groups, such as ALF (Animal Liberation Front): "If one wants to understand the ALF, one must transcend the false rhetoric of 'terrorism' and approach the real purpose of its struggle—animal liberation—through the method of critical pedagogy" (Nocella, 2019, p. 22).

DILEMMA 2

1. Chatsworth is an Indian township in the southwestern part of Durban, not easily accessible from Wentworth without a car.

CHAPTER 3

1. The institute was at the time of apartheid one of the centers of (White) liberal thinking that opposed the apartheid policies of the Nationalist Party government and advocated "bridging the gap" between South Africa's racial groups; some of its views were, however, influenced by the racial ideologies of the time and it sometimes clashed with the ANC and other representative bodies of the non-White majority (Everatt, 2010).

2. The change was to reflect what the commission perceived to be the essential features of India's history and culture: "The two most characteristic features of Indian civilisation have been the ethical approach to life's problems and broad tolerance of differences, and these are attitudes which are not irrelevant today but more than ever needed" (Planning Commission of India, 1958, p. 2). The commission's essentializing of "civilisation" reflected an Orientalist, top-down approach to educational development.

3. While the vision reflected in the report was dominant at this time, other viewpoints circulated within the government and proposed alternative definitions of education, including those rooted in the ideas of Tagore and Gandhi. Elsewhere I have analyzed some of these competing educational visions, as they manifested in government propaganda films of the era (Sutoris, 2018a).

4. The difference between "environmentalism of the poor" and "First World environmentalism" or "environmentalism in the North" has been dealt with extensively in the literature

on environmental movements, with Ramachandra Guha being one of the key figures in this debate. According to Guha and Martinez-Alier (1997, p. 16), "[E]nvironmental movements in the North have . . . been convincingly related to the emergence of a post-materialist or post-industrial society." In India—and elsewhere in low-income countries—"environmentalism has emerged at a relatively early stage in the industrial process. Nature-based conflicts . . . are at the root of the environmental movement in countries such as India. These conflicts have their root in a lopsided, iniquitous and environmentally destructive process of development" (p. 17).

5. For a discussion of how such historical narratives have been used by Indian nationalists in mobilizing support for their movement before India's independence, see Liu and Khan (2014). Such a "golden age" was arguably an invention of orientalists rather than a historical fact; such ideas, however, in many cases outlived the period of colonial rule, as discussed by a number of contemporary historians of India, including Prakash (1990) and Singh (2003).

6. Gandhi's resistance to industrialization is captured perhaps most powerfully in his manifesto *Hind Swaraj or Indian Home Rule* (1921).

7. Mokshagundam Visvesvaraya was India's chief civil engineer and politician in the early twentieth century.

8. This does not mean, however, that Ambedkar won. While independent India embraced industrial modernity as a path toward development, it would be difficult to argue that this has benefited Dalits and other marginalized groups in the way Ambedkar hoped for, especially given the current political climate that in many ways reinforces caste hierarchies (Komireddi, 2019).

9. Limited attempts have been made to advance the theory of Gandhian economics since Gandhi's death, but they have not received much attention in the field of economics; see, for example, Das (1979).

10. Here I refer to the reverence with which Nehru is often addressed in public life, as experienced through my own observations and informal conversations with Indian journalists and scholars.

11. By "depoliticization of environment" I mean the evacuation of Arendtian politics from the shared imaginaries, discourses, and practices related to the natural environment.

12. Estimates range widely, however, with thirty-eight hundred being the conservative government figure. Crematorium and cemetery officials in the Bhopal area, for example, claimed at least eight thousand dead (Kurzman, 1987, p. ix), and some estimates put the figure as high as sixteen thousand, counting the eight thousand who died within weeks of the disaster and the approximately eight thousand who have died since as a direct consequence of their exposure to methyl isocyanate (Eckerman, 2005).

13. Tens of thousands are affected to this day, having had to live with their injuries without fair compensation or rehabilitation for more than three decades.

14. *Parens patriae*, Latin for "parent of the nation," refers to a state's power to intervene on behalf of citizens unable to protect themselves. It is commonly invoked in cases of parental abuse of

minors. In this case, the Indian government decided that hundreds of thousands of women, men, and children could not defend themselves against Union Carbide, which prevented the victims from independently suing the company and defending themselves on their own terms. Arguably, this served the purposes of Union Carbide (and the Indian government, which was interested in minimizing the fallout from the disaster in the form of a decline in foreign investment if the price Union Carbide paid was too high) rather than the purposes of the victims and those seeking justice for them.

15. In his book *Bhopal: The Inside Story*, T. R. Chouhan (1994), a former UCIL worker, enumerated the many ways that UCID and its mother company, Union Carbide, failed to maintain a secure environment at the plant: through negligence, underinvestment and lack of training, and by flat out breaking industrial rules and regulations. Many of these accusations have been independently corroborated (Varma & Varma, 2005), which gave the workers' claims credibility (Fortun, 2001).

16. Pesticides were also seen as central to the Green Revolution (Shiva, 2016), which was to raise India's agricultural productivity and liberate it from its dependence on American food imports. The idea of "development," in other words, was seen as central to the welfare of India's people, but this could only happen on the back of specific technological innovations (such as fertilizers needed to support the Green Revolution, which were made at Bhopal).

17. The colonial past shaped the notion that the lives of people of color are worth less than White lives and the belief in humankind's ability to master nature, including human nature (cf. J. C. Scott, 2008). It also gave rise to the assertion that human progress is equivalent to "development" in its post-Enlightenment, postindustrial revolution rendition, along with the associated paternalistic theory of state in which the citizen was to serve the country rather than the country catering to its citizens' needs (cf. S. Roy, 2007).

18. At the press conference following a seminar on the changing investment climate in post-liberalization India in 1991, "reporters were reminded that the handling of the Bhopal case was evidence that India is an amiable site for foreign investment, symbolizing Indian commitment to the New World Order" (Fortun, 2001, p. 148).

19. The ideological contradictions at the heart of the newly born Indian state call attention to the agency of intrastate actors in shaping educational policy and delivery, as recognized in some of the most recent research into the role state bureaucrats played in educational development in India (Mangla, 2015, 2017).

20. Modi's political awakening can be traced back to his time in RSS youth camps, which "introduced volunteers to the vast pantheon of villains who had plundered and emasculated India down the ages and exhorted them to shed their Hindu impotence"; heeding this call, Modi "wandered through India as a catechist for the Hindu nationalist cause" (Komireddi, 2019, p. 98).

21. Many contemporary proponents of *Hindutva* argue that the assassination of Gandhi was an act of a rogue ex-member of RSS and that the organization is not to blame. Such views are captured in Anand Patwardhan's film *Reason* (2018); in one of the documentary's scenes, the filmmaker enters a heated debate with participants in a political rally who make this argument

and confronts them with what he sees as historical facts about RSS's involvement in the assassination plot. While there is no consensus on direct links between the organization and the killing, a number of historians argue that the RSS, at the very least, spread an ideology that was conducive to such an act (Ramachandran, 2016).

22. See P. S. Ghosh (2000) for the evolution of Hindu nationalism over time.

23. There is also evidence of Hindu nationalism's interference with judicial and state inquiries into the incident, as discussed by Jaffrelot (2012).

24. In another twist of irony, one of the preoccupations of Indian newspapers at the time was how the health of one individual—Barack Obama—would be affected by inhaling Delhi's polluted air during his three days in India; according to scientists' calculations, it would likely shorten his life by approximately six hours ("World's Worst Air," 2015).

25. INC led the government following the 1991 election, but this was a minority government with the support of smaller political parties on the left.

26. This style of government has been dubbed "Moditva," as discussed by Mehta (2010) in the context of a legal battle between the state of Gujarat (at the time Modi served as its chief minister) and the Indian sociologist Ashish Nandy. Mehta uses this case to point to both the personality cult surrounding Modi and the associated suppression of free speech and academic freedom.

27. As Ishizaka (2006) points out, since the 1980s, the construction of large dams has decreased considerably. Based on Singh's (2002) and Khagram's (2004) work, Ishizaka (2006, p. 79) identifies three key reasons for this: "Firstly, the problems of large-scale dams (for example, low level of cost-benefit ratio, adverse influence upon the environment, problem of evacuation, and so on) came to be widely known. Secondly, many anti dam movements started to join forces with each other. Thirdly, notions of environmental protection and preservation of human rights (especially of tribes) came to have much more power in the process of policy making in India." However, as Tehri Dam attests, the age of the large dam is not yet over.

28. Following the earthquake, Sunderlal Bahuguna, the leader of Chipko, went on an indefinite fast, which led the Indian government to order a review of the project, ultimately concluding the dam design was safe (Verghese, 1994, p. 85).

29. According to Bisht, "The rural population displaced by the Tehri Dam is mainly Hindu and is organised on the basis of the caste system. The patrilineal, patrilocal joint family is the functional unit and the basis of the organisation of property and land . . . Prior to displacement, village communities were mainly subsistence farming communities" (Bisht, 2009, p. 304).

30. While the work by Mawdsley (1999) is more than two decades old at the time of this book's publication, these descriptions of the socioeconomic situation of the area resonate with my own fieldwork observations and the insights shared by my interlocutors.

31. The Chipko's history is complex, and it is not my goal in this book to heroize the movement or its leader. It is important to note that the "protests gained wider audiences through simple, populist narratives that pitted peasants against the state and markets, but glossed over the

heterogeneity of classes, interests, and constituencies within the movement. This skilled interweaving of state discourse and populist rhetoric made Chipko the unquestioned icon of grassroots environmentalism in India and international environmental circles" (Rangan, 2004, p. 382). As a result of these limitations, Chipko's actual successes do not necessarily live up to the enthusiasm with which journalists, academics, and environmentalists spoke and wrote of the movement at the time. See Dogra (1993) for further detail. Sunderlal Bahuguna has been "diversely acclaimed as the father of the Chipko movement, a freedom fighter, a true disciple of Gandhi and Vinoba Bhave, an environmental thinker and writer, a gentle crusader, an unobstructive messiah, a rishi, the face of TBVSS, convenor of Himalaya Bachao Andolan [The Save the Narmada Movement]" (Sharma, 2009, p. 36). I met Bahuguna and his wife, fellow activist leader Vimla Bahuguna, in their house in Dehradun during my fieldwork in Pashulok in 2017. While we could not engage in a detailed discussion about the anti-Tehri Dam movement, because of the Bahugunas' advanced age, their charisma and unwavering commitment to protecting the natural environment of the Garhwal Himalayas shone through their eyes as they talked to me about the future challenges they foresee for the region. See James (2013, pp. 171–186) for an overview of the Bahugunas' struggle against Tehri Dam.

32. According to Rakesh, the land was previously owned by Mirabehn, a British woman who moved to India in order to devote her life to advancing Gandhi's principles and India's independence struggle. She later donated the land to local people, who used it for animal grazing until it was converted into a rehabilitation site for Tehri Dam oustees.

33. As Chikane (2018) points out, even though South Africa's president announced a zero percent increase in student fees on October 21, 2015, this did not put an end to the activist struggle. "Eventually, #FeesMustFall 2015 ended, but the search for economic freedom did not" (Chikane, 2018, p. 192).

34. Chari (2005, p. 15) provides a detailed account of this apartheid-era activist history: "Steve Biko was once resident at the Alan Taylor Residence [in Wentworth], black student housing for medical students at the University of Natal. Biko had drawn a wide group of young people to transform Alan Taylor into a hub of political activity in the early 1970s, but its connections were primarily into the city centre and, subsequently, to Indian youth from the township of Merebank. It was only after the assassination of Steve Biko and the suppression of Black Consciousness, and after a period of quiet in the late 1970s that Alan Taylor would become a hotbed of activity again in the early 1980s." Nelson Mandela's connection to activism in Wentworth is explained in chapter 5.

35. The situation in the country in recent years has led Julian Brown (2015) to call South Africa a "country of protest" and refer to its people as "insurgent citizens." In his view, which agrees with my findings, "these small insurgencies might be instigated by a recognition of the gap between the lived realities of inequality and the messianic expectations of the immediate past—by the gap between contemporary reality, and the utopian vision of social and economic redress that thrived in an earlier [postapartheid] moment" (p. 149).

36. Struggles over land have led to a number of farmers' murders in the years leading up to my fieldwork in South Africa. Steinberg's (2015) account of one such case in KwaZulu-Natal exposes just how polarizing this issue can be in the context of South Africa's apartheid history.

37. Arendt here quotes directly from one of the judges in the Eichmann case.

38. Excerpted from Arthur Nortje's (2000, p. 37) poem, "Evil Assumes the Guise of Emptiness."

39. As a consequence of the Act, more than half a million Coloured people were forcibly relocated to residential and sometimes business areas, mostly on the periphery of cities and towns (Adhikari, 2005, p. 4). Other pieces of legislation—including the Population Registration Act of 1950, the Prohibition of Mixed Marriages Act of 1949, the Immorality Amendment Act of 1950, and the Separate Amenities Act of 1953—also severely constrained the civil rights of Coloured people.

40. Scott's PhD dissertation (1994) is an important source of historical knowledge about South Durban, as are many of her subsequent publications (Barnett & Scott, 2007a, 2007b; Brooks et al., 2010; D. Scott, 2003a, 2003b; D. Scott et al., 2002; D. Scott & Barnett, 2009; D. Scott & Oelofse, 2005).

41. As Dianne Scott pointed out to me in her interview, the labor reserve of South Durban supported the rise of industrial activity around the Durban port in the early decades of the twentieth century. At the same time, the perception of people of color as racially inferior, disposable workers whose health did not matter conveniently allowed for forcibly moving them to South Durban to provide cheap labor to fuel the engine of economic development.

42. As Trapido (2011) points out, this military effort involved not only securing harbors necessary for trade but also inland agricultural land to supply them. The British thus sought to control large swathes of territory to advance their economic interests.

43. For example, Britain pursued its "scorched earth" policy not only against the Afrikaners but also against Black South Africans; as many as 116,000 were moved to concentration camps, of which fourteen thousand died (Thompson, 2014, p. 143). It also used Black South Africans for military purposes, with an estimated ten to thirty thousand fighting with the British Army. After the war, Milner [British colonial governor] introduced measures restricting the Black Africans' movement, lowering their wages and generally making life more difficult for them (Thompson, 2014, p. 144).

44. An example of the ways in which these paternalistic ideas affected the thinking of educationalists of the time can be found in C. T. Loram's (1917) *The Education of the South African Native*.

45. The goals of the movement can be gleaned from those Biko (1979b, 1979a) expressed in public prior to his untimely death. In his analysis of the movement's political strategy, Hirschmann (1990, p. 22) argues that, "given the predicaments that faced black political leaders in the 1960s, and the cruel responses that their opposition consistently drew from Pretoria, to have confronted some of these issues head-on and in public would have been self-destructive. In other words, the early stress on the psychological, the cultural, and the historical, and on mobilisation and conscientisation, made tactical sense and, more importantly, worked."

46. Biko delivered this statement as a defense witness at the trial of Sathasivan Cooper and eight others in Pretoria in May 1976.

47. In 2016, four decades after the release of the book, the crisis of governance under ANC's Jacob Zuma prompted R. W. Johnson (2016) to write a follow-up titled *How Long Will South Africa Survive? The Looming Crisis,* in which he once again raised the question of fundamental unsustainability of the country's political regime.

48. Not all impacts of globalization are necessarily negative, however. Cock and Fig (2001) have, for example, pointed to the emergence of a global civil society that helped "regalvanise environmental and developmental movements in contemporary South Africa" (p. 15).

49. Among the key arguments of this book is that South Africa at the time of democratic transition was heavily dependent on foreign investment and export for sustaining its economy, which meant the government needed to ensure the country would be seen as an attractive destination for foreign investment. In problematizing this perspective, Freund (2010, p. 7) has sought to put "into a somewhat new light much of the critical literature on the African National Congress governments under Mandela and Mbeki . . . The chief weakness of this thrust of thinking in my view, apart from an idealisation of what the ANC was like before 1994, lies in a tendency to encourage conspiracy theories of subversion." Wolpe's (1972) analysis suggests that, in order to prop up the apartheid regime, the South African government needed to create "Bantustans" to keep Black people from the cities. This strand of scholarship, in other words, traces the economic divide to apartheid-era policies rather than the neoliberalism of the 1990s and beyond.

50. As Bond and Hallowes (2002, p. 40) note, "The settler-colonial and apartheid divisions of South Africa's land, codified by the 1913 Land Act and numerous subsequent policies and laws, left 87% of the land under white ownership and control, with millions of African people displaced to overcrowded 'bantustans.'"

51. See Steyn (2005) for an in-depth analysis of the continuities in environmental management practices from the apartheid era into the democratic period.

52. There were multiple reasons for this, but the performance of the economy was arguably a key factor. According to Chipkin and Swilling, "The economic policies of the Mbeki period were widely slated as a self-imposed programme of structural adjustment inspired by neoliberal economic policies. In the wake of Polokwane, and especially after the 2009 election, a search began in earnest for a more 'radical' model of transformation. At the time, the Zuma presidency was applauded in 'left-wing' circles for promising a break with the 'neoliberal' policies of the Mbeki years" (2018, p. 4).

53. The use of rhetoric and propaganda was important in sustaining this political project. "In addition to Zuma's new slogan 'radical economic transformation,' the term 'white monopoly capital' started surfacing all over social media where it was wielded mainly by his supporters . . . British PR firm Bell Pottinger, which was retained by the Guptas [a powerful business family with links to Jacob Zuma] to burnish their image . . . was allegedly the mastermind behind this aggressive social-media campaign, according to numerous media reports. The

firm reportedly made use of fake bloggers, commentators and Twitter bots to manipulate public opinion and divert outrage away from the Gupta family towards other imagined examples of state capture by white monopoly capital" (Bisseker, 2017, p. 33).

54. This report by Chipkin and Swilling (2018), titled *Betrayal of Promise: How South Africa Is Being Stolen*, was originally made public in May 2017 and is widely seen as a key source in understanding the phenomenon of state capture. The report showed that "the struggle today was between those who sought change within the framework of the Constitution and those who were ready to jettison the terms of the transition to democracy" (Chipkin & Swilling, 2018, p. 7). It was the latter group that sought to advance the political project of state capture.

55. "Milner's Kindergarten" refers to "the name popularly given to the young British civil servants who served under High Commissioner, Alfred Lord Milner" (Chipkin & Swilling, 2018, p. 1).

56. ANC's support in this election stood at 57.50 percent of the vote, down from 62.15 percent in 2014 ("South Africa's Election Results Reflect Widespread Disillusion," 2019).

57. For the Coloured people of South Africa, the Act was a double-edged sword. "The Group Areas Act was something of a blessing in that it offered improved housing to coloureds, and, therefore, it would seem, drew them into a structural relationship of complicity with the planners of apartheid," Chari (2006b, p. 427) notes. "These contradictions allowed some to seek to exploit the levers of the apartheid state, and others to paint coloureds as intrinsically complicit with apartheid" (Chari, 2009, p. 524).

58. According to Desai (2017, p. 88), "There is a plethora of churches, with some estimates putting the number at 81, in an area of approximately 30 000 residents."

59. This, however, does not mean that the inhabitants of Wentworth lacked political agency. In this regard, Chari's (2006a, pp. 523–524) observations echo some of the findings of my fieldwork: "On my initial trip to Wentworth in 2002, I thought that this was a subaltern population without a bourgeoisie to represent them. I have since found residents tremendously innovative in using governmental mechanisms to leverage resources from corporate capital and local government, through what Chatterjee (2004) calls a 'politics of the governed.'"

60. Chari here references Wacquant's (2004) definition of "ghetto" in the *International Encyclopedia of the Social & Behavioral Sciences*. "Recognizing that it is a product and instrument of group power makes it possible to appreciate that, in its full-fledged form, the ghetto . . . serves opposite functions for the two collectives that it binds in a relation of asymmetric dependency," Wacquant (2004, p. 3) writes. "For the dominant category, its rationale is to confine and control, which translates into what Max Weber calls the 'exclusionary closure' of the dominated category. For the latter, however, it is an integrative and protective device insofar as it relieves its members from constant contact with the dominant and fosters consociation and community building within the constricted sphere of intercourse that it creates" (2004, p. 3).

61. While this historical narrative is consistent with the oral history interviews I undertook here, I would hesitate to use the word "ghetto" in connection with today's Wentworth. The solidarity

between people within the township—including in the form of environmental activism that cuts across racial lines—is palpable, and at odds with Wacquant's notion of a ghetto.

62. For a discussion of the violence of forced removals and the subsequent fate of Cato Manor, see Edwards (1994) and Popke (2000).

63. Although Chari had written a decade before my fieldwork in Wentworth and there may have been demographic shifts since his research took place, the figures he cited resonated with my experience and the information shared by my interlocutors.

64. "Takkie" is Afrikaans slang for branded sport shoes.

65. This was not the case with everyone, however. In an interview, the parents of one of the students who participated in the observational filmmaking workshop told me that they did not feel strongly affected by air pollution or by crime. They lived in a part of Wentworth not immediately adjacent to the refinery and their small house was surrounded by a large fence. The creation of "islands of security" through (electric) fencing, barbed wire, alarms, and private security firms was visible all over urban South Africa, including in Wentworth.

66. At least when it comes to natural environment; if we adopt a broader definition in which the fast violence of crime becomes central to experiencing "the environment," it may be possible to speak of politicization of the environmental through the spectacles of fast violence. This, however, still comes at the expense of politicization around issues of environmental sustainability related to natural resources, pollution, and the destruction of ecosystems.

67. The students' questions to the woman in the scene indeed strongly suggested that they disapproved of smoking; for example, they asked her why she thought smoking was prohibited in public spaces.

CHAPTER 4

1. Later, I started recognizing the limitations of this interpretation as I began to understand the rituals of discipline within the school, which, I believe, had more to do with the children's propensity to please the teacher.

2. A number of scholars of Indian education have pointed in particular to teachers' authoritarian tendencies. According to Vasavi (2015, p. 45), "What marks most of the transactions between teachers and children is the socialisation of children into a culture of obedience, of silence and quiet, and of passive hearing, copying and repeating, doing the bidding of the teacher (including under-taking errands and/or acting as the monitor in the absence of the teacher) as the ideal student. These acts and relationships make and force each child to become an obedient child subject. At the end of these transactions and under the imprint of such relationships, the average GES [Government Elementary School] pupil is typically rendered excessively docile, often incapable of independent thinking, and marked for life to being a subservient subject." Majumdar and Mooji (2011) express a similar view. This phenomenon is also related to the "colonisation of the mind," as discussed by Ashish Nandy (2015).

3. It is important to point out, however, that neither site was meant to be representative of state-sponsored education in its respective country. Schools in South Africa and India both have complicated hierarchies with varying degrees of state involvement, and my observations from Pashulok and Wentworth cannot capture this complexity. Many of the social and cultural patterns I observed in the two schools would, however, be likely to manifest in many other schools serving disadvantaged groups in both countries. It is also important to note that these were not boarding schools, so the idea of a "total institution" could not fully apply as children did not spend all their time here.

4. This trend is confronted in some of the literature critical of depoliticization and individualization of responsibility for the natural environment. Maniates (2001, p. 37), for example, notes that his "students argue that the best way to reverse environmental degradation is to educate the young children now in school. When pressed, they explain that only a sea-change in the choices individual consumers are making will staunch the ecological bleeding we're now facing—and it's too late to make much of dent in the consumer preferences of young adults like themselves."

5. I address my relationship with Rakesh and the ways in which he intervened in my fieldwork in India in dilemma 3.

6. There appeared to be an uneven political geography of time as these forces interacted in complex ways with the histories of both dispossession and accelerated discontinuous time (what we may call postcolonial time or Gregory's [2004] "the colonial present") that shaped the school's context and exposed students to contrasting messages about the "temporal arc" of their lives.

7. Hindu monk who lived in the nineteenth century and is credited with spreading Hindu teachings in the West.

8. Hindu mystic and saint who lived in nineteenth-century Bengal, Swami Vivekananda's teacher.

9. Religious leader whose teachings form the core of Buddhism. It is disputed whether he was born in India or Nepal, as both countries claim to be his birthplace.

10. The founder of Sikhism who lived in the fifteenth to sixteenth centuries.

11. In the mountain regions, both Hinduism and Buddhism are practiced by a significant number of people, many of whom see Buddha as a Hindu god. Even though the list may appear diverse, I believe it reflects a Brahmanical cosmology (one rooted in the Vedas) rather than acceptance of religious diversity.

12. With the exception of one teacher, who was a Rajput, a people historically associated with being warriors.

13. On one level, this observation reflected my own values and the privileged gaze of a researcher from the "Global North." On another level, however, what I was witnessing also contradicted the values of equality and fraternity in the context of a casteist society encoded in India's constitution (Jaffrelot, 2005) and the lower castes' countless struggles for equality and justice

throughout the colonial and postcolonial periods (see, e.g., Ambedkar, 2014; Hardtmann, 2010; King, 2015; Kolge, 2017).

14. A number of scholars of Indian education have pointed to similarities in ideas about education between colonial-era officials and the nationalist elites that governed the country after Independence (S. Basu, 2010; Kumar, 2005; Srivastava, 1998).

15. This seemed to be a rhetorical remark, as I had little sense of the students' academic achievement at this point (given how docile and quiet they were in the presence of teachers, and by extension, me).

16. The idea that the students' agency lies in their "surrendering" to the teachers and that any academic achievements are due to the work of the teachers rather than of the students suggests an almost total dismissal of the children's own initiative and motivation for learning. In trying to understand how pervasive this view was, I tried to establish whether other teachers had a similar attitude. When I asked Pranay whether his views on discipline were shared by his colleagues, he remarked, "We can't create a *mahaul* [environment] of discipline without the support of colleagues . . . We worked hard, for first four or five years . . . You can see the classrooms or you can say gallery you will not see a mark of pencil in the walls, which is a very common thing in schools."

17. The concept of "purity" has a central role in Hinduism; those belonging to the lower castes are considered to be less pure than their upper-caste counterparts.

18. The subject of environmental studies, however, was not conspicuous by its absence. This description of the functioning of Indian government elementary schools by Vasavi (2015, p. 44) seemed apt as I observed how all the subjects were taught at Seema Primary: "Class schedules and teacher-allocated classes are more on paper than in practice. Teachers take classes at times and of durations suitable to them. Children lug all the books to and from home and school, and the class timetable is rarely followed. With lesson plans an idea that is yet to take root, classes predominantly consist of reading from the text, some explanation made on the board, and 'practice' (*abhyas*) sessions for a range of subjects. Where transactions take place at all, they are mostly routinised copying of words, sentences, questions and answers either from the board or the textbook or as dictated by the teacher."

19. By this I mean specializations within education degree programs of the kind available for other subjects. This absence of training came up in a number of interviews with teachers at Seema Primary and was confirmed in a number of my interviews with Indian academics and educationists. It is possible that some programs are available, but neither my informants in India nor I were aware of them.

20. Other subjects in my observation were often seen as routinized to the point that teachers could supervise each other's classes. Teachers' discipline-based identity and subject-specific expertise, in other words, seem to have been lacking across the board, and in this sense environmental studies was not an exception.

21. Padma Sarangapani (2003) explored these cultural landscapes in her ethnography of schooling in a government primary school in "Kasimpur," a village near Delhi. (This is not a real

name, as Sarangapani maintained the anonymity of the community in which she conducted her fieldwork.). Her findings, which echo my own observations in Pashulok, point to a rigid transmission of textbook knowledge from the teacher to the learners who are expected to memorize it, revise it, and later recall it for an exam.

22. They include "A Snake Charmer's Story," which "look[s] at the close relationship between animals and human beings" (NCERT, 2008, p. vi) or "Sunita in Space," which "engages with the challenging concepts of the 'shape of the earth' and 'gravitation' using children's intuitive ideas'" (NCERT, 2008, pp. vi–vii).

23. A "show" lesson could be seen as a narrative of power expressed through culture and may be of value to an ethnographic study. However, participating in such an exercise could have complicated my ability to build trust with the students, as it could have further added to my being perceived as affiliated with the discipline-enforcing teaching staff. It therefore seemed too risky to do this in the early stages of my fieldwork, and the students were preparing for exams by the time I left, at which point arranging such a lesson was no longer an option.

24. The assumption operating here seemed to be that, through hard work, the children will be able to attain a materially higher standard of living than their parents. Given India's highly stratified education system and Seema Primary's position near the bottom in terms of education quality, it is unfortunately unlikely that the kinds of occupations students would imagine for themselves (doctor or engineer) would be available to them. It can be argued that this system was based on peddling a lie of a nonexistent meritocracy.

25. It was the ruling of India's Supreme Court that led to the establishment of environmental studies as a compulsory subject in elementary schools. The judiciary has proven itself to be somewhat immune to being swayed by ideological currents of bureaucratization, statist developmentalism, and Hindu nationalism that shape the Indian state, as discussed in chapter 3. For a comprehensive review, see Sathe's (2003) monograph about judicial activism in India.

26. One reason for these continued deficiencies is a lack of funding for education. According to J. B. G. Tilak, viewing education as a public good and a human right "is not ingrained in the minds of our union or state government functionaries, particularly the economic and educational policymakers and planners" (2009, p. 70). As Rao, Cheng, and Narain (2003) note, the Indian state lacked an integrated approach to primary education after Independence and only committed to this agenda more seriously from the 1980s onward. Although new policy initiatives such as Operation Blackboard took off during this time (Dyer, 1996), budgetary allocations remained insufficient and debate about the "public gap" in education spending continued to rage through the 1990s and 2000s (Shariff & Ghosh, 2000).

27. These subjects included science and social science in grade VI and above. The reasons why I was not allowed observation at Seema Primary seemed multiple and complex. The teacher of these subjects repeatedly said she was "not ready" to be observed.

28. Given the sensitive nature of these comments, I am not including any additional information about this particular teacher nor am I using a pseudonym so that these remarks could not be linked to this teacher's remarks (if any) quoted elsewhere in the book.

29. From these comments, it was clear that—whether any genuine censorship by the government was operating in Pashulok—at least one teacher would self-censor her views about the dam out of fear of possible repercussions.

30. This was visible, for example, in the detail with which they observed and filmed *aarti* rituals performed on the banks of the Ganges. As the children explained to me, the intention behind this was to point to the contradiction between the rituals of worship local people engaged in and the sewage and trash with which they polluted the river.

31. The adult who appears in this photograph is one of the translators who helped me with the observational filmmaking workshop.

32. After all, at the time the films were being made, I myself was not aware that intergenerational knowledge transfer would become an important theme in my research. The learners did this in spite of the obvious difficulties in engaging with people beyond their immediate social circles. They often shared with me that they were shy and found it difficult to approach strangers for permission to film them. Intergenerational dialogue clearly mattered to them.

33. Given that Durban is home to many South Africans of Indian origin and that a number of the teachers at Durban South Primary fell into this group, I am using mostly Indian names for teacher pseudonyms in this section.

34. She expressed this perspective in our conversations, but in light of this belief, I often struggled to make sense of her teaching practices. As I discuss later in this section, some of these practices were similar to Pranay's.

35. In 2017 the South African government spent 18.73 percent of its budget, or 6.1 percent of its GDP, on education (UNESCO, 2019b)—the sixth-highest percentage in the world—which compares to India's 14.1 percent of the government budget, or 3.8 percent of GDP (UNESCO, 2019a). This figure, the most recent available for India, is for 2013, whereas the South African figure is for 2018. In 2013 the South African government expenditure on education stood at 19.17 percent.

36. Historically, however, the school had exclusively served the Coloured population of Wentworth, which changed after the fall of apartheid, opening up opportunities for Black children from nearby townships to attend the school.

37. This could be seen as the continuation of an apartheid-era trend of schools serving non-White pupils having deliberately substandard levels of quality and performance.

38. As secondary education was not within the scope of my project, this point is based on conversations with teachers and academics rather than systematic research.

39. Treasure Beach is one of the most affluent areas in South Durban, separated from the oil refineries by a hill and overlooking the Indian ocean.

40. Intergenerational knowledge transfer played little role in these aspirations, as did any concept of the environment that did not see it as a site of exploitation for economic growth.

41. They were also often aware of how slow violence affected them personally. For example, in one of my conversations with one of the students who made *Pollution Kills*, the student told

me about an LO lesson in which the topic of pollution came up. "He [the teacher] said that's why he doesn't want to live in Wentworth, . . . That's why he went to another place because it's much safer because in Wentworth things happen; fire comes out any time."

42. Joseph Skido, who had a history of anti-apartheid activism, was one of the artisanal labor unionists who founded the Metalworkers' Cooperative in Wentworth (Chari, 2007, p. 260). Chari (2008, pp. S68–S69) recalled: "I drove around with the late Skido Joseph as he put together his portfolio as a 'development consultant,' to transform his situation as an unemployed person who seemed genuinely interested in helping the lot of his neighbourhood. [. . .] What was clear, as he drove around Wentworth in his old car blaring anti-Apartheid 'struggle music,' was that he was bitter about not being able to use his struggle credentials to access jobs in the post-Apartheid state, as many of his former comrades had."

43. For above-ground political activity in Wentworth during apartheid through unions and other organized groups, see Chari (2005, p. 16).

44. By this I do not mean apartheid politics but the kind of politics that emerged as a result of the antiapartheid struggle and extended into the early days of the post-1994 dispensation.

45. The process indeed led to many disagreements among the students—from everyday logistics of arranging where and when to meet to go filming, to deciding who would keep the camera overnight, to figuring out how to translate the broad theme of the film into shots that could realistically be captured. The students also had to find a way to harmonize their visions during the editing process, which was sometimes tedious, but ultimately the two groups were able to reach internal consensus on the final edit of each film. This is how Collin described the process within his group, which made *Pollution Kills*: "We spoke in a group and then if one person didn't like it then we wouldn't film it. And if all of us liked it then we would film it because we can't put something in the film that we're making that somebody like Tanya [another member of the group], if she didn't like something we wanted to film we couldn't because we don't know if what if her opinion is better? What if she wants to take us to a better place?"

46. Luke lived in Wentworth but did not go to Durban South Primary; the drawings and quotes come from one of the focus groups I conducted at another school in the community. These focus groups did not seem to point to any systematic differences between the perspectives of students at Durban South and the other school, and the two schools were similar in terms of size, the demographic they catered to and their exposure to social and environmental issues in Wentworth.

CHAPTER 5

1. The Democratic Alliance (DA) was, at the time of my fieldwork, the largest opposition party in South Africa.

2. One of the speakers at the event was a scientist from the University of KwaZulu-Natal's Department of Occupational and Environmental Health, who highlighted SDCEA's commitment to science and its ability to bring scientists on board its agendas.

3. SDCEA sometimes asked me to participate in its events, including as a speaker at the People's Economic Forum, an alternative event organized during the World Economic Forum on Africa that took place in Durban in May 2017; this exacerbated my dilemma about how much involvement was appropriate. Being seen as too closely aligned with the activists could affect the way I was perceived in local schools and how much access I would be allowed.

4. Including terrorism in the name of environmentalism (J. V. Carson et al., 2012; Vanderheiden, 2005).

5. Here the concept of ecotopia refers to an aggressive pursuit of a utopian world (a radical political project), as coined in Callenbach's (1978) novel by the same name.

6. With the exception of those explicitly identified as scholars or journalists.

7. Including New Delhi, Ahmedabad, and rural areas of Maharashtra state in India, and Johannesburg, Pietermaritzburg, and Cape Town in South Africa.

8. In this context, it is useful to think of a generation as people alive at a particular point in time. By applying this definition, intergenerational agonism becomes a bridge to the dead and intragenerational agonism a force unifying those alive in the present across lots of often rigid divides.

9. This logic became visible to me thanks to the comparative dimension of my work. The Indian activists' conscious effort to preserve the cultural heritage of their now submerged worlds to allow the past to shape the future alerted me to agonizing with the dead as crucial to activism that seeks to heal intergenerational trauma. The activists of South Durban, on the other hand, with their history of organizing across groups that had been pitted against each other by the apartheid regime brought into sharp relief the importance of agonizing with living others who are socially constructed as fundamentally different from ourselves. It was only after leaving one research site and reflecting on it from the vantage point of my other site that these patterns became visible, allowing me to deepen my understanding of both the vertical and the horizontal on my follow-up visits and to understand that the two kinds of cultural logic operated in both spaces.

10. While Chipko has been characterized by scholars as a powerful critique of the Indian state's project of modernizing India (Gadgil & Guha, 1992; T. Weber, 1988), concerns with employment and local economic development were also an integral part of the movement (Rangan, 2004; see also Mawdsley, 1998), a complexity also reflected in the struggles against the Tehri Dam.

11. Some of my interlocutors disagreed with the activist perspective. Apart from the representatives of the Tehri Hydro Development Corporation (THDC, which operates the dam) who praised the project in an interview with me, teachers at Seema Primary and a number of people I spoke to in the community approved of the project. The most common reason offered for supporting the project was the need for India to keep developing, and many conversations reflected a good deal of national pride in India's economic progress since the 1990s.

12. The issue of culture loss is not merely of concern to anthropologists; it has been conceptualized within legal frameworks with respect to "cultural property rights" (Kirsch, 2001).

13. Bigha is a customary unit of measurement used in Nepal and across a number of Indian states. Its size varies by location.

14. The activist narratives directly contradicted the statements of a representative of THDC, the government-controlled company that built the dam and was in charge of operating it, who claimed in an interview that the rehabilitation of the resettled population in Tehri was not only carried out in accordance with all legal frameworks and that all promises were met, but that this effort was in fact so exemplary that the Indian government based its nationwide rehabilitation policies on the example of Tehri. Indeed, some of the community members I interviewed in Pashulok who had no history of involvement with the activist movement claimed that the compensation was generous, one even going so far as to liken it to "a true Marxist revolution" because oustees received the same amount of compensation regardless of their caste, class, and wealth before resettlement.

15. A veteran of antidam protests in different parts of India, Rakesh offered a perspective that reflected a long history of working with local communities. Yet his engagement with the Pashulok community had been sporadic, which made him simultaneously an insider and an outsider among local activists. Rakesh appeared to be motivated by his convictions about social and environmental justice; to him, Tehri Dam was a manifestation of a larger system he has dedicated his life to fighting against.

16. The activist groups I interacted with did not appear to be concerned with the rich history of struggle against dams on the holy river Ganges on religious grounds by Hindu activists (Drew, 2017; Mawdsley, 2005; Sharma, 2009, 2012).

17. Organized resistance to the project is almost as old as the idea of the dam itself. In the late 1960s, shortly after the project was conceived, the emerging antidam movement had the support of Kamlendumati Shah, the local member of Parliament and wife of the Maharaja of Tehri-Garhwal Narendra Shah (James, 2013). A "massive antidam rally" took place in 1977, one activist told me, and the *Tehri Bandh Virodhi Sangharsh Samiti* (Anti-Tehri Dam Struggle Committee) was formed. It was, however, not until after the death of Indira Gandhi in 1984 and Gorbachev's visit to India in 1986 that the project took off, to a large extent because of Soviets' interest in the dam and their provision of technical expertise to build it (Dogra, 1992). As construction moved ahead in November 1989, Sunderlal Bahuguna and his wife set up a *kuti* (a small hut) near the construction site and remained there in *satyagraha* (nonviolent resistance), insisting that theirs would be the first submerged dwelling if the dam proceeded, which helped attract nationwide media attention to the struggle against the dam (James, 2013, p. 175). In his foreword to an edited volume on environmental protection, written while living in the kuti, Bahuguna (2000, p. v) observed: "I am writing these lines sitting on the bank of the River Bhagirathi (Holy Ganga). About 200 metres downstream, the construction of the 263-metre high Tehri Dam, the highest in Asia, is proceeding on a war footing. The running of trucks, moving of bulldozers and the thundering sounds of heavy blasting, day and night, makes me feel as if I am sitting in a battlefield, where man is at war with Nature in the name of development." While resistance continued well into the 1990s, the movement ultimately did not manage to stop the dam project.

18. It is possible this timing had something to do with the election season. As one of my activist informants told me in March 2017, "in Pashulok they fight for land rights in last 5–6 months, I feel that was also supported by some, one political party . . . because the election is happening." Remembering events preceding the local election, another activist noted that "the Election Day was also nearing, and we had said that if we are not given land ownership then we will boycott the elections and no one from us will vote. We had a slogan, 'No Land Ownership, No Votes,' and we took out a huge rally."

19. New Tehri was affected by the construction of the dam in different ways from Pashulok. Being located in the vicinity of the dam, many of the complaints mentioned to me in interviews were related to poor water quality (which was pumped from the dam) and the spreading of disease, as bodies were often cremated on the banks of the dam. For a more comprehensive overview of the difficulties suffered by oustees who were moved to New Tehri, see Newton (2008).

20. *Purana* is an ancient literary text of the Hindus; the Puranic literature consists mostly of myths, legends, and traditional folklore.

21. *Yaksha* is the name of a broad class of nature-spirits, usually benevolent, who are caretakers of the natural treasures hidden in the earth and tree roots. They appear in Hindu, Jain, and Buddhist texts.

22. *Gandharva* is a name used for distinct heavenly beings in Hinduism and Buddhism.

23. It could be argued that what was happening in Pashulok was likely to lead over time to the "tragedy of the commons," a situation in which individuals who act in their self-interest end up undermining the common good by damaging shared resources (Hardin, 1968). This is one lens through which the emergence and continuance of slow violence can be viewed.

24. Even Rakesh, an "outsider" in this community, recalled personal experiences of shared solidarity. He told me that at the time of the Gujarat riots of 2002 (discussed in chapter 3), he was campaigning in Tehri. Scared about the possibility of an outbreak of communal violence, he braced himself for the worst. But he felt heartened when "one person, he said, he assured me, he's from a Brahman family, if something will happen, this will happen on our shoulders, these are our brothers, nothing will happen with them. Such a big thing."

25. The idea of "progress" being not fully forward-looking and partly rooted in looking back was first suggested to me by Newton LaJuan in 2010, when he was the director of the Alele Museum in Majuro, Marshall Islands, and I was working on my documentary film *The Undiscovered Country* about development and education in the islands. Newton invited me to his property on a remote island, where we spent several days talking about how quickly the place was changing and what progress meant in this context, and where he demonstrated to me how he was combining agricultural practices of the old with lifestyles of the new. Newton convinced me that it was possible to get away from the modernity/tradition dichotomy often seen in academic texts, and that his version of "looking back" was very different from the romanticism and Orientalism (Said, 1979) of the colonial gaze. These insights, for which I remain grateful, have accompanied me through my work and research ever since; at times

during my interactions with activists in both Pashulok and Wentworth, I felt as though I was speaking to Newton. For all the place-based wisdom of his words, they seemed to transcend place and reverberate across space.

26. Botanical Survey of India conducted a survey of flora affected by Tehri Dam prior to flooding the valley and concluded that twelve rare species were likely to be "disturbed." The government certainly was not disturbed about the flora: "None of these have any medicinal or commercial use. In any case, a botanical garden is being developed to preserve these rare species of plants" (Govardhan, 1993, p. 293).

27. As it is the activists of today who are engaging in the hermeneutics of memory, they are identifying values in past worlds that they see as relevant to the challenges they (and their children) face today or are imagined to face in the future. The "surplus meaning" therefore lies not only in the "hidden ontology" of the past (i.e., the values the dead possessed without being consciously aware of them) but also in contemporary interpretation of the past, as captured in memory through the "detour" of distanciation. The latter has the potential to generate meanings independent of the ontology of past worlds or historical "truth."

28. The pace of sociocultural change was arguably slower for many generations who lived in Tehri before resettlement than for the current generation, which went through the trauma of relocation and the related cultural dislocation. It is therefore possible that the dead were not fully aware of some of the values and beliefs that now appear lost, as they only became conspicuous by their absence (or, rather, the absence of material and social environments needed to nurture them) after the damming of Tehri and resettling of the local populations.

29. The history of racial discrimination indeed shaped South African environmentalism well before 1994. As Beinart and Coates (1995) point out in their comparative study of the rise of environmentalism in the United States and South Africa, "in South Africa, opposition to the older resource-based conservation policies did not originate initially from American-derived 1960s environmentalism with its accent on amenity and 'rights of nature.' Rather it was expressed in black popular movements opposing government conservationist measures in the African reserve areas" (p. 99). See Carruthers (1995) chapter, "'The Other Side of the Fence': Africans and the Kruger National Park," pp. 89–102, for an overview of the impact of early government conservation efforts on the Black population and the work of the historian Farieda Khan (1994, 2000, 2014) for a wider overview of the impact of the end of apartheid on South Africa's environmental movement.

30. My informants often referred to groundWork as SDCEA's sister organization. It was founded in 1999 by activists with a view toward influencing the international discourse on development. "The mandate of groundWork has been to address three major concerns: oil and air pollution with regard to chemical industries, health-care waste and incineration, and hazardous waste" (Chari, 2006b, p. 435).

31. Culture has also played a role, although it is difficult to assess this in depth as my data only allows tracing cultural change back in time to a limited extent, through the memory of my participants.

32. Countercultural, in this context, does not mean antistate, as I argue later in this section.

33. Not all countries on the continent are, of course, plagued by all these issues, and my preconceived notions about "Africa" were among the assumptions challenged by my fieldwork.

34. The working definition of "sustainable development" at the conference was "development which doesn't destroy its own future" (Hallowes, 1993, p. ix). But the point of the conference in some ways was to find a new definition, as national and international figures were brought together in an effort to understand what the concept may mean in the context of a rapidly changing South Africa.

35. Yet, elsewhere in his essay, Albertyn's writing betrays a growing realization of what this critique may mean in the context of 1992 South Africa. "Francis Bacon's injunctions with regard to our relationship with nature also said much about the position of women and the poor in this reality," he wrote. "Nature was to be 'bound into service,' made a 'slave' and our purpose was to 'torture nature's secrets from her.' These injunctions to dominate, divide, control, and compete have become the very fabric of the Western way of life" (Albertyn, 1993, p. 217). In this part of the essay, Albertyn continues his attack on an essentially high modernist (J. C. Scott, 2008) view of development, albeit with an emphasis on "women and the poor." This perspective could be seen to mirror the environmental movement's growing openness to the agendas of the groups fighting for the rights of the poor, women, and other marginalized groups at this time.

36. See Cock (2006), Koch (1991), and Crompton and Erwin (1991) for analysis of the coalitions formed within the environmental movement after the fall of apartheid.

37. This type of activist mobilization appears to have operated separately (through different actors, at different times and in different spaces) from the antiapartheid mobilizations in South Durban linked to Biko, the African National Congress (ANC), and *uMkhonto we Sizwe* (MK). Sparks (2006, p. 207) has traced the contours of this history: "Earlier civic mobilisations around public health and civic amenities by white landowners on the Bluff found newer, more powerful expressions in the 1950s with the establishment of Stanvac. Landowner interests, founded on a conception of the Bluff as a neighbourhood with an attractive 'natural' character, conducive to comfortable living, leisure and a high standard of civic amenities, informed the character of mobilisations from the beginning, though health concerns (still vaguely articulated) became increasingly prominent. This civic culture also had traces of a critique of corporate greed and powerful layman discourses which betrayed its roots among white railway and municipal workers on the Bluff."

38. In Sparks' (2006, p. 218) account, "President Mandela's ribbon-cutting visit in late March 1995 to dedicate the new expansion of the refinery, was a watershed in the controversy. He was greeted at the gates by a protest organised by the WDF [Wentworth Development Forum]. Mandela stopped to speak with them, and refinery pollution was thrust onto the national stage in a way that had not occurred since the 1950s. Three days later, a government delegation, led by Mandela, met with leaders of the area's civic organisations and the refinery's management. The Deputy Minister of Environment and Tourism (DEAT), Bantu Holomisa,

was tasked by Mandela to convene a 'multi-stakeholder' *indaba* [conference of principal men of the Zulu people] in May."

39. More than two decades on, this story figured prominently in the consciousness of activists across South Durban. Sometimes they would invoke it with a tinge of nostalgia, as if they were missing the times when the government was listening to the activists; at other times it served to legitimize the activist struggle which aimed to fulfill the promise of the constitution.

40. The term "rainbow nation" is attributed to Archbishop Desmond Tutu and represented a key political goal of Nelson Mandela while president.

41. Along with groundWork and other organizations, including the Centre for Environmental Rights, which has been active in recent years in the realm of judicial activism and has worked with both SDCEA and groundWork.

42. Aside from the Settlers epidemiological study, SDCEA collaborated on a range of scholarly investigations. For example, a 2002 report, "Comparison of Refineries in Denmark and South Durban in an Environmental and Societal Context" (Danmarks Naturfredningsforening & SDCEA, 2002), highlighted Shell's double standards of acceptable environmental footprint, with its Danish refineries being much "cleaner" than Sapref in South Durban, also owned by Shell. Another study that compared the asthma rates of children in South and North Durban found a statistically significant relationship between attending a school in the south of the city and suffering from respiratory illnesses including asthma (R. Naidoo et al., 2007).

43. SDCEA regularly offers "toxic tours" of the area. These involve driving to several viewpoints around the industrial basin and listening to SDCEA staff recount the history and current state of the struggle. In my fieldnotes from the tour I went on in the beginning of my fieldwork, I wrote, among other observations, "Stopping in front of the chemical storage facility on the Bluff; Bongani asked me to park the car across the road from the entrance gate, as we got out he says this industrial complex still under 'apartheid' laws for objects of 'national importance' that almost turns it into its own 'sovereign state'; Bongani visibly afraid that he might get spotted and get in trouble; he whispers to me that he is known to the management of the facility and it's better they don't see him."

44. While "conflict" mostly remained confined to marches, demonstrations or words uttered in conference rooms behind closed doors, sometimes it got much more serious. During one of our conversations, Des recalled an incident in which "they petrol-bombed the flat after midnight . . . So I still bear the scars of it, and fighting the fire off. Lucky enough I was trained, so I fought the fire off, put the electricity off. My kitchen was completely burned, the lounge was burned somewhere at the bottom—I didn't really care. After I went to hospital, I came back the same morning and walked back and showed those that I wasn't scared of them. And show them that now I'm still going to fight even harder."

45. Historically, systemic constraints have limited such participation (Leonard, 2014a), something SDCEA has challenged, with some success.

46. My observations were consistent with Chari's (2007, p. 264), based on his fieldwork over a decade before mine, suggesting a consistent pattern of a mixture of engagement and

confrontation: "Given that SDCEA does not have a mass base but that it can bring together a strong crowd around issues like incineration and relocation, it has found it necessary to deepen the links between campaigning and episodic militancy. One of the challenges the alliance faces is to forge a tighter link between labour and fenceline communities, to bring together questions of environmental pollution and jobless growth in the expansion of the South Durban industrial basin."

47. John Dunn House was originally founded as an assisted living residence named after a local reverend by the Durban Senior Citizens Association.

48. The "bucket brigade" is SDCEA's way of involving the community while collecting scientific evidence of pollution levels in the industrial basin. It involves a bucket, a sealed plastic bag, and a bicycle pump. The pump, attached to a hole in the bucket's lid, fills the plastic bag with air, upon which the bag is sealed and sent to an independent laboratory for examination. When Bongani demonstrated this to me, he noted that SDCEA used to have to send samples all the way to California, because there were no laboratories within South Africa that were not owned or controlled by industry or industry-associated groups. At the time of my fieldwork, the samples were being sent to a domestic laboratory, which was deemed reliable and independent by SDCEA.

49. If my initial goal was to, in the language of economics, examine the impact of my independent variable (air pollution) on the dependent variable (activism), my fieldwork forced me to contend with the many confounding variables that influence both.

50. The film was made in 2006 by Greg Streak, a South African visual artist. This viewpoint offers a stark vista juxtaposing the ocean, beach, and hill on the one side (which, as Bongani shared with me, was the "beauty" referred to in the title of the documentary) and the smokestacks rising on the other side of the hill (representing the "beasts").

CHAPTER 6

1. The original quote is from Tagore (1991, p. 71).

2. As Bonneuil and Fressoz (2017, p. 32) argue, "the Anthropocene, as the reunion of human (historical) time and Earth (geological) time, between human agency and non-human agency, gives the lie to this—temporal, ontological, epistemological and institutional—great divide between nature and society that widened in the nineteenth and twentieth centuries."

3. The poorest are likely to be the most impacted by climate change. According to modeling by Rozenberg and Hallegatte (2019, p. 24), the world is likely to see between 3 and 122 million additional people living in poverty by 2030 (the variation is due to the many possible scenarios of the severity of climate change and other variables influencing poverty). Poor people, particularly in Africa, are also vulnerable to natural disasters such as floods and droughts (Winsemius et al., 2015). Small, low-income island countries, such as the Marshall Islands and the Maldives, are also among the most vulnerable (S.-A. Robinson, 2017), and their inhabitants might soon have, in the words of the Marshallese poet Kathy Jetnil-Kijiner (2014), "only a passport to call home."

4. Interviews with German citizens in the immediate aftermath of World War II suggest that, while the public at large knew of the concentration camps, they did not know their true purpose or the number of people sent there (Janowitz, 1946).

5. Here I mean action rooted in freedom (which arises through participation) and spontaneity (Schell, 2010, pp. 251–254).

6. This point also echoes the work of Dewey, who reminds us of education's important role in the functioning of democracies. While this theme was explored across a range of Dewey's writings, perhaps the most significant in this regard is his monograph *Democracy and Education* (1916).

7. One such dominant paradigm is "innovation." The barons of Silicon Valley are, perhaps, correct in assuming that the solutions to the challenges of our era lie in innovation (Musk, 2017), in charting paths previously unknown. But excluding billions of people from the process of finding these innovations (which may in fact be rooted in existing knowledge and practices) would be like having billions of supercomputers at our fingertips and not engaging them in solving the most complex of problems—except that humans have much more to offer than mere computing power: a mosaic of their subjective experiences, cultures, and languages, their emotions, their poetry, their genius, their intrinsic care for the species and the planet (however suppressed these may be by the forces of bureaucratization and depoliticization).

8. Such pretense of neutrality is often present in discourses of education in the context of international development, where terms like "access," "enrollment," "literacy and numeracy," and others are used to describe the goals and effects of education without acknowledging the political dimension of schooling. One of the most vocal critics of this trend is Manish Jain (2013), who in his writings refers to education for all as "McEducation for All" and emphasizes the effect of "westernizing" students through schooling and interfering with the transmission of Indigenous knowledge. This theme is also explored in the 2010 documentary film *Schooling the World*.

9. It may well be that, in some spheres of human endeavor, aiming for "the political" may not be the most pragmatic goal in the face of the Anthropocene's challenges, but when it comes to education, pragmatism and politics are on the same side—not least because when Amartya Sen wrote that the aim of development (and education) ought to be ensuring that people lead lives they have a reason to value (Sen, 1999), he was very much imagining a world that embraces politics. This link is evident in much of the literature about the "capability approach" to development coined by Amartya Sen and Martha Nussbaum, specifically in the links between the approach's focus on agency and sense of belonging (Deneulin & McGregor, 2010; Glassman & Patton, 2014; Robeyns, 2005) and Arendt's concept of politics. Mathias and Herrera (2006) have, through hermeneutic analysis, pointed to further links to Arendt and Ricœur, especially between the notion of capability and Arendt's conception of "action" and "power."

10. Bobby Peek made a similar observation about SDCEA's school visits when I interviewed him. Arguably, the age of the students in this particular session had to do with the depoliticized

content, as the class was aimed at lower-grade pupils. But SDCEA activists also shared with me in interviews that, in order to be able to work with schools, the narratives they shared could not be beyond what educators were prepared to accept as part of the schooling process—and this was in turn influenced by the state-sanctioned depoliticized curriculum.

11. Faces of pupils have been blurred in this photograph to protect their identity, as this was a general school assembly and not all students were participating in my research or had granted informed consent.

12. This is consistent with the literature about cultural concepts such as *ubuntu* ("humanity"). Le Grange (2012) has, for example, argued that *ubuntu* is intrinsically linked to the *ukama* ethic of the Shona people in Zimbabwe—which is concerned with the well-being of future generations (Murove, 2007). Therefore, "to become more fully human does not mean caring only for the self and other human beings but also for the entire biophysical world" (Grange, 2012, p. 329). In a similar vein, Behrens (2012, p. 180) has argued that a traditional "African" cultural notion exists, according to which "land is not something that can be individually owned. It belongs to the community, which comprises *past, present and future generations.* Since the ancestors are the guardians of the community, they are also the guardians of the land. The land, broadly understood to mean the environment, is consequently not something we can treat in any way we choose. This entails a direct obligation to future persons, to preserve the environment, since the land is a resource that must be shared with others, including posterity . . . the living need to demonstrate gratitude to their ancestors by following their example and ensuring that their descendants also inherit an environment capable of providing for their basic needs" (emphasis added). Some of this literature could be, however, seen as essentializing culture and generalizing arguments across diverse groups of people, which is why I do not rely on it in advancing my arguments in this book.

13. Including those others we may have never known in the past or the present.

References

Adhikari, M. (2005). *Not white enough, not black enough: Racial identity in the South African coloured community*. University of Ohio Press.

Albertyn, C. (1993). The effluent of affluence: How I came to see the dirt on Adam Smith's invisible hand. In D. Hallowes (Ed.), *Hidden faces: Environment, development, justice: South Africa and the global context* (pp. 213–221). Earthlife Africa.

Alier, J. M. (2002). *The environmentalism of the poor: A study of ecological conflicts and valuation*. Edward Elgar.

Alier, J. M. (2009). Socially sustainable economic de-growth. *Development and Change, 40*(6), 1099–1119. https://doi.org/10.1111/j.1467-7660.2009.01618.x

Allen, J. S., & Jobson, R. C. (2016). The decolonizing generation: (Race and) theory in anthropology since the eighties. *Current Anthropology, 57*(2), 129–148. https://doi.org/10.1086/685502

Ambedkar, B. R. (2014). *Annihilation of caste*. Verso.

Anderson, B. (2009). "I'm not so into gangs anymore. I've started going to church now": Coloured Boys Resisting Gangster Masculinity. *Agenda, 23*(80), 55–67. https://doi.org/10.1080/10130950.2009.9676241

Angus, I. (2016). *Facing the Anthropocene: Fossil capitalism and the crisis of the Earth system*. Monthly Review Press.

Ansoff, H. I. (1975). Managing strategic surprise by response to weak signals. *California Management Review, 18*(2), 21–33. https://doi.org/10.2307/41164635

Appadurai, A. (2013). The capacity to aspire: Culture and the terms of recognition. In *The future as cultural fact: Essays on the global condition* (pp. 179–195). Verso.

Arendt, H. (1961). *Between past and future: Six exercises in political thought*. Viking Press.

Arendt, H. (1962). *The origins of totalitarianism*. World Publication Company.

Arendt, H. (1970). *On violence*. Harcourt.

Arendt, H. (1984). Thinking and moral considerations: A lecture. *Social Research, 51*(1/2), 7–37. https://www.jstor.org/stable/40970069

Arendt, H. (1998). *The human condition*. University of Chicago Press.

Arendt, H. (2006). *Eichmann in Jerusalem: A report on the banality of evil*. Penguin.

Arendt, H. (2007). *The promise of politics*. Schocken.

Arendt, H. (2018). *Thinking without a banister: Essays in understanding, 1953–1975*. Schocken.

Armitage, D. (2000). *The ideological origins of the British Empire*. Cambridge University Press.

Asthana, V. (2018). Forced displacement: A gendered analysis of the Tehri Dam project. In S. I. Rajan (Ed.), *India migration report 2017: Forced migration* (pp. 46–63). Routledge. https://doi.org/10.4324/9781351188753-4

Atkinson, P. (2001). *Handbook of ethnography*. SAGE.

Au, W., & Ferrare, J. (Eds.). (2015). *Mapping corporate education reform: Power and policy networks in the neoliberal state*. Routledge.

Aylett, A. (2010a). Conflict, collaboration and climate change: Participatory democracy and urban environmental struggles in Durban, South Africa. *International Journal of Urban and Regional Research, 34*(3), 478–495. https://doi.org/10.1111/j.1468-2427.2010.00964.x

Aylett, A. (2010b). Participatory planning, justice, and climate change in Durban, South Africa. *Environment and Planning A: Economy and Space, 42*(1), 99–115. https://doi.org/10.1068/a4274

Badat, S., & Sayed, Y. (2014). Post-1994 South African education: The challenge of social justice. *The ANNALS of the American Academy of Political and Social Science, 652*(1), 127–148. https://doi.org/10.1177/0002716213511188

Baer, H. A. (2018). *Democratic eco-socialism as a real utopia: Transitioning into an alternative world system*. Berghahn Books.

Bahuguna, S. (2000). Foreword. In V. Chaudhary (Ed.), *Environmental protection* (pp. v–vi). Pointer Publishers.

Ball, S. (2012). *Global Education Inc.: New policy networks and the neo-liberal imaginary*. Routledge.

Bangay, C., & Blum, N. (2010). Education responses to climate change and quality: Two parts of the same agenda? *International Journal of Educational Development, 30*(4), 359–368. https://doi.org/10.1016/j.ijedudev.2009.11.011

Barkdull, J., & Harris, P. G. (2015). Climate-induced conflict or hospice Earth: The increasing importance of eco-socialism. *Global Change, Peace & Security, 27*(2), 237–243. https://doi.org/10.1080/14781158.2015.1019442

Barker, H. M. (2013). *Bravo for the Marshallese: Regaining control in a post-nuclear, post-colonial world*. Wadsworth.

Barnett, C. (2003). Media transformation and new practices of citizenship: The example of environmental activism in post-apartheid Durban. *Transformation: Critical Perspectives on Southern Africa, 51*(1), 1–24. https://doi.org/10.1353/trn.2003.0017

Barnett, C., & Scott, D. (2007a). Spaces of opposition: Activism and deliberation in post-apartheid environmental politics. *Environment and Planning, 39*(11), 2612–2631. https://doi.org/10.1068/a39200

Barnett, C., & Scott, D. (2007b). The reach of citizenship. *Urban Forum, 18*(4), 289–309. https://doi.org/10.1007/s12132-007-9015-4

Basu, K. (2004). The Indian economy: Up to 1991 and since. In K. Basu (Ed.), *India's emerging economy: Performance and prospects in the 1990s and beyond* (pp. 3–31). The MIT Press.

Basu, S. (2010). The dialectics of resistance: Colonial geography, Bengali Literati and the racial mapping of Indian Identity. *Modern Asian Studies, 44*(1), 53–79. https://doi.org/10.1017/S0026749X09990060

Behar, R. (1996). *The vulnerable observer: Anthropology that breaks your heart.* Beacon Press.

Behrens, K. G. (2012). Moral obligations towards future generations in African Thought. *Journal of Global Ethics, 8*(2–3), 179–191. https://doi.org/10.1080/17449626.2012.705786

Beinart, W., & Coates, P. (1995). *Environment and history: The taming of nature in the USA and South Africa.* Routledge.

Bencze, L., & Carter, L. (2020). Capitalism, nature of science and science education: Interrogating and mitigating threats to social justice. In H. A. Yacoubian & L. Hansson (Eds.), *Nature of science for social justice* (pp. 59–78). Springer. https://doi.org/10.1007/978-3-030-47260-3

Berners-Lee, M. (2021). *There is no Planet B: A handbook for the make or break years* (updated ed.). Cambridge University Press.

Bickford-Smith, V. (2016). *The emergence of the South African metropolis: Cities and identities in the twentieth century.* Cambridge University Press.

Biko, S. (1979a). *Black consciousness in South Africa.* Vintage Books.

Biko, S. (1979b). *The testimony of Steve Biko* (M. Arnold, Ed.). Maurice Temple Smith.

Bisht, T. C. (2009). Development-induced displacement and women: The case of the Tehri Dam, India. *The Asia Pacific Journal of Anthropology, 10*(4), 301–317. https://doi.org/10.1080/14442210903271312

Bisseker, C. (2017). *On the brink: South Africa's political and fiscal cliff-hanger.* NB Publishers.

Bloch, G. (2009). *The toxic mix: What's wrong with South Africa's schools and how to fix it.* Tafelberg.

Blom Hansen, T. (2019). Democracy against the law: Reflections on India's illiberal democracy. In A. P. Chatterji, T. Blom Hansen, & C. Jaffrelot (Eds.), *Majoritarian state: How Hindu nationalism is changing India* (pp. 19–40). Hurst.

Bond, P. (2004). *Talk left, walk right: South Africa's frustrated global reforms.* University of KwaZulu-Natal Press.

Bond, P. (2014). *Elite transition—Revised and expanded edition: From apartheid to neoliberalism in South Africa.* Pluto Press.

Bond, P., & Hallowes, D. (2002). The environment of apartheid-capitalism: Discourses and issues. In P. Bond (Ed.), *Unsustainable South Africa: Environment, development and social protest* (pp. 25–46). Merlin.

Bonneuil, C., & Fressoz, J.-B. (2017). *The shock of the Anthropocene*. Verso.

Booysen, S. (2015). *Dominance and decline: The ANC in the time of Zuma*. Wits University Press.

Boraine, A. (2000). *A country unmasked*. Oxford University Press.

Bourgois, P. (2008). Foreword. In V. Sanford & A. Angel-Ajani (Eds.), *Engaged observer: Anthropology, advocacy, and activism* (pp. IX–XII). Rutgers University Press.

Bradshaw, C. J. A., Ehrlich, P. R., Beattie, A., Ceballos, G., Crist, E., Diamond, J., Dirzo, R., Ehrlich, A. H., Harte, J., Harte, M. E., Pyke, G., Raven, P. H., Ripple, W. J., Saltré, F., Turnbull, C., Wackernagel, M., & Blumstein, D. T. (2021). Underestimating the challenges of avoiding a ghastly future. *Frontiers in Conservation Science, 1*(9). https://doi.org/10.3389/fcosc.2020.615419

Branson, N., Hofmeyr, C., & Lam, D. (2014). Progress through school and the determinants of school dropout in South Africa. *Development Southern Africa, 31*(1), 106–126. https://doi.org/10.1080/0376835X.2013.853610

Brooks, S., Sutherland, C., Scott, D., & Guy, H. (2010). Integrating qualitative methodologies into risk assessment: Insights from South Durban. *South African Journal of Science, 106*(9–10), 1–10.

Broughton, E. (2005). The Bhopal disaster and its aftermath: A review. *Environmental Health, 4*(6). https://doi.org/10.1186/1476-069X-4-6

Brown, J. (2015). *South Africa's insurgent citizens: On dissent and the possibility of politics*. Zed Books.

Burke, J. (2012, October 22). UK government ends boycott of Narendra Modi. *The Guardian*. https://www.theguardian.com/world/2012/oct/22/uk-ends-boycott-narendra-modi

Callenbach, E. (1978). *Ecotopia: A novel about ecology, people and politics in 1999*. Pluto Press.

Caradonna, J. L. (2014). *Sustainability: A history*. Oxford University Press.

Caradonna, J. L. (2017). An incompatible couple: A critical history of economic growth and sustainable development. In I. Borowy & M. Schmelzer (Eds.), *History of the future of economic growth: Historical roots of current debates on sustainable degrowth* (pp. 154–173). Routledge.

Carruthers, J. (1995). *The Kruger National Park: A social and political history*. University of Natal Press.

Carson, J. V., LaFree, G., & Dugan, L. (2012). Terrorist and non-terrorist criminal attacks by radical environmental and animal rights groups in the United States, 1970–2007. *Terrorism and Political Violence, 24*(2), 295–319. https://doi.org/10.1080/09546553.2011.639416

Carson, R. L. (1965). *Silent spring*. Penguin.

Carter, N. (2018). *The politics of the environment: Ideas, activism, policy*. Cambridge University Press.

Centre for Environment Education. (2015). *Parampara: India's culture of climate friendly sustainable practices*. Ministry of Environment, Forest and Climate Change, Government of India.

Chari, S. (2005). *Political work: The Holy Spirit and the labours of activism in the shadows of Durban's refineries* (Research Report No. 30). Centre for Civil Society, University of KwaZulu Natal. https://ccs.ukzn.ac.za/files/RReport_30.pdf

Chari, S. (2006a). Life histories of race and space in the making of Wentworth and Merebank, South Durban. *African Studies, 65*(1), 105–130. https://doi.org/10.1080/00020180600771808

Chari, S. (2006b). Post-apartheid livelihood struggles in Wentworth, South Durban. In V. Padayachee (Ed.), *The development decade?: Economic and social change in South Africa, 1994–2004* (pp. 427–443). HSRC Press.

Chari, S. (2007). How do activists act? Conceiving counterhegemony in Durban. In J. Chalcraft & Y. Noorani (Eds.), *Counterhegemony in the colony and postcolony* (pp. 252–274). Palgrave Macmillan.

Chari, S. (2008). The antinomies of political evidence in post-apartheid Durban, South Africa. *The Journal of the Royal Anthropological Institute, 14*, S61–S76.

Chari, S. (2009). Photographing dispossession, forgetting solidarity: Waiting for social justice in Wentworth, South Africa. *Transactions of the Institute of British Geographers, 34*(4), 521–540. https://doi.org/10.1111/j.1475-5661.2009.00360.x

Checker, M. (2005). *Polluted promises: Environmental racism and the search for justice in a southern town*. New York University Press.

Chikane, R. (2018). *Breaking a rainbow, building a nation: The politics behind #MustFall movements*. Picador Africa.

Chipkin, I., & Swilling, M. (2018). *Shadow state: The politics of state capture*. Wits University Press.

Chomsky, N. (2016). The multiple crises of neoliberal capitalism and the need for a global working class response. *International Socialist Review.* https://isreview.org/issue/101/multiple-crises -neoliberal-capitalism-and-need-global-working-class-response

Chouhan, T. R. (1994). *Bhopal, the inside story: Carbide workers speak out on the world's worst industrial disaster*. The Other India Press.

Cianchi, J. (2015). *Radical environmentalism: Nature, identity and more-than-human agency*. Palgrave Macmillan. https://cam.ldls.org.uk/vdc_100062228176.0x000001

Cock, J. (2006). Connecting the red, brown and green: The environmental justice movement in South Africa. In R. Ballard, A. Habib, & I. Valodia (Eds.), *Voices of protest: Social movements in post-apartheid South Africa* (pp. 203–224). University of KwaZulu-Natal Press.

Cock, J., & Fig, D. (2001). The impact of globalisation on environmental politics in South Africa, 1990–2002. *African Sociological Review, 5*(2), 15–35.

Connell, R. (2007). *Southern theory: The global dynamics of knowledge in social science*. Polity.

Cooper, D. E., Palmer, J., & Bresler, L. (Eds.). (2001). *Fifty major thinkers on education: From Confucius to Dewey*. Routledge.

Costanza, R., Graumlich, L., & Steffen, W. L. (Eds.). (2007). *Sustainability or collapse?: An integrated history and future of people on Earth*. The MIT Press.

Craig, S. R. (2020). *The ends of kinship: Connecting Himalayan lives between Nepal and New York*. University of Washington Press.

Crompton, R., & Erwin, A. (1991). Reds and greens: Labour and the environment. In J. Cock & E. Koch (Eds.), *Going green: People, politics and the environment in South Africa* (pp. 78–91). Oxford University Press.

Cross, M., Mungadi, R., & Rouhani, S. (2002). From policy to practice: Curriculum reform in South African education. *Comparative Education*, *38*(2), 171–187. https://doi.org/10.1080 /03050060220140566

Crutzen, P. J. (2002). Geology of mankind. *Nature*, *415*, 23. https://doi.org/10.1038/415023a

Crutzen, P. J., & Stoermer, E. F. (2000). The "Anthropocene." *Global Change Newsletter*, *41*, 17–18.

Dalby, S. (2016). Framing the Anthropocene: The good, the bad and the ugly. *The Anthropocene Review*, *3*(1), 33–51. https://doi.org/10.1177/2053019615618681

Danmarks Naturfredningsforening, & SDCEA. (2002). *Comparisons of refineries in Denmark & South Durban in an environmental societal context: A 2002 snapshot.*

Das, A. (1979). *Foundations of Gandhian economics*. Allied.

Datt, G., & Ravallion, M. (2002). Is India's economic growth leaving the poor behind? *Journal of Economic Perspectives*, *16*(3), 89–108. https://doi.org/10.1257/089533002760278730

Dauvergne, P. (2016). *Environmentalism of the rich*. The MIT Press.

Davie, T. B. (1955). *Education and race relations in South Africa: The interaction of educational policies and race relations in South Africa*. South African Institute of Race Relations.

Davies, J. (2016). *The birth of the Anthropocene*. University of California Press.

Demmer, U., & Hummel, A. (2017). Degrowth, anthropology, and activist research: The ontological politics of science. *Journal of Political Ecology*, *24*(1), 610–622.

Deneulin, S., & McGregor, J. A. (2010). The capability approach and the politics of a social conception of wellbeing. *European Journal of Social Theory*, *13*(4), 501–519. https://doi.org/10 .1177/1368431010382762

Denny, M. (2017). *Making the most of the Anthropocene: Facing the future*. Johns Hopkins University Press.

Desai, A. (2017). Service delivery and the war within: Wentworth, Durban, South Africa. *South African Review of Sociology*, *48*(1), 85–99. https://doi.org/10.1080/21528586.2016.1204245

Dewey, J. (1916). *Democracy and education: An introduction to the philosophy of education*. Macmillan.

Dias, A. (2002). Development-induced displacement and its impact. In S. Tharakan (Ed.), *The nowhere people: Responses to internally displaced persons* (pp. 1–23). Books for Change.

Dillabough, J.-A., Wang, E., & Kennelly, J. (2005). "Ginas," "thugs," and "gangstas": Young people's struggles to "become somebody" in working-class urban Canada. *Journal of Curriculum Theorizing*, *21*(2), 83–108.

Dogra, B. (1992). *The debate on large dams.* B. Dogra.

Dogra, B. (1993). *Living for others: Vimla and Sunderlal Bahuguna.* B. Dogra.

Drew, G. (2017). *River dialogues: Hindu faith and the political ecology of dams on the Sacred Ganga.* University of Arizona Press.

Dryzek, J. S. (2016). Institutions for the Anthropocene: Governance in a changing earth system. *British Journal of Political Science, 46*(4), 937–956. https://doi.org/10.1017/S0007123414000453

Dubow, S. (1995). *Scientific racism in modern South Africa.* Cambridge University Press.

Duflo, E., & Pande, R. (2007). Dams. *The Quarterly Journal of Economics, 122*(2), 601–646. https://doi.org/10.1162/qjec.122.2.601

Dukes, P. (2011). *Minutes to midnight: History and the Anthropocene era from 1763.* Anthem.

Dunne, J. (2007). Beyond sovereignty and deconstruction: The storied self. In R. Kearney (Ed.), *Paul Ricœur: The hermeneutics of action* (pp. 137–157). SAGE.

Dyer, C. (1996). *The improvement of primary school quality in India: Successes and failures of "Operation Blackboard."* Centre for South Asian studies at the University of Edinburgh.

Eckerman, I. (2005). *The Bhopal saga: Causes and consequences of the world's largest industrial disaster.* Universities Press.

Edwards, I. (1994). Cato Manor: Cruel past, pivotal future. *Review of African Political Economy, 21*(61), 415–427. https://doi.org/10.1080/03056249408704069

Ellis, E. (2011). The planet of no return: Human resilience on an artificial Earth. *The Breakthrough Journal, 2,* 37–44.

Elon, A. (2006). Introduction: The excommunication of Hannah Arendt. In H. Arendt, *Eichmann in Jerusalem: A report on the banality of evil.* Penguin.

Engelbrecht, P., Nel, M., Smit, S., & van Deventer, M. (2016). The idealism of education policies and the realities in schools: The implementation of inclusive education in South Africa. *International Journal of Inclusive Education, 20*(5), 520–535. https://doi.org/10.1080/13603116.2015.1095250

Engineer, A. A. (2002). Gujarat riots in the light of the history of communal violence. *Economic and Political Weekly, 37*(50), 5047–5054.

Escobar, A. (2008). *Territories of difference: Place, movements, life, redes.* Duke University Press.

Etymonline. (n.d.). Anthropo-. *Online Etymology Dictionary.* https://www.etymonline.com/word/anthropo-

Evans, M. S. (1906). *The native problem in Natal.* P. Davis & Sons.

Everatt, D. (2010). *The origins of non-racialism: White opposition to apartheid in the 1950s.* Wits University Press.

Fearnside, P. M. (1995). Hydroelectric dams in the Brazilian Amazon as sources of "greenhouse" gases. *Environmental Conservation, 22*(1), 7–19. https://doi.org/10.1017/S0376892900034020

Fearnside, P. M. (2005). Do hydroelectric dams mitigate global warming? The case of Brazil's CuruÁ-una Dam. *Mitigation and Adaptation Strategies for Global Change, 10*(4), 675–691. https://doi.org/10.1007/s11027-005-7303-7

Ferguson, J. (1994). *The anti-politics machine: "Development," depoliticization, and bureaucratic power in Lesotho.* University of Minnesota Press.

Ferguson, J., & Gupta, A. (2005). Spatializing states: Toward an ethnography of neoliberal governmentality. In X. Inda (Ed.), *Anthropologies of modernity: Foucault, governmentality, and life politics* (pp. 105–134). Blackwell.

Field, S. (2012). *Oral history, community, and displacement: Imagining memories in post-apartheid South Africa.* Palgrave Macmillan.

Fortun, K. (2001). *Advocacy after Bhopal: Environmentalism, disaster, new global orders.* University of Chicago Press.

Foster, J. B. (2002). The ecological tyranny of the bottom line: The environmental and social consequences of economic reductionism. In *Ecology against capitalism* (pp. 26–43). Monthly Review Press.

Foucault, M. (1979). *Discipline and punish: The birth of the prison.* Penguin.

Fournier, V. (2008). Escaping from the economy: The politics of degrowth. *International Journal of Sociology and Social Policy, 28*(11/12), 528–545. https://doi.org/10.1108/01443330810915233

Freire, P. (1972). Education: Domestication or liberation? *Prospects, 2*(2), 173–181. https://doi.org/10.1007/BF02195789

Freire, P. (1998). *Pedagogy of hope: Reliving pedagogy of the oppressed.* Continuum.

Freire, P. (1999). Reprint: Cultural action for freedom. *Harvard Educational Review, 68*(4), 471–521. https://doi.org/10.17763/haer.68.4.656ku47213445042

Freund, B. (2001). Brown and green in Durban: The evolution of environmental policy in a post-apartheid city. *International Journal of Urban and Regional Research, 25*(4), 717–739. https://doi.org/10.1111/1468-2427.00341

Freund, B. (2010). Development dilemmas in post-apartheid South Africa: An introduction. In B. Freund & H. Witt (Eds.), *Development dilemmas in post-apartheid South Africa.* University of KwaZulu-Natal Press.

Friedlingstein, P., O'Sullivan, M., Jones, M. W., Andrew, R. M., Hauck, J., Olsen, A., Peters, G. P., Peters, W., Pongratz, J., Sitch, S., Le Quéré, C., Canadell, J. G., Ciais, P., Jackson, R. B., Alin, S., Aragão, L. E. O. C., Arneth, A., Arora, V., Bates, N. R., . . . Zaehle, S. (2020). Global carbon budget 2020. *Earth System Science Data, 12*(4), 3269–3340. https://doi.org/10.5194/essd-12-3269-2020

Gadgil, M., & Guha, R. (1992). *This fissured land: An ecological history of India.* Oxford University Press.

Gandhi, M. K. (1921). *Hind Swaraj or Indian home rule.* G. A. Natesan & Co.

Ganguly-Scrase, R., & Scrase, T. J. (2008). *Globalisation and the middle classes in India: The social and cultural impact of neoliberal reforms.* Routledge.

Garland, D. (2014). What is a "history of the present"? On Foucault's genealogies and their critical preconditions. *Punishment & Society, 16*(4), 365–384. https://doi.org/10.1177/1462474514541711

Gates, B. (2021). *How to avoid a climate disaster: The solutions we have and the breakthroughs we need.* Allen Lane.

Geertz, C. (1973). Thick description: Toward an interpretive theory of culture. In *The interpretation of cultures* (pp. 3–30). Basic Books.

Geertz, C. (1988). *Works and lives: The anthropologist as author.* Stanford University Press.

Geertz, C. (2001). *Available light: Anthropological reflections on philosophical topics.* Princeton University Press.

Gerhardt, E. (2004). A return on the repressed: The debt of history in Paul Ricœur's time and narrative. *Philosophy Today,* 245–254.

Ghosh, A. (2016). *The great derangement: Climate change and the unthinkable.* Penguin.

Ghosh, P. S. (2000). *BJP and the evolution of Hindu nationalism: From periphery to centre.* Manohar.

Ghosh, S. C. (2012). "English in taste, in opinions, in words and intellect": Indoctrinating the Indian through textbook, curriculum and education. In J. A. Mangan (Ed.), *The imperial curriculum* (pp. 175–193). Routledge.

Giroux, H. A. (1988). *Teachers as intellectuals: Toward a critical pedagogy of learning.* Bergin & Garvey.

Giroux, H. A. (2004). Cultural studies, public pedagogy, and the responsibility of intellectuals. *Communication and Critical/Cultural Studies, 1*(1), 59–79. https://doi.org/10.1080/1479142042000180926

Glassman, M., & Patton, R. (2014). Capability through participatory democracy: Sen, Freire, and Dewey. *Educational Philosophy and Theory, 46*(12), 1353–1365.

Glăveanu, V. P., & de Saint Laurent, C. (2015). Political imagination, otherness and the European crisis. *Europe's Journal of Psychology, 11*(4), 557–564. https://doi.org/10.5964/ejop.v11i4.1085

Goffman, E. (1961). *Asylums: Essays on the social situation of mental patients and other inmates.* Doubleday.

Govardhan, V. (1993). *Environmental impact assessment of Tehri Dam.* Ashish Publishing House.

Grear, A. (2015). Deconstructing anthropos: A critical legal reflection on 'anthropocentric' law and anthropocene 'humanity.' *Law and Critique, 26*(3), 225–249. https://doi.org/10.1007/s10978-015-9161-0

Gregory, D. (2004). *The colonial present: Afghanistan, Palestine, Iraq.* Blackwell.

Griggs, D., Stafford-Smith, M., Gaffney, O., Rockström, J., Öhman, M. C., Shyamsundar, P., Steffen, W., Glaser, G., Kanie, N., & Noble, I. (2013). Policy: Sustainable development goals for people and planet. *Nature, 495,* 305–307. https://doi.org/10.1038/495305a

Grusin, R. (2017). *Anthropocene feminism*. University of Minnesota Press.

Gudyanga, R., & Jita, L. C. (2018). Mapping physical sciences teachers' concerns regarding the new curriculum in South Africa. *Issues in Educational Research, 28*(2), 405–421.

Guha, R. (2000). *Environmentalism: A global history*. Longman.

Guha, R. (2011). *India after Gandhi: The history of the world's largest democracy*. Macmillan.

Guha, R., & Martinez-Alier, J. (1997). *Varieties of environmentalism: Essays north and south*. Earthscan.

Gunkel, G. (2009). Hydropower—a green energy? Tropical reservoirs and greenhouse gas emissions. *CLEAN—Soil, Air, Water, 37*(9), 726–734. https://doi.org/10.1002/clen.200900062

Håkansson, M., Östman, L., & Van Poeck, K. (2018). The political tendency in environmental and sustainability education. *European Educational Research, 17*(1), 91–111. https://doi.org/10.1177/1474904117695278

Hale, C. R. (2006). Activist research v. cultural critique: Indigenous land rights and the contradictions of politically engaged anthropology. *Cultural Anthropology, 21*(1), 96–120.

Hall, M. (2011). Beyond the human: Extending ecological anarchism. *Environmental Politics, 20*(3), 374–390. https://doi.org/10.1080/09644016.2011.573360

Hallowes, D. (Ed.). (1993). *Hidden faces: Environment, development, justice: South Africa and the global context*. Earthlife Africa.

Hardin, G. (1968). The tragedy of the commons. *Science, 162*(3859), 1243–1248. https://doi.org/10.1126/science.162.3859.1243

Hardtmann, E.-M. (2010). *The Dalit movement in India: Local practices, global connections*. Oxford University Press.

Harvey, D. (2007). Neoliberalism as creative destruction. *The ANNALS of the American Academy of Political and Social Science, 610*(1), 21–44. https://doi.org/10.1177/0002716206296780

Heller, P. (2001). Democratic deepening in India and South Africa. In I. Hofmeyr & M. Williams (Eds.), *South Africa & India: Shaping the Global South* (pp. 150–175). Wits University Press.

Hertwich, E. G. (2013). Addressing biogenic greenhouse gas emissions from hydropower in LCA. *Environmental Science & Technology, 47*(17), 9604–9611. https://doi.org/10.1021/es401820p

Hickel, J. (2020a). *Less is more: How degrowth will save the world*. Random House.

Hickel, J. (2020b). What does degrowth mean? A few points of clarification. *Globalizations, 18*(7), 1105–1111. https://doi.org/10.1080/14747731.2020.1812222

Hirsch, A. (2005). *Season of hope: Economic reform under Mandela and Mbeki*. University of KwaZulu-Natal Press.

Hirsch, F. (1977). *Social limits to growth*. Routledge and Kegan Paul.

Hirschmann, D. (1990). The Black consciousness movement in South Africa. *The Journal of Modern African Studies, 28*(1), 1–22.

Hodson, D. (2011). Making it happen. In *Looking to the future: Building a curriculum for social activism* (pp. 295–307). Sense Publishers. https://doi.org/10.1007/978-94-6091-472-0

Hodson, D. (2014). Becoming part of the solution: Learning about activism, learning through activism, learning from activism. In J. Bencze & S. Alsop (Eds.), *Activist science and technology education* (pp. 67–98). Springer Netherlands. https://doi.org/10.1007/978-94-007-4360-1_5

Holfelder, A.-K. (2019). Towards a sustainable future with education? *Sustainability Science, 14*(4), 943–952. https://doi.org/10.1007/s11625-019-00682-z

Holmes, S. M. (2013). *Fresh fruit, broken bodies: Migrant farmworkers in the United States.* University of California Press.

Holopainen, M., & Toivonen, M. (2012). Weak signals: Ansoff today. *Futures, 44*(3), 198–205. https://doi.org/10.1016/j.futures.2011.10.002

Hunter, M. (2010). Racial desegregation and schooling in South Africa: Contested geographies of class formation. *Environment and Planning A: Economy and Space, 42*(11), 2640–2657. https://doi.org/10.1068/a439

Hunter, S. (2017, March 27). *Massive Durban fire filmed from the sky.* 2 Oceans Vibe News. https://www.2oceansvibe.com/2017/03/27/massive-durban-fire-filmed-from-the-sky-video/

Hursh, D., Henderson, J., & Greenwood, D. (2015). Environmental education in a neoliberal climate. *Environmental Education Research, 21*(3), 299–318. https://doi.org/10.1080/13504622.2015.1018141

Illich, I. (2018). *Deschooling society.* Camas Books.

IPCC (Intergovernmental Panel on Climate Change). (2018). *Global warming of 1.5°C* [An IPCC special report on the impacts of global warming of 1.5°C above pre-industrial levels and related global greenhouse gas emission pathways, in the context of strengthening the global response to the threat of climate change, sustainable development, and efforts to eradicate poverty]. Cambridge University Press.

IPCC (Intergovernmental Panel on Climate Change). (2021). *Climate change 2021: The physical science basis* [Contribution of Working Group I to the Sixth Assessment Report of the Intergovernmental Panel on Climate Change]. Cambridge University Press.

Ishizaka, S. (2006). The anti Tehri Dam movement as a new social movement and Gandhism. *Journal of the Japanese Association for South Asian Studies, 18,* 76–95.

Ivanova, D., Stadler, K., Steen-Olsen, K., Wood, R., Vita, G., Tukker, A., & Hertwich, E. G. (2016). Environmental impact assessment of household consumption. *Journal of Industrial Ecology, 20*(3), 526–536. https://doi.org/10.1111/jiec.12371

Jacques, P. J. (2009). *Environmental skepticism: Ecology, power and public life.* Routledge. https://doi.org/10.4324/9781315580050

Jaffrelot, C. (2005). *Dr Ambedkar and untouchability: Analysing and fighting caste* (Rev. ed.). Hurst & Co.

Jaffrelot, C. (2012). Gujarat 2002: What justice for the victims? The Supreme Court, the SIT, the police and the state judiciary. *Economic and Political Weekly, 47*(8), 77–89.

Jagadeesan, S. (2015). *The Sardar Sarovar Project: Assessing economic and social impacts.* Sage.

Jain, M. (2013). McEducation for all: Whose agenda does global education really serve? *Critical Literacy: Theories and Practices, 7*(1), 84–90.

Jalal, A. (2009). *Democracy and authoritarianism in South Asia.* Cambridge University Press. https://doi.org/10.1017/CBO9780511559372

James, G. A. (2013). *Ecology is permanent economy: The activism and environmental philosophy of Sunderlal Bahuguna.* SUNY Press.

Janowitz, M. (1946). German reactions to Nazi atrocities. *American Journal of Sociology, 52*(2), 141–146. https://doi.org/10.1086/219961

Jaspers, K. (1953). *The origin and goal of history.* Yale University Press.

Jefferess, D. (2009). The limits of dissent: Arundhati Roy and the struggle against the Narmada dams. In R. Ghosh & A. Navarro Tejero (Eds.), *Globalizing dissent: Essays on Arundhati Roy* (pp. 157–179). Routledge.

Jetnil-Kijiner, K. (2014). *A poem to my daughter* (recited at the opening of the UN General Assembly in September 2014). https://jkijiner.wordpress.com/2014/09/24/united-nations-climate-summit-opening-ceremony-my-poem-to-my-daughter/

Jickling, B. (1994). Why I don't want my children to be educated for sustainable development. *Trumpeter, 11*(3), 114–116.

Johnson, G. A., Pfister, A. E., & Vindrola-Padros, C. (2012). Drawings, photos, and performances: Using visual methods with children. *Visual Anthropology Review, 28*(2), 164–178. https://doi.org/10.1111/j.1548-7458.2012.01122.x

Johnson, R. W. (1977). *How long will South Africa survive?* Macmillan.

Johnson, R. W. (2016). *How long will South Africa survive?: The looming crisis.* Hurst & Company.

Johnston, J. S. (1998). Nietzsche as educator: A reexamination. *Educational Theory, 48*(1), 67–83.

Jovchelovitch, S., Priego-Hernandez, J., & Glăveanu, V. P. (2017). Imagination in children entering culture. In T. Zittoun & V. P. Glăveanu (Eds.), *Handbook of imagination and culture* (pp. 113–135). Oxford University Press.

Kahn, R. (2010). *Critical pedagogy, ecoliteracy, & planetary crisis: The ecopedagogy movement.* Peter Lang.

Kallis, G. (2011). In defence of degrowth. *Ecological Economics, 70*(5), 873–880. https://doi.org/10.1016/j.ecolecon.2010.12.007

Kallis, G., Paulson, S., D'Alisa, G., & Demaria, F. (2020). *The case for degrowth.* John Wiley & Sons.

Kanjee, A., & Sayed, Y. (2013). Assessment policy in post-apartheid South Africa: Challenges for improving education quality and learning. *Assessment in Education: Principles, Policy & Practice, 20*(4), 442–469. https://doi.org/10.1080/0969594X.2013.838541

Kateb, G. (1977). Freedom and worldliness in the thought of Hannah Arendt. *Political Theory*, 5(2), 141–182. https://doi.org/10.1177/009059177700500202

Katz, E., Light, A., & Rothenberg, D. (2000). *Beneath the surface: Critical essays in the philosophy of deep ecology*. The MIT Press.

Kearney, R. (2004). *On Paul Ricœur: The owl of Minerva*. Ashgate.

Khagram, S. (2004). *Dams and development: Transnational struggles for water and power*. Cornell University Press.

Khan, F. (1994). Rewriting South Africa's conservation history—The role of the Native Farmers Association. *Journal of Southern African Studies*, 20(4), 499–516.

Khan, F. (2000). Environmentalism in South Africa: A sociopolitical perspective. *Macalester International*, 9(11), 156–181.

Khan, F. (2014, August 27–29). *Race, politics and the environment in South Africa—Trends in the history of environmental civil society organisations* [paper presentation]. Dialogue on Environmental History: BRICS, History Institute, University of Rio de Janeiro, Brazil.

Khilnani, S. (2012). *The idea of India*. Penguin.

King, M. E. (2015). *Gandhian nonviolent struggle and untouchability in South India: The 1924–25 Vykom Satyagraha and mechanisms of change*. Oxford University Press.

Kirsch, S. (2001). Lost worlds. *Current Anthropology*, 42(2), 167–198. https://doi.org/10.1086/320006

Kistnasamy, E. J., Robins, T. G., Naidoo, R., Batterman, S., Mentz, G. B., Jack, C., & Irusen, E. (2008). The relationship between asthma and ambient air pollutants among primary school students in Durban, South Africa. *International Journal of Environment and Health*, 2(3/4), 365–385.

Klausen, S. M. (2018). Eugenics and the maintenance of white supremacy in modern South Africa. In D. B. Paul, J. Stenhouse, & H. G. Spencer (Eds.), *Eugenics at the edges of empire: New Zealand, Australia, Canada and South Africa* (pp. 289–309). Palgrave Macmillan.

Klein, D., Carazo, M. P., Doelle, M., Bulmer, J., & Higham, A. (Eds.). (2017). *The Paris Climate Agreement: Analysis and commentary*. Oxford University Press.

Klein, N. (2014). *This changes everything: Capitalism vs. the climate*. Allen Lane.

Klingensmith, D. (2007). *One valley and a thousand: Dams, nationalism, and development*. Oxford University Press.

Koch, E. (1991). Rainbow alliances: Community struggles around ecological problems. In J. Cock & E. Koch (Eds.), *Going green: People, politics and the environment in South Africa* (pp. 20–32). Oxford University Press.

Kohli, A. (2006). Politics of economic growth in India, 1980–2005: Part II: The 1990s and beyond. *Economic and Political Weekly*, 41(14), 1361–1370.

Kolbert, E. (2015). *The sixth extinction: An unnatural history*. Bloomsbury.

Kolbert, E. (2021). *Under a white sky: The nature of the future*. Random House.

Kolge, N. (2017). *Gandhi against caste*. Oxford University Press.

Komatsu, H., Rappleye, J., & Silova, I. (2019). Culture and the independent self: Obstacles to environmental sustainability? *Anthropocene, 26*, 100198. https://doi.org/10.1016/j.ancene.2019 .100198

Komireddi, K. S. (2019). *Malevolent republic: India under Modi*. Hurst & Co.

Komljenovic, J., & Robertson, S. L. (2017). Making global education markets and trade. *Globalisation, Societies and Education, 15*(3), 289–295. https://doi.org/10.1080/14767724.2017 .1330140

Kumar, K. (1988). Origins of India's "textbook culture." *Comparative Education Review, 32*(4), 452–464. https://doi.org/10.1086/446796

Kumar, K. (2005). *Political agenda of education: A study of colonialist and nationalist ideas*. Sage Publications.

Kurzman, D. (1987). *A killing wind: Inside Union Carbide and the Bhopal catastrophe*. McGraw-Hill.

Lassiter, L. E. (2001). From "Reading over the Shoulders of Natives" to "Reading Alongside Natives," literally: Toward a collaborative and reciprocal ethnography. *Journal of Anthropological Research, 57*(2), 137–149. https://doi.org/10.1086/jar.57.2.3631564

Latouche, S. (2010). Degrowth. *Journal of Cleaner Production, 6*(18), 519–522.

Latour, B. (2004). Why has critique run out of steam? From matters of fact to matters of concern. *Critical Inquiry, 30*(2), 225–248. https://doi.org/10.1086/421123

Le Grange, L. (2012). Ubuntu, ukama, environment and moral education. *Journal of Moral Education, 41*(3), 329–340. https://doi.org/10.1080/03057240.2012.691631

Leonard, L. (2013). The relationship between the conservation agenda and environmental justice in post-apartheid South Africa: An analysis of Wessa KwaZulu-Natal and environmental justice advocates. *South African Review of Sociology, 44*(3), 2–21. https://doi.org/10.1080/21528586 .2013.817059

Leonard, L. (2014a). Participatory democracy against industrial risks: Environmental justice in Durban, South Africa. *Politikon, 41*(2), 311–329. https://doi.org/10.1080/02589346.2014 .905263

Leonard, L. (2014b). The network society, power and the print media in post-apartheid South Africa: The case of media contestation in Durban for environmental justice. *Media, Culture & Society, 36*(7), 966–981. https://doi.org/10.1177/0163443714536080

Leonard, L., & Pelling, M. (2010). Mobilisation and protest: Environmental justice in Durban, South Africa. *Local Environment, 15*(2), 137–151. https://doi.org/10.1080/13549830903527654

Levy, B. L. M., & Zint, M. T. (2013). Toward fostering environmental political participation: Framing an agenda for environmental education research. *Environmental Education Research*, *19*(5), 553–576. https://doi.org/10.1080/13504622.2012.717218

Lewis, S. L., & Maslin, M. A. (2018). *Human planet: How we created the Anthropocene*. Pelican.

Lieder, M., & Rashid, A. (2016). Towards circular economy implementation: A comprehensive review in context of manufacturing industry. *Journal of Cleaner Production, 115*, 36–51. https://doi.org/10.1016/j.jclepro.2015.12.042

Litfin, K. (2016). Person/planet politics: Contemplative pedagogies for a New Earth. In S. Nicholson & S. Jinnah (Eds.), *New Earth politics: Essays from the Anthropocene* (pp. 115–134). The MIT Press.

Liu, J. H., & Khan, S. S. (2014). Nation building through historical narratives in pre-independence India: Gandhi, Nehru, Savarkar, and Golwalkar as entrepreneurs of identity. In M. Hanne, W. D. Crano, & J. S. Mio (Eds.), *Warring with words: Narrative and metaphor in politics* (pp. 221–247). Psychology Press.

Loram, C. T. (1917). *The education of the South African native*. Longmans, Green, And Co.

Lotz-Sisitka, H., Ali, M. B., Mphepo, G., Chaves, M., Macintyre, T., Pesanayi, T., Wals, A., Mukute, M., Kronlid, D., Tran, D. T., Joon, D., & McGarry, D. (2016). Co-designing research on transgressive learning in times of climate change. *Current Opinion in Environmental Sustainability*, *20*, 50–55. https://doi.org/10.1016/j.cosust.2016.04.004

Lotz-Sisitka, H., Wals, A. E., Kronlid, D., & McGarry, D. (2015). Transformative, transgressive social learning: Rethinking higher education pedagogy in times of systemic global dysfunction. *Current Opinion in Environmental Sustainability, 16*, 73–80. https://doi.org/10.1016/j.cosust.2015.07.018

Ludden, D. (1992). India's development regime. In N. Dirks (Ed.), *Colonialism and culture* (pp. 247–287). University of Michigan Press.

Lundegård, I., & Wickman, P.-O. (2007). Conflicts of interest: An indispensable element of education for sustainable development. *Environmental Education Research, 13*(1), 1–15. https://doi.org/10.1080/13504620601122566

MacDougall, D. (2006). *The corporeal image: Film, ethnography, and the senses*. Princeton University Press.

Macintyre, T., Lotz-Sisitka, H., Wals, A., Vogel, C., & Tassone, V. (2018). Towards transformative social learning on the path to 1.5 degrees. *Current Opinion in Environmental Sustainability, 31*, 80–87. https://doi.org/10.1016/j.cosust.2017.12.003

Majumdar, M., & Mooij, J. E. (2011). *Education and inequality in India: A classroom view*. Routledge.

Malinowski, B. (1922). *Argonauts of the western Pacific: An account of native enterprise and adventure in the archipelagoes of Melanesian New Guinea*. Routledge & Kegan Paul.

Malm, A., & Hornborg, A. (2014). The geology of mankind? A critique of the Anthropocene narrative. *The Anthropocene Review, 1*(1), 62–69. https://doi.org/10.1177/2053019613516291

Mandela, N. (2013). *Long walk to freedom*. Abacus.

Mangla, A. (2015). Bureaucratic norms and state capacity in India: Implementing primary education in the Himalayan region. *Asian Survey, 55*(5), 882–908. https://doi.org/10.1525/as.2015.55.5.882

Mangla, A. (2017). Elite strategies and incremental policy change: The expansion of primary education in India. *Governance, 31*, 381–399. https://doi.org/10.1111/gove.12299

Maniates, M. F. (2001). Individualization: Plant a tree, buy a bike, save the world? *Global Environmental Politics, 1*(3), 31–52. https://doi.org/10.1162/152638001316881395

Maniates, M. F. (2016). Make way for hope: A contrarian view. In S. Nicholson & S. Jinnah (Eds.), *New earth politics: Essays from the Anthropocene* (pp. 135–154). The MIT Press.

Mann, J. (2014, May 2). Why Narendra Modi was banned from the U.S. *Wall Street Journal*. https://www.wsj.com/articles/why-narendra-modi-was-banned-from-the-u-s-1399062010

Manteaw, O. O. (2012). Education for sustainable development in Africa: The search for pedagogical logic. *International Journal of Educational Development, 32*(3), 376–383. https://doi.org/10.1016/j.ijedudev.2011.08.005

Marcus, G. E. (1995). Ethnography in/of the world system: The emergence of multi-sited ethnography. *Annual Review of Anthropology, 24*, 95–117.

Marcuse, H. (1965). *Repressive tolerance*. Berkeley Commune.

Mathias, N., & Herrera, R. T. (2006). A hermeneutic of Amartya Sen's concept of capability. *International Journal of Social Economics, 33*(10), 710. https://doi.org/10.1108/03068290610689741

Matthews, H. D., & Tokarska, K. (2021, January 18). New research suggests 1.5C climate target will be out of reach without greener COVID-19 recovery plans. *The Conversation*. http://theconversation.com/new-research-suggests-1-5c-climate-target-will-be-out-of-reach-without-greener-covid-19-recovery-plans-151527

Matu Jansangthan. (2002). *Tehri Dam Fourth document: Towards failure and devastation*. Matu Peoples' Organisation.

Mawani, R. (2010). *Colonial proximities: Crossracial encounters and juridical truths in British Columbia, 1871–1921*. UBC Press.

Mawdsley, E. (1998). After Chipko: From environment to region in Uttaranchal. *The Journal of Peasant Studies, 25*(4), 36–54. https://doi.org/10.1080/03066159808438683

Mawdsley, E. (1999). A new Himalayan state in India: Popular perceptions of regionalism, politics, and development. *Mountain Research and Development, 19*(2), 101–112. https://doi.org/10.2307/3674251

Mawdsley, E. (2005). The abuse of religion and ecology: The Visha Hindu Parishad and Tehri Dam. *Worldviews: Global Religions, Culture, and Ecology, 9*(1), 1–24. https://doi.org/10.1163/1568535053628427

McKenzie, M. (2012). Education for y'all: Global neoliberalism and the case for a politics of scale in sustainability education policy. *Policy Futures in Education, 10*(2), 165–177. https://doi.org/10.2304/pfie.2012.10.2.165

McKibben, B. (2019). *Falter: Has the human game begun to play itself out?* Wildfire.

McNeill, J. R., & Engelke, P. (2014). *The great acceleration: An environmental history of the Anthropocene since 1945.* The Belknap Press of Harvard University Press.

Meadows, D. H. (1972). *The limits to growth: A report for the Club of Rome's Project on the Predicament of Mankind.* Pan Books.

Meadows, D. H., Randers, J., & Meadows, D. L. (2006). *The limits to growth: The 30-year update.* Earthscan.

Mebratu, D. (1998). Sustainability and sustainable development: Historical and conceptual review. *Environmental Impact Assessment Review, 18*(6), 493–520. https://doi.org/10.1016/S0195-9255(98)00019-5

Mehta, N. (2010). Ashis Nandy vs. the state of Gujarat: Authoritarian developmentalism, democracy and the politics of Narendra Modi. *South Asian History and Culture, 1*(4), 577–596. https://doi.org/10.1080/19472498.2010.507028

Misiaszek, G. W. (2016). Ecopedagogy as an element of citizenship education: The dialectic of global/local spheres of citizenship and critical environmental pedagogies. *International Review of Education, 62*(5), 587–607. https://doi.org/10.1007/s11159-016-9587-0

Modi, N. (2015). Foreword. In Centre for Environmental Education (Ed.), *Parampara: India's culture of climate friendly sustainable practices* (pp. i–ii). Ministry of Environment, Forest and Climate Change, Government of India.

Moore, J. W. (2017). The Capitalocene, Part I: On the nature and origins of our ecological crisis. *The Journal of Peasant Studies, 44*(3), 594–630. https://doi.org/10.1080/03066150.2016.1235036

Moran, K. A. (2009). Can Kant have an account of moral education? *Journal of Philosophy of Education, 43*(4), 471–484. https://doi.org/10.1111/j.1467-9752.2009.00721.x

Morgan, C. (2016). Testing students under cognitive capitalism: Knowledge production of twenty-first century skills. *Journal of Education Policy, 31*(6), 805–818. https://doi.org/10.1080/02680939.2016.1190465

Morris, P. (2015). Comparative education, PISA, politics and educational reform: A cautionary note. *Compare: A Journal of Comparative and International Education, 45*(3), 470–474. https://doi.org/10.1080/03057925.2015.1027510

Mouffe, C. (2000). Deliberative democracy or agonistic pluralism. In *Political Science Series 72.* Institute for Advanced Studies.

Murove, M. F. (2007). The Shona Ethic of Ukama with reference to the immortality of values. *Mankind Quarterly, 48*(2), 179–190.

Musk, E. (2017). Making humans a multi-planetary species. *New Space, 5*(2), 46–61. https://doi.org/10.1089/space.2017.29009.emu

Nachowitz, T. (1988). The Tehri Dam, India—Stumbling toward catastrophe. *Cultural Survival Quarterly, 12*(2), 9–12.

Naidoo, R., Gqaleni, N., Batterman, S., & Robins, T. (2007). *Multipoint plan: Project 4: Health study and health risk assessment*. University of KwaZulu-Natal, Centre for Occupational and Environmental Health and the University of Michigan.

Naidoo, R. N., Robins, T. G., Batterman, S., Mentz, G., & Jack, C. (2013). Ambient pollution and respiratory outcomes among schoolchildren in Durban, South Africa. *South African Journal of Child Health*, *7*(4), 127–134.

Nambissan, G. B. (2010). The global economic crisis, poverty and education: A perspective from India. *Journal of Education Policy*, *25*(6), 729–737. https://doi.org/10.1080/02680939.2010.508180

Nambissan, G. B., & Ball, S. (2010). Advocacy networks, choice and private schooling of the poor in India. *Global Networks*, *10*(3), 324–343. https://doi.org/10.1111/j.1471-0374.2010.00291.x

Nandy, A. (2015). *The intimate enemy: Loss and recovery of self under colonialism*. Oxford University Press.

National Council of Educational Research and Training. (2005). *Environment education as infused in NCERT syllabus for Classes I to XII*.

National Council of Educational Research and Training. (2008). *Looking around: Environmental textbook for Class V*.

Nehru, J. (1962). *India's freedom [Essays, letters, and speeches]*. Allen & Unwin.

Newton, J. (2008). Displacement and development: The paradoxes of India's Tehri dam. *Geographical Bulletin—Gamma Theta Upsilon*, *49*(1), 19–32.

Nilsen, A. G. (2010). *Dispossession and resistance in India: The river and the rage*. Routledge.

Nixon, R. (2011). *Slow violence and the environmentalism of the poor*. Harvard University Press.

Nocella, A. (2019). Unmasking the animal liberation front using critical pedagogy: Seeing the ALF for who they really are. In A. Nocella, C. Drew, A. George, S. Ketenci, J. Lupinacci, I. Purdy, & J. L. Schatz (Eds.), *Education for total liberation: Critical animal pedagogy and teaching against speciesism* (pp. 15–25). Peter Lang.

Nolan, C. (2012). *Shaping the education of tomorrow: 2012 report on the UN decade of education for sustainable development, abridged*. UNESCO.

Nortje, A. (2000). *Anatomy of dark: Collected poems of Arthur Nortje* (D. Klopper, Ed.). University of South Africa.

Nriagu, J., Robins, T., Gary, L., Liggans, G., Davila, R., Supuwood, K., Harvey, C., Jinabhai, C. C., & Naidoo, R. (1999). Prevalence of asthma and respiratory symptoms in south-central Durban, South Africa. *European Journal of Epidemiology*, *15*(8), 747–755. https://doi.org/10.1023/A:1007653709188

Palmer, J., & de Klerk, D. (2012). Power relations: Exploring meanings in the Curriculum and Assessment Policy Statement (2011). *Communitas*, *17 (special ed.)*, 61–79.

Palshikar, S. (2019). Toward hegemony: The BJP beyond electoral dominance. In A. P. Chatterji, T. Blom Hansen, & C. Jaffrelot (Eds.), *Majoritarian State: How Hindu nationalism is changing India* (pp. 101–116). Hurst.

Panagariya, A. (2005). India in the 1980s and the 1990s: A triumph of reforms. In W. Tseng & D. Cowen (Eds.), *India's and China's recent experience with reform and growth* (pp. 170–200). Palgrave Macmillan UK.

Parrique T., Barth J., Briens F., C. Kerschner, Kraus-Polk A., Kuokkanen A., & Spangenberg J. H. (2019). *Decoupling debunked: Evidence and arguments against green growth as a sole strategy for sustainability*. European Environmental Bureau.

Patel, B. N., & Nagar, R. (2018). *Sustainable development and India: Convergence of law, economics, science, and politics*. Oxford University Press.

Patkar, M., & Kothari, S. (2017). The struggle for participation and justice: A historical narrative. In W. Fisher (Ed.), *Toward sustainable development?: Struggling over India's Narmada River* (pp. 157–178). Routledge.

Patnaik, U. (2007). Neoliberalism and rural poverty in India. *Economic and Political Weekly*, *42*(30), 3132–3150.

Patwardhan, A. (2016). Anand Patwardhan's chronicles of socio-political realities. *ANTYAJAA: Indian Journal of Women and Social Change*, *1*(2), 257–274. https://doi.org/10.1177/2455632717690602

Paxton, R. O. (2002). *Europe in the twentieth century* (4th ed.). Harcourt College Publishers.

Pellow, D. N. (2014). *Total liberation: The power and promise of animal rights and the Radical Earth Movement*. University of Minnesota Press.

Pels, P. (2008). What has anthropology learned from the anthropology of colonialism? *Social Anthropology*, *16*(3), 280–299. https://doi.org/10.1111/j.1469-8676.2008.00046.x

Pepper, D. (2005). Utopianism and environmentalism. *Environmental Politics*, *14*(1), 3–22. https://doi.org/10.1080/0964401042000310150

Peterson, D. J. (1993). *Troubled lands: The legacy of Soviet environmental destruction*. Westview Press.

Phasha, T., Bipath, K., & Beckmann, J. (2016). Teachers' experiences regarding continuous professional development and the Curriculum Assessment Policy Statement. *International Journal of Educational Sciences*, *14*(1–2), 69–78. https://doi.org/10.1080/09751122.2016.11890480

Planning Commission of India. (1958). *Reorientation of curricular content of elementary schools: Note prepared by the Education Division of the Planning Commission* (Education Department, SEUI Branch, Progs., Nos. 1–17 B.2). National Archives of India.

Popke, E. J. (2000). Violence and memory in the reconstruction of South Africa's Cato Manor. *Growth and Change*, *31*(2), 235–254. https://doi.org/10.1111/0017-4815.00127

Potts, K. & Brown, L. (2005). "Becoming an anti-oppressive researcher." In L. Brown and S. Strega (Eds.), *Research as resistance: Critical, indigenous and anti-oppressive approaches* (pp. 255–86). Canadian Scholars' Press.

Potts, R. (2015). A conversation with David MacDougall: Reflections on the childhood and modernity workshop films. *Visual Anthropology Review, 31*(2), 190–200. https://doi.org/10.1111/var.12081

Prakash, G. (1990). Writing post-Orientalist histories of the Third World: Perspectives from Indian historiography. *Comparative Studies in Society and History, 32*(2), 383–408. https://doi.org/10.1017/S0010417500016534

Prakash, M. S., & Esteva, G. (2008). *Escaping education: Living as learning within grassroots cultures.* Peter Lang.

Prozesky, M. (2009). Well-fed animals and starving babies: Environmental and developmental challenges in process and African perspectives. In M. F. Murove (Ed.), *African ethics: An anthology of comparative and applied ethics* (pp. 298–307). University of KwaZulu-Natal Press.

Rabinow, P. (1977). *Reflections on fieldwork in Morocco.* University of California Press.

Rabinow, P. (2007). Anthropological observation and self-formation. In J. Biehl, B. Good, & A. Kleinman (Eds.), *Subjectivity: Ethnographic investigations* (pp. 98–118). University of California Press.

Raj, D. S. (2002). Big dams—boon or burden?: An overview. In S. Tharakan (Ed.), *The nowhere people: Responses to internally displaced persons* (pp. 61–81). Books for Change.

Rajagopal, A. (2005). And the poor get gassed (1987). In B. Hanna, W. Morehouse, & S. Sarangi (Eds.), *The Bhopal reader: Remembering twenty years of the world's worst industrial disaster* (pp. 24–27). Apex Press.

Ralph, L. (2020). *The torture letters: Reckoning with police violence.* University of Chicago Press.

Ramachandran, S. K. (2016, July 21). RSS didn't kill Gandhi but created an ideology against him, say historians. *Hindustan Times.*

Ramatlapana, K., & Makonye, J. P. (2012). From too much freedom to too much restriction: The case of teacher autonomy from National Curriculum Statement (NCS) to Curriculum and Assessment Statement (CAPS). *Africa Education Review, 9*(suppl), S7–S25. https://doi.org/10.1080/18146627.2012.753185

Rana, N., Sati, S. P., Sundriyal, Y. P., Doval, M. M., & Juyal, N. (2007). Socio-economic and environmental implications of the hydroelectric projects in Uttarakhand Himalaya, India. *Journal of Mountain Science, 4*(4), 344–353. https://doi.org/10.1007/s11629-007-0344-5

Rangan, H. (2000). *Of myths and movements: Rewriting Chipko into Himalayan history.* Oxford University Press.

Rangan, H. (2004). From Chipko to Uttaranchal. In M. Watts & R. Peet (Eds.), *Liberation ecologies: Environment, development, social movements* (pp. 371–389). Routledge.

Rao, N., Cheng, K.-M., & Narain, K. (2003). Primary schooling in China and India: Understanding how socio-contextual factors moderate the role of the state. *International Review of Education, 49*, 153–176.

Rao, T. S. (1992). *Tehri Dam is a time bomb: A case study in anti-environmentalism.* T. Lavanya Lata.

Räthzel, N., & Uzzell, D. (2009). Transformative environmental education: A collective rehearsal for reality. *Environmental Education Research, 15*(3), 263–277. https://doi.org/10.1080 /13504620802567015

Rawat, R. (2012). Development, displacement and its impact on rural women: A case study of oustees of Tehri dam. *Eastern Anthropologist, 65*(2), 141–155.

Rawat, R. (2013). Tehri Dam and its environmental impacts on the people of fringe villages. *Guru Nanak Journal of Sociology, 34*(1–2), 63–81.

Rembert, R. B. (1995). Socrates, discussion and moral education. *International Review of Education, 41*(1), 97–108. https://doi.org/10.1007/BF01099293

Renwick, R. (2018). *How to steal a country: State capture and hopes for the future in South Africa.* Jacana.

Republic of South Africa. (2015). *The Constitution of the Republic of South Africa, 1996: As adopted on 8 May, 1996 and amended on 11 October, 1996 by the Constituent Assembly.* Department of Justice and Constitutional Development.

Ricœur, P. (1984). *Time and narrative.* University of Chicago Press.

Ricœur, P. (2010). Asserting personal capacities and pleading for mutual recognition. In B. Treanor & H. Venema (Eds.), *A passion for the possible: Thinking with Paul Ricœur* (1st ed., pp. 22–26). Fordham University Press.

Robertson, S. L., & Komljenovic, J. (2016). Non-state actors, and the advance of frontier higher education markets in the global south. *Oxford Review of Education, 42*(5), 594–611.

Robeyns, I. (2005). The capability approach: A theoretical survey. *Journal of Human Development, 6*(1), 93–117. https://doi.org/10.1080/146498805200034266

Robin, L., & Steffen, W. (2007). History for the Anthropocene. *History Compass, 5*(5), 1694–1719. https://doi.org/10.1111/j.1478-0542.2007.00459.x

Robinson, J. (2004). Squaring the circle?: Some thoughts on the idea of sustainable development. *Ecological Economics, 48*(4), 369–384. https://doi.org/10.1016/j.ecolecon.2003.10.017

Robinson, S.-A. (2017). Climate change adaptation trends in small island developing states. *Mitigation and Adaptation Strategies for Global Change, 22*(4), 669–691. https://doi.org/10.1007 /s11027-015-9693-5

Rockström, J., Steffen, W., Noone, K., Persson, Å., Chapin Iii, F. S., Lambin, E. F., Lenton, T. M., Scheffer, M., Folke, C., Schellnhuber, H. J., Nykvist, B., de Wit, C. A., Hughes, T., van der Leeuw, S., Rodhe, H., Sörlin, S., Snyder, P. K., Costanza, R., Svedin, U., . . . Foley, J. A. (2009). A safe operating space for humanity. *Nature, 461*, 472–475. https://doi.org/10.1038/461472a

Rosaldo, M. Z. (1982). The things we do with words: Ilongot speech acts and speech act theory in philosophy. *Language in Society, 11*(2), 203–237.

Rosaldo, R. (1994). Subjectivity in social analysis. In S. Seidman (Ed.), *The postmodern turn: New perspectives on social theory* (pp. 171–184). Cambridge University Press. https://doi.org/10.1017 /CBO9780511570940.012

Rostron, B. (1991). *Till Babylon falls*. Coronet.

Routledge, P. (2003). Voices of the dammed: Discursive resistance amidst erasure in the Narmada Valley, India. *Political Geography, 22*(3), 243–270. https://doi.org/10.1016/S0962-6298(02)00095-1

Rowell, A. (1996). *Green backlash: Global subversion of the environmental movement*. Routledge.

Roy, A. (1999). *The greater common good*. India Book Distributors.

Roy, A. (2003). *War talk*. South End Press.

Roy, S. (2007). *Beyond belief: India and the politics of postcolonial nationalism*. Duke University Press.

Rozenberg, J., & Hallegatte, S. (2019). Poor people on the front line: The impacts of climate change on poverty in 2030. In R. Kanbur & H. Shue (Eds.), *Climate justice: Integrating economics and philosophy* (pp. 24–42). Oxford University Press.

Ruparelia, S. (2015). 'Minimum government, maximum governance': The restructuring of power in Modi's India. *South Asia: Journal of South Asian Studies, 38*(4), 755–775. https://doi.org/10.1080/00856401.2015.1089974

Russell, A. (2010). *After Mandela: The battle for the soul of South Africa*. Windmill.

Säfström, C. A., & Östman, L. (2020). Transactive teaching in a time of climate crisis. *Journal of Philosophy of Education, 54*(4), 989–1002. https://doi.org/10.1111/1467-9752.12477

Said, E. (1979). *Orientalism*. Vintage Books.

Samuel, R. (1994). *Theatres of memory*. Verso.

Sarangapani, P. (2003). *Constructing school knowledge: An ethnography of learning in an Indian village*. Sage Publications.

Sarkar, S. (1993). The fascism of the Sangh Parivar. *Economic and Political Weekly, 28*(5), 163–167.

Sathe, S. P. (2003). *Judicial activism in India: Transgressing borders and enforcing limits* (2nd ed.). Oxford University Press.

Schell, J. (2010). In search of a miracle: Hannah Arendt and the atomic bomb. In S. Benhabib, R. T. Tsao, & P. J. Verovšek (Eds.), *Politics in dark times: Encounters with Hannah Arendt* (pp. 247–258). Cambridge University Press.

Schensul, D., & Heller, P. (2011). Legacies, change and transformation in the post-apartheid city: Towards an urban sociological cartography. *International Journal of Urban and Regional Research, 35*(1), 78–109. https://doi.org/10.1111/j.1468-2427.2010.00980.x

Schneider, F., Kallis, G., & Martinez-Alier, J. (2010). Crisis or opportunity? Economic degrowth for social equity and ecological sustainability. *Journal of Cleaner Production, 18*(6), 511–518. https://doi.org/10.1016/j.jclepro.2010.01.014

Schudel, I. (2017). Deliberations on a changing curriculum landscape and emergent environmental and sustainability education practices in South Africa. In H. Lotz-Sisitka, O. Shumba, J. Lupele, & D. Wilmot (Eds.), *Schooling for sustainable development in Africa* (pp. 39–54). Springer International Publishing. https://www.springer.com/gp/book/9783319459875

Schwab, K. (2016). *The fourth industrial revolution*. World Economic Forum.

Scott, D. (1994). *Communal space construction: The rise and fall of Clairwood and district* [PhD thesis]. University of Natal.

Scott, D. (2003a). The destruction of Clairwood: A case study on the transformation of communal living space. In D. M. Smith (Ed.), *The apartheid city and beyond: Urbanization and social change in South Africa* (pp. 89–100). Routledge.

Scott, D. (2003b). "Creative destruction": Early modernist planning in the South Durban industrial zone, South Africa. *Journal of Southern African Studies, 29*(1), 235–259. https://doi.org/10.1080/0305707032000060458A

Scott, D., & Barnett, C. (2009). Something in the air: Civic science and contentious environmental politics in post-apartheid South Africa. *Geoforum, 40*(3), 373–382. https://doi.org/10.1016/j.geoforum.2008.12.002

Scott, D., & Oelofse, C. (2005). Social and environmental justice in South African cities: Including 'invisible stakeholders' in environmental assessment procedures. *Journal of Environmental Planning and Management, 48*(3), 445–467. https://doi.org/10.1080/09640560500067582

Scott, D., Oelofse, C., & Guy, C. (2002). Double trouble: Environmental injustice in South Durban. *Agenda: Empowering Women for Gender Equity, 52*, 50–57. https://doi.org/10.2307/4066473

Scott, J. C. (2008). *Seeing like a state: How certain schemes to improve the human condition have failed*. Yale University Press.

Scranton, R. (2015). *Learning to die in the Anthropocene: Reflections on the end of a civilization*. City Lights Books.

Seekings, J., & Nattrass, N. (2005). *Class, race, and inequality in South Africa*. Yale University Press.

Seekings, J., & Nattrass, N. (2015). *Policy, politics and poverty in South Africa*. Palgrave Macmillan.

Sekulova, F., Kallis, G., Rodríguez-Labajos, B., & Schneider, F. (2013). Degrowth: From theory to practice. *Journal of Cleaner Production, 38*, 1–6. https://doi.org/10.1016/j.jclepro.2012.06.022

Sen, A. (1999). *Development as freedom*. Oxford University Press.

Seth, S. (2007). *Subject lessons*. Duke University Press.

Shabazz, A. (2015). Foreword. In M. X & A. Haley, *The autobiography of Malcolm X* (pp. IX–XXIV). Ballantine Books.

Shariff, A., & Ghosh, P. K. (2000). Indian education scene and the public gap. *Economic and Political Weekly, 35*(16), 1396–1406.

Sharma, M. (2009). Passages from nature to nationalism: Sunderlal Bahuguna and Tehri Dam opposition in Garhwal. *Economic and Political Weekly, 44*(8), 35–42.

Sharma, M. (2012). *Green and Saffron: Hindu nationalism and Indian environmental politics*. Permanent Black.

Shiva, V. (2016). *The violence of the green revolution: Third world agriculture, ecology and politics*. University Press of Kentucky.

Shrivastava, A., & Kothari, A. (2012). *Churning the Earth: The making of global India*. Penguin.

Shugar, D. H., Jacquemart, M., Shean, D., Bhushan, S., Upadhyay, K., Sattar, A., Schwanghart, W., McBride S., Van Wyk De Vries, M., Mergili, M., Emmer, A., Deschamps-Berger, C., McDonnell, M., Bhambri, R., Allen, S., Berthier, E., Carrivick, J. L., Clague, J. J., Dokukin, M., Dunning, S. A. . . . Westoby, M. J. (2021). A massive rock and ice avalanche caused the 2021 disaster at Chamoli, Indian Himalaya. *Science, 373*(6552), 300–306. https://doi.org/10.1126 /science.abh4455

Simon, R. I., & Dippo, D. (1986). On critical ethnographic work. *Anthropology & Education Quarterly, 17*(4), 195–202.

Singh, J. (2003). *Colonial narratives/cultural dialogues: "Discoveries" of India in the language of colonialism*. Routledge.

Singh, S. (2002). *Taming the waters: The political economy of large dams in India*. Oxford University Press.

Sitze, A. (2013). *The impossible machine: A genealogy of South Africa's Truth and Reconciliation Commission*. The University of Michigan Press.

Smith, B. D., & Zeder, M. A. (2013). The onset of the Anthropocene. *Anthropocene, 4*, 8–13. https://doi.org/10.1016/j.ancene.2013.05.001

Smith, C. J. (2018). *Decolonising the South African art curriculum* [MA thesis]. University of Witwatersrand. http://wiredspace.wits.ac.za/handle/10539/25963

Smith, M. (2005). Ecological citizenship and ethical responsibility: Arendt, Benjamin and political activism. *Environments, 33*(3), 51–64.

Smith, W. C., & Joshi, D. K. (2016). Public vs. private schooling as a route to universal basic education: A comparison of China and India. *International Journal of Educational Development, 46*(Suppl. C), 153–165. https://doi.org/10.1016/j.ijedudev.2015.11.016

Sneddon, C., Howarth, R. B., & Norgaard, R. B. (2006). Sustainable development in a postBrundtland world. *Ecological Economics, 57*(2), 253–268. https://doi.org/10.1016/j.ecolecon.2005 .04.013

Somerville, K. (2016). *Africa's long road since Independence: The many histories of a continent*. Hurst & Co.

South Africa's election results reflect widespread disillusion. (2019, May 16). *The Economist*.

Sparks, S. (2006). Civil society, pollution and the Wentworth Oil Refinery. *Historia, 51*(1), 201–233.

Sriprakash, A. (2016). Modernity and multiple childhoods: Interrogating the education of the rural poor in global India. In L. Hopkins & A. Sriprakash (Eds.), *The 'Poor Child:' The cultural politics of education, development and childhood* (pp. 151–167). Routledge.

Sriprakash, A., Sutoris, P., & Myers, K. (2019). The science of childhood and the pedagogy of the state: Postcolonial development in India, 1950s. *Journal of Historical Sociology, 32*(3), 345–359. https://doi.org/10.1111/johs.12246

Srivastava, S. (1998). *Constructing post-colonial India: National character and the Doon School*. Routledge.

Statistics South Africa. (2019). *Youth graduate unemployment rate increases in Q1: 2019*. http://www .statssa.gov.za/?p=12121

Steffen, W., Crutzen, P. J., & McNeill, J. R. (2007). The Anthropocene: Are humans now overwhelming the great forces of nature? *Ambio, 36*(8), 614–621.

Steffen, W., Grinevald, J., Crutzen, P., & McNeill, J. (2011). The Anthropocene: Conceptual and historical perspectives. *Philosophical Transactions: Mathematical, Physical and Engineering Sciences, 369*(1938), 842–867.

Steffen, W., Persson, Å., Deutsch, L., Zalasiewicz, J., Williams, M., Richardson, K., Crumley, C., Crutzen, P., Folke, C., Gordon, L., Molina, M., Ramanathan, V., Rockström, J., Scheffer, M., Schellnhuber, H. J., & Svedin, U. (2011). The Anthropocene: From global change to planetary stewardship. *Ambio, 40*(7), 739–761.

Steffen, W., Richardson, K., Rockström, J., Cornell, S. E., Fetzer, I., Bennett, E. M., Biggs, R., Carpenter, S. R., Vries, W. de, Wit, C. A. de, Folke, C., Gerten, D., Heinke, J., Mace, G. M., Persson, L. M., Ramanathan, V., Reyers, B., & Sörlin, S. (2015). Planetary boundaries: Guiding human development on a changing planet. *Science, 347*(6223), 1259855. https://doi.org/10.1126 /science.1259855

Steinberg, J. (2015). *Midlands: A very South African murder*. Jonathan Ball Publishers.

Stevenson, R. B. (2007). Schooling and environmental education: Contradictions in purpose and practice. *Environmental Education Research, 13*(2), 139–153. https://doi.org/10.1080 /13504620701295726

Steyn, P. (2002). Popular environmental struggles in South Africa, 1972–1992. *Historia, 47*(1), 125–158.

Steyn, P. (2005). The lingering environmental impact of repressive governance: The environmental legacy of the apartheid era for the new South Africa. *Globalizations, 2*(3), 391–402. https://doi .org/10.1080/14747730500367983

Sterling, S. (1996). Education in change. In J. Huckle & S. Sterling (Eds.), *Education for sustainability* (pp. 18–39). Earthscan Publications.

Stratford, R. (2019). Educational philosophy, ecology and the Anthropocene. *Educational Philosophy and Theory, 51*(2), 149–152. https://doi.org/10.1080/00131857.2017.1403803

Sund, L., & Ohman, J. (2014). On the need to repoliticise environmental and sustainability education: Rethinking the postpolitical consensus. *Environmental Education Research, 20*(5), 639–659.

Sutoris, P. (2016). *Visions of development: Films division of India and the imagination of progress, 1948–75*. Oxford University Press.

Sutoris, P. (2018a). Elitism and its challengers: Educational development ideology in postcolonial India through the prism of film, 1950–1970. *International Journal of Educational Development, 60*, 1–9. https://doi.org/10.1016/j.ijedudev.2017.10.017

Sutoris, P. (2018b). Ethically scaling up interventions in educational development: A case for collaborative multi-sited ethnographic research. *Comparative Education, 54(3)*, 390–410. https://doi.org/10.1080/03050068.2018.1481622

Sutoris, P. (2019). Politicising ESE in postcolonial settings: The power of historical responsibility, action and ethnography. *Environmental Education Research, 25(4)*, 601–612. https://doi.org/10.1080/13504622.2019.1569204

Sutoris, P. (2021). Environmental futures through children's eyes: Slow observational participatory videomaking and multi-sited ethnography. *Visual Anthropology Review, 37(2)*, 310–332. https://doi.org/10.1111/var.12240

Tagore, R. (1991). *Nationalism*. Ruppa.

Taylor, B. (2008). The tributaries of radical environmentalism. *Journal for the Study of Radicalism, 2*(1), 27–61.

Thapliyal, N. (2016). Privatized rights, segregated childhoods: A critical analysis of neoliberal education policy in India. In K. P. Kallio, S. Mills, & T. Skelton (Eds.), *Politics, citizenship and rights* (pp. 21–37). Springer Singapore. https://doi.org/10.1007/978-981-4585-57-6_14

Thomashow, M. (2020). *To know the world: A new vision for environmental learning*. The MIT Press.

Thomassen, B. (2009). The uses and meanings of liminality. *International Political Anthropology, 2*(1), 5–27.

Thomassen, B. (2013). Anthropology and social theory: Renewing dialogue. *European Journal of Social Theory, 16*(2), 188–207. https://doi.org/10.1177/1368431012463809

Thomassen, B. (2016). *Liminality and the modern: Living through the in-between*. Routledge.

Thompson, L. (2014). *A history of South Africa*. Yale University Press.

Tilak, J. B. G. (2009). Public expenditure in education in two educationally backward states. In R. Sharma & V. Ramachandran (Eds.), *The elementary education system in India* (pp. 70–108). Routledge.

Tillmanns, J. (2009). Can historical responsibility strengthen contemporary political culture? *The American Journal of Economics and Sociology, 68*(1), 127–152.

Tlaba, G. M. (1987). *Politics and freedom: Human will and action in the thought of Hannah Arendt*. University Press of America.

Tooley, J. (2013). *The beautiful tree: A personal journey into how the world's poorest people are educating themselves*. Cato Institute.

Topdar, S. (2015). Duties of a 'good citizen': Colonial secondary school textbook policies in late nineteenth-century India. *South Asian History and Culture, 6*(3), 417–439. https://doi.org/10.1080/19472498.2015.1030877

Trapido, S. (2011). Imperialism, settler identities, and colonial capitalism: The hundred-year origins of the 1899 South African War. In R. Ross, A. K. Mager, & B. Nasson (Eds.), *The Cambridge history of South Africa, Vol. 2: 1885–1994* (pp. 66–101). Cambridge University Press.

Treanor, B. (2013). Turn around and step forward: Environmentalism, activism and the social imaginary. In T. S. Mei & D. Lewin (Eds.), *From Ricœur to action: The socio-political significance of Ricœur's thinking* (pp. 155–174). Bloomsbury Academic.

Tsing, A. L. (2005). *Friction: An ethnography of global connection.* Princeton University Press.

UNESCO. (2019a). *Sustainable Development Goal (SDG) 4 Country Profile: India.* UNESCO Institute for Statistics. http://tcg.uis.unesco.org/wp-content/uploads/sites/4/2019/03/IN.pdf

UNESCO. (2019b). *Sustainable Development Goal (SDG) 4 Country Profile: South Africa.* UNESCO Institute for Statistics. http://tcg.uis.unesco.org/wp-content/uploads/sites/4/2019/03/ZA.pdf

United Nations. (2015). The Sustainable Development Agenda: What is sustainable development? *United Nations Sustainable Development Goals.* https://www.un.org/sustainabledevelopment/development-agenda/

United Nations. (2018). *The Sustainable Development Goals report 2018.*

United Nations Environment Programme. (1975). *The Belgrade Charter: A framework for environmental education.* https://unesdoc.unesco.org/ark:/48223/pf0000017772

Usher, P. J. (2016). Untranslating the Anthropocene. *Diacritics, 44*(3), 56–77. https://doi.org/10.1353/dia.2016.0014

van den Bergh, J. (2007). *Abolishing GDP* (Tinbergen Institute Discussion Paper No. 07–019/3). Tinbergen Institute. https://econpapers.repec.org/paper/tinwpaper/20070019.htm

van Gennep, A. (2019). *The rites of passage* (2nd ed.). University of Chicago Press. https://press.uchicago.edu/ucp/books/book/chicago/R/bo38180827.html

Van Maanen, J. (2011). *Tales of the field: On writing ethnography* (2nd ed.). University of Chicago Press.

VanderDussen Toukan, E. (2017). Expressions of liberal justice? Examining the aims of the UN's Sustainable Development Goals for Education. *Interchange: A Quarterly Review of Education, 48*(3), 293–309. https://doi.org/10.1007/s10780-017-9304-3

Vanderheiden, S. (2005). Eco-terrorism or justified resistance? Radical environmentalism and the "war on terror." *Politics & Society, 33*(3), 425–447. https://doi.org/10.1177/0032329205278462

Vare, P., & Scott, W. (2007). Learning for a change exploring the relationship between education and sustainable development. *Journal of Education for Sustainable Development, 1*(2), 191–198. https://doi.org/10.1177/097340820700100209

Varma, R., & Varma, D. R. (2005). The Bhopal disaster of 1984. *Bulletin of Science, Technology & Society, 25*(1), 37–45. https://doi.org/10.1177/0270467604273822

Varshney, A. (1998). Mass politics or elite politics? India's economic reforms in comparative perspective. *The Journal of Policy Reform, 2*(4), 301–335. https://doi.org/10.1080/13841289808523388

Vasavi, A. R. (2015). Culture and life of government elementary schools. *Economic and Political Weekly, 50*(33), 36–50.

Vaughan, N. E., & Lenton, T. M. (2011). A review of climate geoengineering proposals. *Climatic Change, 109*(3), 745–790. https://doi.org/10.1007/s10584-011-0027-7

Verghese, B. G. (1994). *Winning the future: From Bhakra to Narmada, Tehri, Rajasthan Canal.* Konark Publishers.

Villa, D. (2000). Introduction: The development of Arendt's political thought. In D. Villa (Ed.), *The Cambridge companion to Hannah Arendt* (pp. 1–21). Cambridge University Press.

Voogt, J., & Roblin, N. P. (2012). A comparative analysis of international frameworks for 21st century competences: Implications for national curriculum policies. *Journal of Curriculum Studies, 44*(3), 299–321. https://doi.org/10.1080/00220272.2012.668938

Vora, R. (2009). *The world's first anti-dam movement: The Mulshi satyagraha, 1920–1924.* Permanent Black.

Wackernagel, M., & Rees, W. (1998). *Our ecological footprint: Reducing human impact on the Earth.* New Society Publishers.

Wacquant, L. (2004). Ghetto. In N. J. Smelser & P. B. Baltes (Eds.), *International encyclopedia of the social & behavioral sciences* (pp. 1–7). Pergamon. https://doi.org/10.1016/B0-08-043076 -7/99103-4

Wacquant, L. (2016). Revisiting territories of relegation: Class, ethnicity and state in the making of advanced marginality. *Urban Studies, 53*(6), 1077–1088. https://doi.org/10.1177 /0042098015613259

Wacquant, L. (1996). The rise of advanced marginality: Notes on its nature and implications. *Acta Sociologica, 39*(2), 121–139. https://doi.org/10.1177/000169939603900201

Walker, K. L. M. (2008). Neoliberalism on the ground in rural India: Predatory growth, agrarian crisis, internal colonization, and the intensification of class struggle. *The Journal of Peasant Studies, 35*(4), 557–620. https://doi.org/10.1080/03066150802681963

Wang, C., & Burris, M. A. (1997). Photovoice: Concept, methodology, and use for participatory needs assessment. *Health Education & Behavior, 24*(3), 369–387. https://doi.org/10.1177 /109019819702400309

The World Commission on Environment and Development. (1987). *Our common future.* Oxford University Press.

Weber, H. (2017). Politics of 'leaving no one behind': Contesting the 2030 Sustainable Development Goals agenda. *Globalizations, 14*(3), 399–414. https://doi.org/10.1080/14747731.2016 .1275404

Weber, T. (1988). *Hugging the trees: The story of the Chipko movement.* Viking.

Wendland, C. L. (2010). *A heart for the work: Journeys through an African medical school.* University of Chicago Press.

Wigley, T. M. L. (2006). A combined mitigation/geoengineering approach to climate stabilization. *Science, 314*(5798), 452–454. https://doi.org/10.1126/science.1131728

Williams, C., Gannon, S., & Sawyer, W. (2013). A genealogy of the 'future': Antipodean trajectories and travels of the '21st century learner.' *Journal of Education Policy*, *28*(6), 792–806. https://doi .org/10.1080/02680939.2013.776117

Williams, J., & Crutzen, P. J. (2013). Perspectives on our planet in the Anthropocene. *Environmental Chemistry*, *10*(4), 269–280. https://doi.org/10.1071/EN13061

Williams, R. (1977). *Marxism and literature*. Oxford University Press.

Winsemius, H. C., Jongman, B., Veldkamp, T. I. E., Hallegatte, S., Bangalore, M., & Ward, P. J. (2015). *Disaster risk, climate change, and poverty: Assessing the global exposure of poor people to floods and droughts*. The World Bank. https://doi.org/10.1596/1813-9450-7480

Wolpe, H. (1972). Capitalism and cheap labour-power in South Africa: From segregation to apartheid. *Economy and Society*, *1*(4), 425–456. https://doi.org/10.1080/03085147200000023

Wood, J. R. (1993). India's Narmada River dams: Sardar Sarovar under siege. *Asian Survey*, *33*(10), 968–984. https://doi.org/10.2307/2645096

Woodhead, M., Frost, M., & James, Z. (2013). Does growth in private schooling contribute to education for all? Evidence from a longitudinal, two cohort study in Andhra Pradesh, India. *International Journal of Educational Development*, *33*(1), 65–73. https://doi.org/10.1016/j.ijedudev .2012.02.005

World's worst air might have taken six hours off President Barack Obama's life. (2015, January 28). *The Economic Times*.

Young, W., Hwang, K., McDonald, S., & Oates, C. J. (2010). Sustainable consumption: Green consumer behaviour when purchasing products. *Sustainable Development*, *18*(1), 20–31. https:// doi.org/10.1002/sd.394

Yusoff, K. (2018). *A billion Black Anthropocenes or none*. University of Minnesota Press.

Zachariah, B. (2005). *Developing India: An intellectual and social history, c. 1930–50*. Oxford University Press.

Zachariah, B. (2012). The "Nehruvian" State, developmental imagination, nationalism, and the government. In R. Samaddar & S. K. Sen (Eds.), *Political transition and development imperatives in India*. (pp. 53–85). Routledge.

Index

Anthropocene (cont.)
  and perception, 50, 132
  philosophical implications of, 50–51,
    55–58
  and public anthropology, 26–29
  semantics of, 7
  and slow violence, 8–9, 132, 135, 199
  and sustainable development, 45
  and totalitarianism, 22–23
  visual representations of, 122–123,
    140–144
anthropology
  colonial legacies of, 65, 214n27
  public, 12, 14, 25–30 (see also activism,
    anthropology and)
  See also ethnography; liminality; thick
    description
apartheid
  and city planning, 86–87, 93
  and democratic transition, 36, 126,
    177–180, 223n49
  and destruction of multiracial communi-
    ties, 94
  and education, 3, 67–68, 126–128, 137
  and elitism, 31–32
  environmentalism at the time of, 173–174,
    234n29, 235n37
  impact on environmental governance of,
    91–92
  legacies of, 65, 85–86, 88–91, 96–97, 152,
    172, 175–176, 185–186
  literary representations of, 85
  state-sponsored violence during, 88
  struggle against, 189, 221n34 (see also
    African National Congress)
  See also Group Areas Act; Mandela, Nelson;
    Biko, Steve; White flight
Arendt, Hannah
  action, 44, 47, 135, 153, 155
  bureaucratization, 21–23, 32, 40, 49, 55,
    63, 76, 102–103, 115, 135–136, 195,
    205–206, 228n25

  and the capability approach, 238n9
  and education, 208
  and freedom, 198
  Homo Faber, 198
  and hope, 37
  and politics, 13, 48, 67, 68, 76, 104, 111,
    154, 197, 206
  practiced ignorance, 116, 144
  relevance to the study of environment of,
    14, 41, 55–56, 196
  and the question of evil, 23, 85
  See also agonistic pluralism; depoliticization;
    Eichmann trial; totalitarianism
asthma. See respiratory disease

Bahuguna, Sunderlal, 81, 147, 157, 160–161,
  220n31, 232n17
Beauty and the Beasts (documentary film),
  185–186
Behar, Ruth, 28, 62
Bharatiya Janata Party (Indian People's Party),
  76–77 (see also Modi, Narendra)
Bhopal disaster, 72–75, 78, 162
Biko, Steve, 84, 87–88, 221n34
biodiversity, 8, 17, 41, 54, 213n12–13
Bluff (Durban), 178, 185, 235n37, 236n43
Boer War, 87, 91, 92
British Empire. See India, history of
Brundtland Commission, 42–43
bureaucratization. See Arendt, Hannah,
  bureaucratization

cancer, 34, 129, 185, 186
Cape Colony, 87, 91
Cape Town, 86, 94, 152, 175
capitalism, 21, 39, 44–45, 72, 74–75, 78, 87,
  108, 175, 177, 185
Capitalocene. See Anthropocene, alternatives to
caste, 68, 79, 106–107, 168, 218n8 (see also
  Ambedkar, B. R.)
Cato Manor, 93–94, 185, 225n62
Centre for Environmental Rights, 236n41

eco-socialism, 45, 153
ecotopia, 153, 231n5
education. *See* Anthropocene, environmental
   learning and; apartheid, education and;
   Arendt, Hannah, education and; Centre
   for Environment Education; curriculum;
   Curriculum Assessment Policy Statements
   (South Africa); depoliticization, education and; development, education and;
   Dewey, John; ecopedagogy; education for
   sustainable development; environmental
   and sustainability education; fast violence,
   education and; handprint (educational
   approach); hidden education; historical responsibility, education and; outlier
   teachers; Ricœur, Paul, educating for
   the Anthropocene and; Socrates; state,
   schooling and; sustainability, education
   and; Tehri Dam, education and; total
   institution (Erving Goffman); transformative intellectuals (Giroux); twenty-first
   century skills
education for sustainable development, 4–6,
   15, 46–48, 55, 211n4, 212n7
Eichmann trial, 23, 37, 85
Electricity, 99, 116, 158–159, 203
Engen (oil refinery), 33, 215n36
environmental activism. *See* activism
environmentalism of the poor, 173–174,
   217n4
environmental multicrisis
   and the Anthropocene, 10, 39, 196
   and disruption, 197–200
   origins of, 196
   proposed solutions to, 41–43, 46–47, 78
   urgency of, 6
environmental racism, 152, 172–173, 200,
   213n20. *See also* air pollution
environmental and sustainability education
   and ageism, 12
   alternative conceptions of, 55–58, 105
   and coloniality, 75–76
   and conceptions of the future, 45–46

criticism of, 15, 26,
and depoliticization, 5, 41, 44, 47–51,
   108–109, 200–201, 211n2
and ethnography, 13–14, 25,
policy, 11
and public anthropology, 28–29
purpose of, 15
environmental justice, 11, 129, 136, 140,
   152, 188, 190, 200, 210
Escobar, Arturo, 153
ethnographic film. *See* MacDougall, David;
   observational filmmaking
ethnography
   critical, 214n30
   engaged, 28
   and extractive research, 100
   and grounded theory, 24
   and knowledge co-creation, 25
   multisited, 25–26, 189, 196
   and nuance, 12–14
   and positionality, 11, 61–66, 147–150
   practice of, 84
   as a process, 4–5, 26–30, 117
   purpose of, 16, 53
   and representation, 65–66, 152, 159, 173
eugenics, 32, 186
e-waste, 213n20
extinction. *See* biodiversity
extractive research. *See* ethnography, extractive
   research and
extractivism, 134. *See also* commodification;
   degrowth

fast violence
   causing slow violence, 154
   definition of, 225n66
   eclipsing slow violence, 97, 132, 137, 190,
      192
   and education, 104, 129–136, 144
   enacted by the state, 162
   narratives of, 188
   targeted at children, 62
   and totalitarianism, 13, 23, 102

Fees Must Fall, 84, 221n33
Films Division of India, 157, 217n3
fossil fuels, 113. *See also* extractivism; sustainability
Foucault, Michel, 62, 69
freedom fighters. *See* African National Congress; Indian National Congress
Freire, Paulo, 41, 53, 200
friction (Anna Tsing), 31
future. *See* activism, alternative futures and; imagination, future worlds of

Gandhi, Indira, 159–160, 232n17
Gandhi, Mohandas Karamchand, 71–72, 76, 147, 196, 217n3, 219n21
the Ganges, 8, 84, 120–121, 160, 229n30, 232n16
Geertz, Clifford, 29, 150, 159
gender, 7, 89, 111, 130, 148, 155, 174, 185
geology. *See* Anthropocene; Crutzen, Paul; Holocene; golden spikes
ghetto, 33, 94, 97, 224n60
Ghosh, Amitav, 18–19, 71
globalization, 23, 35, 154, 212n6, 223n48
golden spikes, 17–18
Goldman Environmental Prize, 174
the great acceleration, 18, 212n6
Green Revolution, 74, 219n16
greenwashing, 58, 136, 191–192
gross domestic product, 34, 229n35
grounded theory. *See* ethnography, grounded theory and
groundWork, 176–177, 180, 196, 234n30
Group Areas Act (apartheid-era legislation), 33, 86, 93, 224n57
Guha, Ramachandra, 69–79, 173, 217n4
Gujarat riots, 76–77

handprint (educational approach), 211n2
hermeneutics, 56, 148, 172, 234n27
hidden education, 136–137
high modernism (James Scott), 19, 157, 235n35

Hindutva, 76–77, 91, 106, 219n21
historical responsibility
  and action, 135
  and activism, 156
  and education, 28–30, 103, 195, 206
  and environmental futures, 14–15
  and intergenerational justice, 197
  and political imagination, 105
  theory of, 56–58
Holocaust, 24, 85, 199
Holocene, 16
hope, 28, 37, 65, 77, 97, 126, 136–140, 144, 205, 210
human rights, 54, 153, 187
hydropower. *See* dams

Illich, Ivan, 54
illness. *See* cancer; respiratory disease
imagination
  activist, 160–161
  Anthropocenic, 198
  of future worlds, 12–13, 26, 56, 104, 134, 140–144
  hermeneutic, 172
  political, 5, 44, 97, 105, 112, 123, 202–203
  radical, 24, 53, 205–207
  suppression of, 135
India
  colonialism and, 106–107
  democratic consolidation of, 31
  history of, 32, 69–78
  schooling in, 30–32, 104–107, 112–116
  See also Bahuguna, Sunderlal; *Bharatiya Janata Party* (Indian People's Party); Bhopal disaster; Centre for Environment Education (Ahmedabad); development, cinematic representations of; Films Division of India; Gandhi, Indira; Gandhi, Mohandas Karamchand; Gujarat riots; *Hindutva*; Indian National Congress; judicial activism; land rights; Modi, Narendra; Mulshi *satyagraha*; Narmada valley; National Council of Educational Research

Ricœur, Paul
and the capability approach, 238n9
crisis of the present, 203
debt to the dead, 41, 56–57, 138, 158, 164,
195, 206
and educating for the Anthropocene,
55–58, 196
horizons of the possible, 13
insolvency paradox, 57–58
storied self, 56–57
surplus meaning, 56, 101, 170, 234n27
temporal arc, 13, 56, 101, 122, 155,
226n6
See also historical responsibility; imagination, hermeneutic

safety, 79, 84, 103–104, 138, 159, 177
Said, Edward. See orientalism
Science, technology, society, environment
(STSE), 51–52
scientism, 55
Sen, Amartya, 238n9
Skido, Joseph, 138, 230n42
slow violence
acceleration of, 10, 69
and the Anthropocene, 8, 156
and bureaucratization, 103, 115
confronting. 140, 153, 206 (see also
activism)
and critique of industrial modernity, 71
eclipsed by fast violence, 97, 123, 129–136,
190
enabling of, 198
history of, 14
and liminality, 31
narratives of, 188
oblivion towards, 85, 158
parallels with fast violence, 23, 102, 132
and perception, 50, 132, 135, 181
and phenomenology, 13, 99, 187
and postcolonial states, 74
recognition of, 196

speed of, 197
turning into fast violence, 162, 186
social justice, 92, 153,
Socrates, 39
South Africa
and citizenship, 68
constitution, 32–33
democratic consolidation of, 31
dependence on foreign capital, 180
education system, 126–127
history of, 65, 84–91, 94
and HIV, 33
and murders of farmers, 222n36
political economy of, 126
racism and, 67–68
securitization within, 225n65
townships, 3–5 (see also Wentworth)
unemployment in, 127
See also activism, end of apartheid and;
African National Congress; air pollution;
Albertyn, Chris; apartheid; Beauty and
the Beasts (documentary film); Biko,
Steve; Bluff (Durban); Boer War; Cape
Colony; Cape Town; Cato Manor; Centre
for Environmental Rights; Clairwood
(Durban); Coloured people; Curriculum
Assessment Policy Statements (South
Africa); Democratic Alliance (political
party); District Six (Cape Town); D'Sa,
Desmond; Earthlife Africa; Engen (oil
refinery); environmental racism; eugen-
ics; Fees Must Fall; Group Areas Act
(apartheid-era legislation); groundWork;
Johannesburg; Kathrada, Ahmed; Man-
dela, Nelson; Milner, Alfred Lord; Nortje,
Arthur; Peek, Bobby; Pietermaritzburg;
Ramaphosa, Cyril; Rhodes, Cecil; Rhodes
Must Fall; Skido, Joseph; South Durban
Community Environmental Alliance;
South Durban Industrial Basin; state
capture; toxic tour; Truth and Reconcili-
ation Commission; uMkhonto we Sizwe